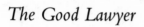
The Good Lawyer

DOUGLAS O. LINDER & NANCY LEVIT

The Good
Lawyer

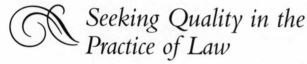 *Seeking Quality in the
Practice of Law*

OXFORD
UNIVERSITY PRESS

OXFORD
UNIVERSITY PRESS

Oxford University Press is a department of the University of
Oxford. It furthers the University's objective of excellence in research,
scholarship, and education by publishing worldwide.

Oxford   New York
Auckland   Cape Town   Dar es Salaam   Hong Kong   Karachi
Kuala Lumpur   Madrid   Melbourne   Mexico City   Nairobi
New Delhi   Shanghai   Taipei   Toronto

With offices in
Argentina   Austria   Brazil   Chile   Czech Republic   France   Greece
Guatemala   Hungary   Italy   Japan   Poland   Portugal   Singapore
South Korea   Switzerland   Thailand   Turkey   Ukraine   Vietnam

Oxford is a registered trademark of Oxford University Press
in the UK and certain other countries.

Published in the United States of America by
Oxford University Press
198 Madison Avenue, New York, NY 10016

Linder, Douglas O., 1951- author.
The good lawyer : seeking quality in the practice of law / Douglas O. Linder,
Nancy Levit.
    p. cm.
ISBN 978-0-19-936023-9 (hardback)
  1. Lawyers.   2. Practice of law.   I. Levit, Nancy, author.   II. Title.
K115.L56 2014
340.023—dc23
2013040066

9 8 7 6 5 4 3 2 1
Printed in the United States of America
on acid-free paper

For the good lawyers who have made our lives better in too many ways to count:

For Cheryl
DOL

For Tim and Jon
NEL

I know that there is nothing better for people than to be happy and to do good while they live.

—Ecclesiastes 3:12

Contents

Preface

You point to something as having Quality and the Quality tends to go away. Quality is what you see out of the corner of your eye.
—Robert M. Pirsig

WHAT DOES IT MEAN TO BE A GOOD LAWYER? THE QUESTION can inspire, nag, or haunt an entire career. If anything has become clear to me from my own attempts to answer that question it is this: being a good lawyer is even harder than being a great one. Winning big cases and earning acclaim is a piece of cake compared to building the set of skills, attitudes, dispositions, and behaviors that characterize the best lawyers.

In the chapters that follow, our inquiry into the meaning of quality in the practice of law will take us in many directions, but in this preface we head to Alaska. What better place to find one's "true north"?

THE WOLF AT LOST LAKE

Douglas O. Linder

One month into our summer clerkships at prominent Anchorage law firms—at least as prominent as Alaskan law firms can be—the three of us planned a backpacking adventure for the upcoming Fourth of July weekend. After a series of day hikes on preceding weekends, we looked forward to a multiday trip to Lost Lake, where we'd have time to relax, enjoy some of the Kenai Peninsula's most spectacular alpine scenery, and share thoughts about our clerking experiences.

Denny, the president of the Environmental Law Society at an East Coast law school and indisputably the most experienced backpacker in our group, warned us that the hike was rated "Difficult" and that we should expect snow at the higher elevations, even during this first week of July. "Difficult," in Denny's mind, was a good thing. It meant we could expect to encounter few, if any, other hikers along the route and that we would be rewarded with the virtuous feeling that comes from meeting and overcoming challenges. Just the sort of thinking you'd expect from a former Outward Bound instructor.

Driving down the Seward Highway toward the trailhead, we talked about the weather—temperatures in the 50s and threatening skies—and about our first weeks of doing "real law." Denny and I clerked at a sixteen-person firm (large by Anchorage standards), and both of us had been asked to help the firm's clients, mostly large energy and mining companies, secure the necessary permits to begin digging minerals out of the public lands or pumping oil from the bottom of the Arctic Ocean. In the mid-1970s, natural resource exploiters of all kinds seemed to be moving into the state, led by developers of the 800-mile Trans-Alaska pipeline, which was then under construction from Prudhoe Bay to Valdez, a seaport on Prince William Sound. Although no one could match Denny's passion for the natural world, all three of us proudly claimed the label "environmentalist." At my law school in California, I had taken the school's first offering of Environmental Law and managed to snag a job as a research assistant for the professor who taught the course. I believed in clean air, clean water, and a happy habitat for every endangered species. Stew, the third member of our band of hikers, was a classmate of Denny's and clerked at the other credential-conscious Anchorage firm, where he also dealt with—who didn't in this place at this time?— environmental issues from a corporate perspective. His interests seemed more catholic than those of Denny or me, but Stew was a steward of the earth. Working for what we had each come to think of as the enemy was troubling each of us, and it quickly became apparent that wrestling with the internal conflicts we were experiencing would be a major theme of conversation over the long weekend.

We celebrated the Fourth climbing for seven and a half miles through a dense spruce forest in a steady rain, then slogging through snow that nearly reached waist level on the north sides of foothills. When we finally reached our campsite on the edge of Lost Lake, we were tired, hungry, and watching for symptoms of hypothermia. In addition to some hard miles, we'd covered some intellectual terrain as well. We had debated whether "loophole finding," which we first agreed was inappropriate when it came to representing resource exploiters, could honestly be distinguished from the normal job of lawyers: to zealously represent the interests of their clients within the bounds of the law and of ethics. As the conversation progressed, we became less and less confident that such a distinction could be made. We also had considered and rejected the standard rationalization for doing work that doesn't align with your own values: "If I don't do this, they'll just find somebody else that will." Thinking of ourselves as easily replaceable commodities in the faceless legal market depressed all three of us. We finished our hot chocolates, swallowed a few handfuls of gorp ("good old raisins and peanuts," a popular trail mix), and headed for our tents.

Early the next morning, around 4 A.M. or so, I peered out of my tent and saw a blue Alaskan sky, with sunlight already brightening the delicate tundra flowers. Nature was calling, so I scrambled out of the tent to answer. Then I saw something that I'll never forget. On the opposite bank of the narrowest portion of the lake, only about twenty yards away, sat an adult gray wolf. I stood frozen, observing this remarkable sight. The wolf seemed to sense that the water separating us meant that I presented no threat. As it too remained motionless, looking at me through its wolf eyes, I wondered whether this was her closest encounter with a human. Curiosity is not an emotion restricted to our species. After a minute or two, the wolf turned and walked away toward the crest of the hill, in the direction of Mount Ascension. It was one of those moments beyond the "I-wish-I-had-a-camera" feeling. I wanted to burn the image of that wolf, that lake, that Alaskan light into my memory forever.

When the others awoke, I shared the story of my wolf encounter. The change in weather and coffee sent our moods soaring. Stew speculated that running barefoot across a snowfield might be great fun, so we trekked off to a snow-covered, north-facing slope along the lake and removed our hiking boots. We took off in all directions across the snowfield, yelping and falling and rolling. There are maybe a handful of days in a life, if you're lucky, where you can say you lived life with an irrepressible intensity. That day on Lost Lake was one of those days.

The emotional intensity of the day seemed somehow to clarify our feelings about the practice of law. Other lawyers with other values can represent oil companies and mining companies, and we should not think less of them for doing so, but it is not for us—not if we want to be lawyers of quality. When you're in your twenties, things have a way of seeming crystal clear even when they really aren't.

Also, during that decade of life, questions about the purpose of life's work have an urgency that fades in midlife and only reappears near career's end. Framing my thinking was a book that I'd been reading that summer in Anchorage. In the summer of my clerkship, Robert Pirsig's *Zen and the Art of Motorcycle Maintenance* remained an unlikely best-seller, with sales approaching five million copies. I, and everyone I knew, read, or was reading, *ZAMM*, and almost all of us took it as something like a sacred text.

The book describes a motorcycle journey from Minnesota to California undertaken by the narrator, his son, and two close friends, punctuated by lectures on the meaning of Quality. Philosophical investigations of Quality—what it means to be good—are tied together by a story to the narrator's past self, whom the author calls "Phaedrus." Phaedrus's obsessive quest to understand the meaning of Quality eventually drives him insane, leading to electric shock therapy and a permanently changed personality. Reconciliation of the narrator with his past comes at book's end. Pirsig tells us that Phaedrus means "wolf" in Greek, an apt fit given Phaedrus's persistent and aggressive effort to understand Quality. My wolf encounter, Phaedrus: the stars seemed to be aligning for a day of insight. (In a later edition of *ZAMM*, Pirsig admits his understanding of Greek was mistaken. Phaedra, the root word, actually means "brilliant" or "radiant.")[1]

To us, in our second law school summers, no question seemed more pressing than "How can I be a quality lawyer?" Or, if there was a more important question, it was "Can I be a quality person and still be a lawyer?" Those were questions that *Zen and the Art of Motorcycle Maintenance* seemed to answer, or partially answer. Although Pirsig wrote about what it took to be a quality motorcycle mechanic, his lessons applied broadly. That day, on Lost Lake, we talked about embracing quality.

I'd be lying if I said I remembered details of our conversations about finding a good life in the law. Looking back now at the underlining in my dog-eared copy of *ZAMM* provides some clues, however. Quality, Pirsig argued, while ultimately undefinable, reconciles two visions of reality, which he labeled the "classic" and "romantic" modes.[2]

Law, with its emphasis on reasoning and logic, is considered to be a field in the classic mode. Lawyers are trained to apply analytic thought—Pirsig called it "the knife"—to experience, always killing something in the process. We learn to take handfuls of sand and sort them into piles and interrelate them, compared to the romantic whose "understanding is directed toward the handful of sand before the sorting begins."[3] The romantic critic views sorting and interrelating as dull and oppressive—"the death force."[4] Law school certainly felt like the death force sometimes. One of my 1L professors warned, "Law school sharpens the mind by narrowing it"—and he was right. All three of us sensed, vaguely, that we were losing our souls through legal education. The idealism that we brought to law school eroded as we were challenged to evaluate this or that fact or consideration that undercut our deeply held, and emotionally based, beliefs. We felt as though we had been given a pair of gray-tinted glasses and doomed to forever see the world through its lenses.

The romantic understanding of the world, with its emphasis on imagination, intuition, and creativity, seemed to have little place in law school. Feelings should be suppressed; facts and rationality should predominate in our decision making. Our professors dismissed our romantic notions as irrational, shallow, and frivolous. "Thinking like a lawyer" meant putting aside feelings and trusting the process of rationality. If you're not up to the task, here's a dime to call your mother and tell her you'll never make it as a lawyer.

In *ZAMM*, Phaedrus grew contemptuous of "the whole rational, intellectual process." He came to lose faith in reason. He denounced intellectuals for not seeing Quality, because they could not snap it into intellectual form. Quality was something that "lay outside the grasp of the methods of the entire Church of Reason."[5] Yet, for Phaedrus, Quality was everything: "My personal feeling is that this is how further improvement of the world will be done: by individuals making Quality decisions and that's all."[6] One year removed from the bar exam and the real beginning of a career in law, we wanted nothing more than to make Quality decisions, but felt law school had left us woefully unprepared to do that.

Like the illusion that is either a goblet or two old women looking at each other, but never both at the same time, the classic and romantic perspectives are equally valid but can't be held simultaneously. We weren't thinking about reforming legal education on Lost Lake; we were thinking about our own careers, but we doubtless would have agreed that the overwhelmingly classic tilt of law schools needed adjustment. Good lawyers, we sensed, used both a romantic and classic perspective to do well for clients—and to preserve their integrity and ideals.

It seemed to us that day that law schools had fallen off the Quality Track. They lacked balance. They overvalued reasoning and undervalued emotions. They wooed and welcomed masters of the LSAT and sent rejection letters to those with superior empathetic capacity, moral courage, and passion. Law firms seemed to fall into the same classic trap. Membership in the Order of the Coif and editorships on law reviews, that's what they looked for in their new associates—not signs of well-developed "soft skills" that some clients might think more important. Could we make it as lawyers and still maintain a sense of wonder? We aimed to find out.

By the time we folded our tents and began the long trek down the Lost Lake trail, we had wrestled with our doubts about law school and about our careers, but we'd also played and smelled the arctic primroses. Quality is not measured so much as it is sensed. When you are doing quality work, you have a direction and the direction feels right.

Later, back on my law school campus, I got a phone call from one of the partners at my Anchorage firm inviting me to join them as an associate beginning the next summer. I asked the partner, one of the most decent and caring lawyers I have ever met, to give me a week to think it over, but I already knew what my decision would be. After law school, I accepted instead a one-year job as a "research associate in environmental law," working on a range of environmental issues for the state of Illinois, from the legality of local measures to reduce airplane noise at O'Hare to strategies for bringing public water supplies into compliance with the recently enacted Safe Drinking Water Act. Not all of what I did was either interesting or important, and the job paid about one quarter of what I might have earned in the Anchorage firm, but at least it aligned with my own values at the time.

Denny took a job clerking for Justice Jay Rabinowitz on the Alaska Supreme Court in Fairbanks. A decade later, when the oil tanker Exxon Valdez slammed into a reef in Alaska's Prince William Sound and sent half a million or more barrels of crude oil pouring into the Sound's pristine waters, a habitat for whales, otters, seals, salmon, and countless seabirds, Denny was the Commissioner of Alaska's Department of Environmental Conservation. For Denny, who assumed leadership of the state's response, the oil spill would take over the next few years of his life.[7] He would see the human tragedy as well as the environmental tragedy. He saw fistfights break out in his office doorway, read reports showing spikes in drug and alcohol abuse, as well as suicide and domestic violence, in affected fishing communities, and empathized with fishermen crying in village streets. And, of course, there were the lawsuits that would fill hundreds of his hours. Exxon is a wealthy company with an army of lawyers—lawyers conditioned to delay and obfuscate if it advanced their client's interests.[8]

Stew accepted a job as an associate in a Seattle law firm, practicing in the areas of real estate and corporate law. At age thirty-seven, Stew became president of the King County Bar Association. After twenty years of practice, including five years ranked as a Top 100 Super Lawyer, Stew left the firm he started to become a founding member of the Alternative Dispute Resolution Roundtable, and has since used his substantial interpersonal skills to arbitrate over 300 cases and mediate another 2,000 plus cases.

OBSESSED WITH QUALITY

Decades have passed since that summer weekend at Lost Lake. There are many times now, having crossed to the safety of a law teaching job, when I feel admiration for the work Denny and Stew and many other dedicated lawyers continue to do, and a twinge of regret for not being with them on the frontlines. Law school teaching is a great gig in many ways, but it sometimes makes you wonder whether you're making a difference.

In my environmental law classes, I'd seen student's eyes glaze over as we plowed through some of the nearly unfathomable provisions of the Clean Air Act (CAA), the Clean Water Act (CWA), the National Environmental Policy Act (NEPA), the Comprehensive Environmental Response, Compensation, and Liability Act (CERCLA), and a host of other alphabet-soup laws enacted mostly in the 1970s. Both the students and I really wanted to talk about values, yet I quizzed them on the interplay of sections 102(b)(3)(ii) and 116(a)(2)(v). I thought often about a satire from an early edition of *Saturday Night Live* in which Don Novello played Father Guido Sarducci, founder of a new educational institution called "the Five Minute University."[9] Father Sarducci's insight, that everything an average college graduate could remember five years later could be repeated in five minutes, led him to establish his school for students who wanted to avoid the hassle and expense of four years on campus. In the Five Minute University, for just "$20 dollars or so," Father Sarducci promised to give—in five minutes—students all the information they would remember if they wasted their time at other colleges. For example, instead of four months of economics, he would just say "supply and demand." Spanish students would learn the meaning of the question "Como esta usted?" (How are you?), and the appropriate response, "Muy bien" (very well), but nothing more. Five years out of law school, would my students remember the subtleties of the Clean Air Act's stationary source provisions? Of course they wouldn't. Even the usual rationalization for close analysis of statutes and case law—that the process would yield for the students a framework for analysis that they could use in practice—seemed a stretch. Frameworks that really serve lawyers well need regular exercise to remain functional, and would any of my students get that exercise? I had my doubts. Why not open the "Five Minute Law School"?

In my early years of teaching, I saw my mission as inspiring law students to work to make a healthier planet, but over time things came to seem less black and white than they did when I was in my twenties, than they did that day at Lost Lake. Increasingly, I came to see the world as a buzzing, complicated place without easy answers. If most legal and policy questions don't have clearly right or wrong answers, if truth is generally beyond our reach, what could I do—what could any law professor do—that makes the world a better place? What is it that transcends politics and goes to the heart of what it means to be a good lawyer? The answer, of course, is Quality: the set of dispositions, virtues, attitudes, behaviors, and skills that enable lawyers to do the best for their clients, their communities, and—ultimately—themselves.

Looking back, my earlier views of legal education and the practice of law now seem naïve. Law cannot be made into something it is not—it is not a playing field that tilts toward humanistic values, as much as some of us might want it to be. Law is the means by which society seeks to achieve some stability in the face of disagreement over just about everything. Lawyers—in order to do their client-centered jobs well—require certain technical skills and facility with law's flattened vocabulary. Having a passion for justice, empathy, humility, and courage is a wonderful thing, but good lawyers need more.

My obsession with the meaning of quality continued to grow and now has become the focus of my work as a law professor. I no longer teach environmental law or natural resources law. Instead, I teach a seminar called "The Quest for a Satisfying Career in Law"[10] and another called "Famous Trials,"[11] in which I try to pull whatever lessons I can from the good—and bad—lawyers participating in those trials. I log many miles in search of answers to the question of what makes a lawyer of quality. Identifying lawyers who made good decisions leads me to living rooms and law offices around the country, places where I ask good lawyers how they managed to do whatever impressive things they did. When, after a number of these far-flung investigations, and my nose for quality began to improve, I turned to the writings of psychologists and neuroscientists to see what light their work might shed on strengths associated with good lawyers. We've learned a lot in just the past two decades or so. The ratio of knowledge to mystery concerning positive abilities and behaviors continues to increase.

In 2010, Oxford University Press published a book I co-authored with my colleague, Nancy Levit. We presented evidence in *The Happy Lawyer: Making a Good Life in the Law* that, for most lawyers, greater career happiness was both possible and within their own power to grasp. In the process of researching and writing that book, we were struck by the strong link between career satisfaction and doing good work. Two hundred lawyers, when asked by us about what made them happiest, almost to a person spoke about times when they accomplished great results for clients who they cared about.[12] However important happiness was, there seemed to us an even more important question we left unanswered that we needed to address: how does one become a good lawyer? All lawyers want to be happy, but happy lawyers do not necessarily make a better world. Quality work, so often circling back to happiness, is what matters most.

Yet, after digging around in books and talking to lawyers about the large and diverse set of skills and attitudes and dispositions that contribute to making a lawyer of quality, the task of defining or describing a good lawyer at first seemed hopeless. But then a path forward appeared. The book will redress the balance, attending largely to the ignored or undervalued characteristics that good lawyers share, or at least wish they had. There will be no chapters entitled "The Good Lawyer Understands the Canons of Statutory Construction" or "The Good Lawyer Uses Proper Citation Format." Those topics are adequately addressed in law schools or bar journals. Also, while it is no doubt true the particular skills and dispositions that matter most to a good patent attorney differ from those most critical to a first-rate criminal defense lawyer, we believe that almost any lawyer can benefit from plunging with us, in the chapters that follow, into the thickets of courage, honesty, empathy, passion, civility, intuitions, and emotional balance.

There will be times when we will appear lost, times when it will seem we are retracing steps. It's all part of the journey. Quality is elusive. As with wolves, you are lucky if you can catch a glimpse out of the corner of your eye. Keep your eyes open.

Introductory Note

WE ARE ABOUT TO EMBARK ON A QUEST FOR QUALITY, AS quixotic as that might seem to some of you (and pardon our occasional quirkiness).

Becoming a good lawyer is not a simple matter of reading this book, though it's a start. The best of lawyers draw on their training, capacities, experiences, and virtues. Most important, perhaps, they have the right attitudes. What's the most important right attitude to have? It's caring enough about the quality of your work to want to make it better. Congratulations: we take your reading these words as a sign you may have the right stuff.

Some of the chapters that follow will focus on capacities or skills that good lawyers tend to have. You will read, for example, about how the capacity to empathize can allow lawyers to better connect with clients and tell their stories, or how good lawyers persuade, or analyze problems and develop litigation strategies, or make realistic predictions about case outcomes. Other chapters focus on what are generally thought of as virtues that a good lawyer has, such as courage, honesty, humility, emotional balance, or a burning passion for justice. While, as you'll see, genetics plays a role in determining our virtues and how they are manifested, there are ways in which you can turn your virtue "weak suits" into "strong suits" and become a much better lawyer for the effort. The set of virtues, dispositions, behaviors, and skills chosen here for inclusion is eclectic and reflects, unavoidably, certain preferences and biases of your authors. That's the nature of the project.

There is no one path to becoming a good lawyer. Each lawyer must carve his or her own way up the mountain. We aim here to describe the terrain your chosen path must cover. It is our hope and our belief that by working toward becoming a better lawyer, by paying attention to the quality of your work, you also work on yourself and will gain personal satisfaction.

Quality, when you seek it, tends—as Robert Pirsig says—"to fan out in waves." It will affect your clients, your profession, and your community. It makes the world a better place.

Note on the use of "we" and "I": References to your authors in your book will generally use the pronoun "we." When "I" is used, as in the Preface and a handful of other places, the reference is to Doug.

The Good Lawyer

CHAPTER I

The Good Lawyer Is Empathetic

You never really understand a person until you consider things from his point of view...until you climb in his skin and walk around in it.
—Harper Lee, *To Kill a Mockingbird*
(Atticus Finch, explaining life to his daughter, Scout)

STEVEN PINKER, IN HIS BOOK *THE BETTER ANGELS OF Our Nature*, suggests that we are living through an "empathy craze."[1] Everywhere we turn, an author, or a television personality, or a teacher, or a spiritual leader is urging us to feel another's pain. In the last few years, we've seen several new books about empathy: *The Empathy Gap, The Empathy Quotient, The Empathetic Civilization*, and *Teaching Empathy*. Neuroscientists have taken an interest in the subject, scanning brains in search of mirror neurons that enable us to connect with the emotions of our fellow human beings. It's only natural, therefore, that some lawyers and law professors picked up the empathy ball and ran with it, and in this chapter we'll meet some who have.

Empathy turns out to be a rather complicated thing. It is often confused with related emotions, such as sympathy and compassion. In fact, empathy is not an emotion at all, but rather a capacity for assessing the internal life of another person. Empathy allows us to stand in someone else's shoes, feel what that person is feeling, appreciate what he or she values, and respond appropriately. It is a necessary precondition to the experience of sympathy, compassion, guilt, and other emotions that push us to take into account the concerns of other people. Empathy is, according to neuroscientist Raymond Dolan of the University College London, the "attribute that underpins a human disposition to altruism and compassion."[2] (Psychopaths, as you might imagine, score very low on measures of empathy.) Empathy can jar us out of thoughtlessness and indifference and focus our attention on the human consequences of our decisions. In his best-selling book *Emotional Intelligence*, Daniel Goleman identifies empathy as one of the five "domains" of emotional intelligence,[3] and in other works he expresses the hope that one day "empathy will hold as valued a place in the curriculum as algebra."[4]

Empathy enables you to understand your clients' interests, tell your clients' stories in a more powerful way, and gain your clients' appreciation for leaving them feeling valued. If we could sprinkle some empathy dust around American law firms, the public's perception of lawyers would doubtless improve. Empathy is not, however, the solution to all our moral problems. As we'll see, empathy has its limitations—and even a dark side.

FEELING CLIENTS' PAIN ON THUNDERHEAD RANCH

If you pick up a rental car at the Jackson Hole airport and head east for two hours, passing through the Teton National Forest on Highway 26, you eventually come to the town of Dubois, Wyoming, population 971. Continuing east on #26 another ten miles, taking a left on a dirt road and driving ten more miles, you descend a slight hill and see an enormous wooden sign that says "Thunderhead Ranch—Registered Simmentals." You cross a bridge and drive along a buck and rail fence, perhaps gazing out as you do on the horses, donkeys, and cows in the pasture. You're there. You have arrived at the office of Trial Lawyers College (TLC), whose founder and director is famed trial attorney Gerry Spence.

You might be impressed that the 34,000-acre ranch on which you stand was paid for by a lifetime of celebrated verdicts for Spence, including a $10.5 million verdict for the Karen Silkwood family in a wrongful death action against plutonium-plant operator Kerr-McGee, and a $52 million verdict against McDonald's on behalf of a small family-owned ice cream company. He also won an acquittal on federal racketeering charges for Filipino First Lady Imelda Marcos (she of the thousand shoes) and successfully defended survivalist Randy Weaver, charged with murdering an FBI agent after a standoff at Ruby Ridge in northern Idaho. Spence, who retired from active practice in 2008, claimed never to have lost a criminal case, either as a prosecutor or as a defense attorney, and not to have lost a civil case since 1969.

Once at the ranch, if you are a registered student, rather than, as you mistakenly might have guessed from the sign, a "registered Simmental" (which is, by the way, a calf of usually Swiss origin), you are assigned to a log cabin and meet your roommate. You are ready to experience a course very different from any you took in law school. For three weeks, you and a few dozen other plaintiffs and criminal defense lawyers from around the country will—as one recent TLC graduate put it—"learn how to crawl into the hides of their clients, to experience their pain, to understand the witness on the witness stand, even to understand and care for their opponent."[5] By the end of the twenty-one days, if all goes well, you might have "entered into the most sacred realm of human experience" (what TLC literature describes as "personhood") and mastered "the power of credibility."[6]

Your first night, sitting in the Big Barn at Thunderhead Ranch, you might hear a story Spence has told a hundred times. It's a story about the wisdom of Spence's Uncle Slim. Spence tells about standing at a corral with his Uncle Slim when the cowboy breaks into a laugh that sounds "like the end note of a bull elk's bugle."[7] Slim points to a dude in the corral trying to saddle a beaten-up nag with a fancy parade saddle, made of black leather with silver spangles. Slim turns to Gerry and says, "Ya can't get nowhere with a thousand-dollar saddle on a ten-dollar horse."[8] For Spence, the thousand-dollar saddle is the expensive, but not particularly helpful, legal education that most lawyers who come to TLC have had. *They* are the horses. He might end his introductory talk with words like, "So tomorrow we begin. We will work on the horse."[9]

The next morning, as you enter the cookhouse for breakfast, you see posted on the day's schedule a single word, "Psychodrama." Psychodrama, you will discover, is a therapy technique in which participants act out traumatic events from their own lives. The technique was developed by Jacob Moreno, a Romanian psychiatrist who was inspired by the richness of children's play. Moreno founded *Stegreiftheater*, the Theater of Spontaneity, in Vienna in the early 1920s, and from its productions emerged the technique that he would bring to the United States when he moved to New York City in 1925. Moreno promoted psychodrama as a means of regaining the lost spontaneity of childhood and learning to run free from the hobbling impediments of the past.[10]

Although psychodrama fell out of favor among therapists, Gerry Spence saw in the technique a way to help lawyers get in touch with themselves. In his first course in 1994, psychodrama was all about "working on the horse" and had no application for trial preparation. Through the use of spontaneous plays in which lawyers pretended to interact with people not actually present, and acted out traumatic events in their lives, Spence took lawyers on a voyage of self-discovery. It seemed to serve its intended purpose, but as one former student pointed out, left a lot of lawyers wondering, "What the heck was that?"[11] Spence's answer would be, "You cannot be credible without first being honest about the self."[12] At today's TLC, psychodrama for self-discovery has a second use: to remake the saddle into something lighter, more suitable for the horse that will wear it, than the fancy saddle provided by a law school education. Psychodrama becomes a way to share the pain and gain insight into the lives of clients and, more importantly, tell their stories to jurors and judges in ways that reveal emotional truths about them (Figure 1.1).

In one psychodrama session, you might find yourself and fellow lawyers sitting in chairs arranged in a circle. Your facilitator encourages you to stand up, walk around the circle, stare deeply into the faces of each of your fellow attorneys, but not to say a word. A few minutes later, you are asked to pretend to take on the physical characteristics—slouches, limps, coughs, mannerisms— of a client who has deeply affected you. After working on your client's physical persona for a while, you are instructed to tell your client's story in the voice of your client. You are asked to tell the story in the present tense—in psychodrama everything

FIGURE 1.1. Gerry Spence in 2008. Credit: Photo by Greg Westfall.

is happening *now*. You might find that the exercise deeply affects you. In a *Los Angeles Times* story about a TLC psychodrama session, one lawyer, who represented asbestos victims, was so overcome with emotion that he had to excuse himself from the session.[13]

Most TLC grads are enthusiastic about putting their newly developed skills into practice. They report connecting better both with their clients and jurors. However, TLC's approach is controversial in legal circles. Critics contend that it is too "touchy-feely" or they question an instructional program that promotes itself as The Way and seems closed to the idea that for some lawyers, the TLC approach might not be the best approach. You don't have to spend much time searching on the Web to find lawyers comparing the Trial Lawyers College to a cult. Some lawyers also worry that the use of psychodrama techniques in the courtroom by TLC-trained lawyers has gone "over the line."[14] Edith Matthai, former president of the Los Angeles Bar Association, cited as an example of inappropriate conduct a lawyer who, during one trial, spoke to dead people as if they were in the courtroom.[15]

Most TLC graduates, however, knew what they were getting into when they went to Wyoming, and they leave Thunderhead Ranch with rave reviews and renewed confidence in their abilities as trial lawyers.

THE IMPORTANCE OF BEING EMPATHETIC

No doubt Gerry Spence and his disciples are on to something when they stress the importance of being empathetic. Empathy is one of the most useful capacities of humans—who are the world empathy champions among all the species on planet earth.[16] Empathy has been defined as "our ability to identify what someone else is thinking or feeling and to respond to their thoughts or feelings with an appropriate emotion."[17] Four primary benefits come from well-honed empathy skills. First, empathy enables you to acknowledge and respect other people's thoughts, so that they feel valued. Second, empathy substantially reduces the likelihood of miscommunications that can lead to wasted effort and counterproductive results. Third, as you become more aware of other people's feelings, you more readily assess their feelings toward you and can make adjustments to smooth things over when necessary. When others think you're being a jerk, at least you know it soon enough to stop your jerk-like behavior and apologize. Fourth, having walked inside another's skin, you'll be better able to compellingly tell that person's story, should the time and place arise for it.[18]

Empathy has too often been lacking in lawyer-client relationships. Lack of lawyer empathy has led to complaints from clients who feel undervalued and misunderstood. Client dissatisfaction surfaced in an American Bar Association (ABA) study in which a majority of respondents (60%) reported negative feelings toward lawyers, even though two-thirds of them thought lawyers were "smart and knowledgeable" about the law. Particularly disturbing was the survey's finding that "the more direct personal contact" a person had with lawyers, "the lower an individual's opinion of them." In particular, contact with lawyers left people feeling "that lawyers lack care and compassion." Most respondents also believed that things were getting worse, with a majority agreeing that lawyers "were less caring and compassionate" than they once were.[19] In general, clients were least happy with lawyers who represented them in adversarial proceedings, and most satisfied with their relationships with lawyers who did transactional work, such as taxes or estate planning.[20]

Clients place a higher value on the "soft skills" of lawyers than lawyers generally imagine. What clients want most from their lawyers is a sense that they really *care* about them and their problem. A survey of Illinois clients of legal services revealed that feeling their lawyer cared was their highest concern—ranking ahead of superior legal skills, reasonable fees for services, and having a proven track record.[21] Clients say they want to be treated with respect, receive regular communication from their lawyers, have a relationship built on trust, and feel that they are being shown empathy and compassion.[22]

Empathy helps you get to the bottom of your clients' concerns. Just as studies show that empathetic physicians are better able to diagnose patient problems, empathetic lawyers are better able to sense what is troubling their clients and imagine better how they would react to possible litigation scenarios. Anthony Kronman, former Yale Law School dean, argues that a good lawyer is able to "place himself in the client's position by provisionally accepting his ends and then imaginatively considering the consequences of pursuing them." In Kronman's view, the lawyer's job is "to see things from the client's point of view, only more clearly."[23]

When lawyers understand the real concerns of their clients, they create improved relationships with clients, who want above all else to know their lawyer cares. Author and poet Maya Angelou observed, "I've learned that people will forget what you said, people will forget what you did, but people will never forget how you made them feel." With better relationships comes improved communication, which creates more realistic expectations among clients about their cases and reduces the likelihood of malpractice suits. Finally, if empathy becomes a more common feature in lawyer-client relationships, the public's perception of lawyers—now abysmally low—will likely improve.

USING EMPATHY TO TELL BETTER STORIES

The human mind is a story processor, not a logic processor.
—Jonathan Haidt

One way to appreciate the importance of empathy is to think of a lawyer as a translator. Above all else, the role of a litigator is to effectively translate the story of his or her client in settlement negotiations or, if it comes to that, to a jury or a judge. To perform the job of translator well requires empathizing not only with the client but also with opposing counsel, jurors, trial judges, appellate judges, and anyone else who might affect the client's fate. A good translation comes in a vocabulary that accurately conveys the client's interests and moves your listeners to respond.

Gerry Spence is fond of saying, "Everything in life is a story: Everything."[24] We are storytelling animals. We carry stories in our head and we use stories, more than anything else, to understand our world. Because this is so, you have to be a good storyteller to be a good lawyer.

In a law school course on juries taught at our law school, students view videotapes of actual jury deliberations. (Yes, on rare occasions, involving juries both in Wisconsin and Arizona, documentary filmmakers have been allowed to enter the sacred precinct of the jury room to record real jurors deliberating the fates of real parties.)[25] What students always find striking is how much deliberation time is taken up with jurors telling—and sometimes picking apart—stories. "They hardly seem to be weighing the evidence at all," a student might say, "they just are trying to construct the most plausible story." Yes, exactly.

Research conducted by psychologists Nancy Pennington and Reid Hastie backs up this conclusion. In one study, Pennington asked subjects taken from a Massachusetts jury pool to view a realistic filmed reenactment of a murder trial and then "be one of the jurors." Pennington found that the assertions of the subjects made clear they employed story structures to reach their conclusions. For example, a subject would say "Johnson was angry so he decided to kill him," rather than assert, "Johnson was a violent man. That makes me think he intended to kill him." The subjects also would make inferences to "fill in" stories. Finally, Pennington showed that the particular story chosen by a subject almost invariably led to a particular verdict.[26] In another study, Pennington and Hastie presented one of two forms of a simulated trial to groups of college students. Although the evidence was the same in both simulations, in one form the defense witnesses were presented in an order that matched the original events (story order) and the prosecution witnesses were presented in a somewhat random, non-story order. For the other simulation, the reverse was true. As expected, when the prosecution witnesses were presented in story order, a much higher percentage of subjects (78%) found the defendant guilty than when defense witnesses, but not prosecution witnesses, were presented in story order (only 31% found the defendant guilty in this situation).[27] Subsequent experiments confirmed that jurors, overwhelmingly, use what Pennington and Hastie described as the "story construction model" to decide cases.

Although the story model of juror behavior is now largely accepted, for years it competed with another model of juror behavior, the evidence-driven model, which posited a sort of dial in the juror's brain, with an indicator that would incline more toward one party or the other as new evidence was presented. Although this evidence-driven model might explain how a small population of jurors behaves, it has been rejected as an inaccurate description of most juror behavior. Stories trump evidence.[28]

From Clarence Darrow to Gerry Spence, successful attorneys have recognized jury trials as battles of competing stories. The story accepted by jurors—the one more consistent with their own experiences, values, emotions, and biases—prevails. Once a juror preliminarily accepts a story, it becomes the framework for analyzing all the evidence and arguments presented later in the trial. It also serves as a sort of filter that is used by the juror to decide what evidence to retain and what evidence to discard, a memory tool for storing more information than would otherwise be possible, and the basis for persuading other jurors when time comes for deliberations. So what makes a good story? It has to be consistent with undisputed facts, plausible given the values and experiences of the juror, and complete enough to account for all that is known to have happened concerning the incident in dispute. It helps if the story can be told in an emotionally compelling way.

The Trial Lawyers College curriculum is based on the assumption that effective storytelling first requires knowing our own stories—which is, of course, the basis for the personal confessions and the reenactments of traumatic events. As the course progresses, the focus shifts from the lawyers to their clients, with the goal being to teach each lawyer to tell the stories of their clients in ways that most powerfully move jurors or judges in their direction. Telling a client's story well, TLC teaches, means understanding in the deepest possible way what the client actually experienced.

Gerry Spence offers instruction on how to interview a client, Danny Patterson, who comes into your office wanting to sue the local police for false arrest.[29] First, Spence advises, get out from behind your desk, potentially "a psychological Berlin Wall" that shouts power to a frightened and self-conscious young man. Next, Spence says to his client, "Danny, take me to the morning they arrested you. Let's actually be there, right now. What are you doing?" When Danny answers in the past tense, "Well, I just let the dog out," Spence jumps in. "No, you are *letting* the dog out." Spence insists on the present tense, which he thinks "brings the event to the here and now instead of a memory." And Danny's story comes out, with the smells, words, pain all captured in a way other interview techniques would not. Danny describes being hauled to jail after an officer, looking for meth, found a plastic bag containing green leaves he used to feed his guinea pig. Spence asks Danny to continue his story after his arrest. Spence says that by the end of the interview, "Already we've seen the jail, its gray miserable walls of concrete and steel. We've felt the tension of people in cages like caged beasts and we've known the fear, and smelled the evil smells of decaying men and lost women. We've heard the screams and the slamming of steel doors and the hateful orders of the jailers. It has been as if we were trapped in the darkest pits of human existence."[30] Notice Spence's use of "we" in his description: Danny and Gerry. The two of them, client and lawyer, have shared the experience, shared the pain. It's an exercise in empathizing designed to enable the lawyer to most compellingly tell Danny's story in settlement negotiations, before a jury, in front of a panel of judges, or wherever else his representation takes him.

THE ORIGINS AND SCIENCE OF EMPATHY

We've discussed in this chapter empathy and its importance for lawyers. It is time to examine more closely what empathy actually is and how it develops in a thriving human being. Empathy is not a tool you either have or you don't have. Most of us lie somewhere between the poles of the empathy spectrum. If you'd like to know where on the spectrum you are positioned, you can take a test (look for it online) and find out your EQ, or "Empathy Quotient."[31] The test asks you to indicate whether you agree with a series of statements such as "I can easily tell if someone wants to enter a conversation" or "It upsets me to see an animal in pain." Based on these responses, you are assigned an EQ somewhere between 0 (no empathy) and 6 (super empathy). Most people score in the 4 to 5 range, with 4 being closer to the average for males and 5 being closer to the average for females.[32]

Humans have different levels of empathy both because they have different "genes for empathy" and have had different sets of experiences. (It's actually not quite accurate to talk about "empathy genes." As empathy researcher Simon Baron-Cohen (cousin of Sacha Baron Cohen, the famous comic actor) points out, "genes cannot code for a high-level construct such as empathy," but rather certain genes are *associated* with higher or lower measures of empathy.)[33] Genetic factors account for between 10% and 50% of the variation in empathy levels between individuals, depending upon which scientist you believe. The genetic contribution to empathetic capacity is revealed in studies showing that identical twins reared apart have much smaller variation in empathy levels than fraternal twins. While recognizing the genetic contribution to empathetic capacity, authorities including sociobiologist E. O. Wilson, anthropologist Margaret Mead, and biologist Stephen J. Gould have all agreed that culture is more important than genetics in determining empathy levels. Wilson, for example, believes that empathy levels are about 90% culturally determined and only 10% genetic.[34]

The ability to empathize begins to develop soon after a baby leaves the womb. Infants instinctively act in ways that encourage mothers to do some serious bonding and provide access to nipples. Babies and parents typically engage in an unconscious dance of emotions, moods, and responses. Hand and facial gestures are made and copied. Looking into her mother's face, a baby sees reflected her own emotions, and through repeated instances of this experience, begins to understand and organize her internal states. It is primarily through this repeated matching of emotions between infants and parents (or other caregivers) that the capacity for empathy grows.

When the early bonding so critical to the development of empathetic capacity doesn't take place, bad things happen. Studies show that when an infant looks at her mother and sees a blank, passive face, she first becomes upset and fussy, and then soon becomes passive and withdrawn. Deprived for months and years of emotional give-and-take with a caregiver, a child can become permanently incapable of a normal range of human emotional response. (This phenomenon has been observed frequently in children raised in stark Romanian orphanages, for example.) When bonding doesn't happen because of distracted, distant, or absent caregivers, and healthy empathetic capacity fails to develop, children are at significantly greater risk of becoming criminals or engaging in other sorts of antisocial conduct. Decreased capacity for empathy in this country helps explain why police and prosecutors report increasing instances of violent crimes committed by teenagers who seem to exhibit no remorse for what they have done. One public defender-turned-prosecutor said, "I just don't know how long I can go on, staring into the vacant eyes of these children who have, without apparent remorse, done the most awful things."[35]

Historically, the United States has been fortunate to score high in measured levels of empathetic reactions among its citizens compared to levels reported in some other regions of the globe. Americans, as a group, feel for each other. Anthropologist Ronald Cohen attributes the intensity of empathetic reactions to the traditional family patterns that have existed here, patterns he describes as involving "intensive, frequent, and durable relations among members, especially when the children are small."[36] These conditions foster the development of deep emotional attachments and empathetic capacity, Cohen contends.

Speculation that certain regions of the brain play key roles in empathizing began with the case of Phineas Gage, an unlucky Vermont construction foreman who, after a blasting accident in 1848, ended up with an iron rod running from his face through his skull. The rod was successfully removed, and Gage lived a fairly healthy life, but the accident caused him to lose his empathy. While before the accident, Gage was widely considered a decent and polite fellow, afterward he became rude, uttered profanities, and showed no social inhibition. A century later, scientists examined Gage's skull and determined the rod had passed through the medial prefrontal cortex, a hub for the processing of social information. Surgical removal of brain structures also can occasionally produce the opposite effect, causing a person, through a reorganizing of neural circuits prompted by the surgery, to develop "hyper empathy"—and begin to report intense empathetic reactions to characters in novels, people seen on television, or people met in person. Mayo Clinic neurologist Dr. Joseph Sirven notes, "Neural substrates of complex emotions such as empathy are poorly understood."[37] But more is being learned about anatomical correlates of empathy all the time. With advances in imaging technology, researchers can now peer inside heads and observe the functioning of the "empathy circuit" of the brain. Magnetic resonance imaging (MRI) shows that at least ten interconnected regions of the brain are active during empathizing. Scans reveal less activity in these ten regions for low empathizers.[38]

Neuroscientists report that we understand others primarily by feeling what they are feeling, not because we are able to develop good theories to explain their actions. Recent research shows that neural networks in the brain of an empathizing person become activated when the person *mentally imitates* the actions of another. Remarkably, these networks fire in almost exactly the same way they would if the mental imitator were actually *performing* the observed act himself. Perception and evaluation, sometimes thought to be separate activities within the brain, are mixed together as a single process. As David Brooks notes in *The Social Animal*, the research suggests that "loops exist between brains" and that "invisible networks" can "fill the space" between thoughts and feelings in different minds.[39]

On average, women are better empathizers than men. In experiments in which subjects are given visual clues and then asked to guess a person's emotional states, women typically outperform men. Brain imaging shows that partial emotional clues set off a crazed flurry of activity in male brains as they struggle to make sense of them, while female brains light up in more defined places and generate answers with relative ease.[40] Research also suggests that women are the superior listeners. Women in conversations interrupt each other less than men and are more likely than men to talk about others.[41] (It's not at all clear, by the way, that the gender differences have a biological basis. Parents socialize their daughters to be more empathetic, and because women play a disproportionate role in child care, they develop better nurturance skills.)

While sex does seem to matter, intelligence does not. No more than 5% of a person's emotional perceptiveness, according to the results of one study, can be explained by IQ scores or other traditional measures of cognitive intelligence.[42]

CAN LAWYERS LEARN TO BE MORE EMPATHETIC?

We've seen that empathy allows lawyers to better understand their clients' problems, reduces miscommunication, and provides the basis for telling the stories of clients in more effective and compelling ways. Lawyers short on empathy might well ask whether they can increase their empathy, or whether their bad "empathy genes" or deficient family bonding have set their empathy quotient in stone. The honest answer is that the jury is still out on that question. Role-playing techniques, such as the psychodrama used at the Trial Lawyers College, might well increase empathy over the longer term, but there have been few, if any, controlled studies to justify drawing that conclusion with confidence. Sure, many graduates of TLC might *say* they now have more empathy, but do they really?

Research provides stronger evidence that emotion recognition, one of the two main components of empathy, can be improved than exists for the other component, empathetic response.[43] It seems that it is easier to teach people to pick up on the emotions another is experiencing than it is to teach them to respond to that person with an appropriate emotion of their own. Better emotion recognition will reduce miscommunications between a lawyer and client, but without appropriate emotional responses, your client might still think you an insensitive jerk.

Even though no training program can guarantee that it will turn a low empathizer into a high empathizer, there are simple steps to make the most of the empathy we do have and become better lawyers in the process. Below is a list of suggestions for improving your empathetic abilities.

How to Make the Most of Your Empathy: A Checklist

1. Give your client your full attention. Do not multitask when meeting with clients. Take steps to avoid interruptions and external distractions, such as noise.

2. Listen actively. Avoid thinking about what you will say next when your client is talking. Understanding should precede being understood.

3. Pay close attention to clients' clues (body language, tone of voice) so as to appropriately respond to their concerns.

4. Reflect your understanding of your client's emotional state. Acknowledge how your client's legal problem makes him feel.

5. Think of your client as a person, not just as a source of income, and be curious about your client's entire story.

6. Think of yourself as a coach as well as a provider of legal services. Recognize that part of your job is to move clients toward more positive emotions.

7. Avoid legal jargon, lectures, and long-winded answers. Pause between paragraphs to give clients time to process your explanations and their own emotions.

8. Ask clients open-ended questions. Ask for explanations and examples. Don't just ask leading questions.

9. If possible, meet clients in their environment rather than in a sterile law office.

10. Role-play and engage in simulation scenarios with colleagues to improve your empathetic response.

11. Communicate regularly with clients. Respond to their emotions and their expressed regrets. Ask them frequently if you are accurately perceiving their concerns and desires.

12. Use resources such as personality inventories to become more aware of your own strengths and weaknesses as a communicator.

THE CHALLENGE OF DEVELOPING EMPATHY IN LAW SCHOOLS

> *What we really experienced in law school was a lobotomy of sorts, one that anesthetizes the law student against his emotions and attempts to reduce law to some sort of science.*
>
> —Gerry Spence[44]

Recent studies, such as one showing precipitous drops in empathy among American college students, raise alarms. Whether it is increased social isolation, changing family patterns, Facebook, or a media emphasis on self-gratification, something is threatening our capacity for empathy, and the problem seems to be more acute in the United States than in some other countries. In the past decade, for example, while empathy levels fell dramatically among American college students, researchers in Denmark reported that measures of empathy among residents of that nation actually rose 9%.[45] The study of American college students, published in 2011, reported that empathy has declined dramatically among college students since 2000 and that empathy levels in today's college students are about 40% lower than those of college students two or three decades ago. The results were based on an extensive questionnaire that has been the basis for the Interpersonal Reactivity Index since it was first established in 1979. Over a period of more than thirty years, students responded to statements such as "I sometimes try to understand my friends better by imagining how things look from their perspective," or "I often have tender, concerned feelings for people less fortunate than me."[46]

Study author Sara H. Konrath of the University of Michigan said that the study provided no reason for the empathy decline, but she offered the theory that increased social isolation might be a major culprit.[47] Other studies have shown that people who live alone and don't join groups tend to exhibit less empathy than more socially connected people, she noted. A study conducted at Keele University in England, for example, showed that lonely people are more likely to cheat in laboratory games by taking advantage of the trust of others. Another study, conducted at the University of Iowa, indicated that socially isolated people, compared to more connected people, are apt to evaluate others more negatively after interacting with them.[48]

Konrath observed that the results of the college student study may not come as a surprise. "Many people," she said, "see the current group of college students, sometimes called 'Generation Me,' as one of the most self-centered, narcissistic, competitive, confident, and individualistic in recent history."[49] A University of Michigan graduate student who assisted with the study, Edward O'Brien, made the obvious connection: "It is not surprising that this growing emphasis on self is accompanied by a corresponding devaluation of others."[50] O'Brien suggested that the drop in empathy might also be related to the rise of Facebook. "The ease of having 'friends' online might make people more likely to just tune out when they don't feel like responding to others' problems, a behavior that could carry offline," he noted.[51] Members of the University of Michigan research team speculated that unrealistic expectations of success and increased competitiveness in the job market might be other factors in declining empathy levels. Students just might be too worried about their own problems to pay much attention to the problems of others.

If empathy levels are declining in American college students, they probably are among law students as well. When combined with studies showing the importance clients place on lawyers caring about them and their problems, that's bad news.

Young people entering law schools have never been particularly empathetic, especially when compared to, for example, people choosing to enter nursing schools or the ministry. Law students, when scored on the Myers-Briggs assessment, a commonly used personality test, generally turn out to be Thinkers, not Feelers. Although placement on the Thinkers-Feelers spectrum does not directly correlate with empathy quotients, there is a strong correspondence. Thinkers, more likely to be thick-skinned and perceived to be insensitive, often strive to base their decisions on logic and objective principles. Feelers, on the other hand, are typically thin-skinned and sensitive to the feelings of others, and focus in their decision making on how their actions will affect other people. For the Thinker, justice is applying neutral principles, while for Feelers, justice means doing right for a particular person. While most people in the general population are Feelers (52.5%), Feelers constitute only 26.5% of law students. Among male law students, the percentage of Feelers is a paltry 19%. The Feelers who do go to law school generally receive lower grades than the Thinkers and are four times more likely to drop out. If Feelers become a larger segment of the law school population, there will be a need to reconsider both current classroom environments and how schools evaluate student performance.[52]

If law schools wanted to turn out more empathetic lawyers, there are simple ways to achieve that goal. They could, for example, seek to admit a closer balance between Thinkers and Feelers by accepting more female applicants and fewer male applicants—although there are reasons (including constitutional ones) why a gender preference might not be a good idea. Law schools could also, of course, adopt an affirmative action policy for applicants qualifying as Feelers on the Myers-Briggs—but there's not a snowball's chance in hell of that happening. Most likely, extending preferences based on Myers-Briggs results is an unethical use of the instrument. A third, less controversial approach, would be to reduce the role LSAT scores play in admission decisions. The LSAT rewards—above all else—logical thinking skills, and the test is largely responsible for making law schools even more into enclaves for Thinkers than they otherwise would be. What seems likely, at most, on the admissions front is that some schools will be persuaded to tinker with the weight given LSAT scores, allowing for somewhat more consideration for experiences of applicants demonstrating what is commonly called "emotional intelligence."

With entering student populations that are likely to continue to tilt slightly toward the lower end of the empathy spectrum, law schools will not suddenly start cranking out highly empathetic graduates. Turning a bunch of Thinkers into Feelers is not easy; many would say it is inadvisable. Rather than try to change personality types, which tend to be fairly consistent over a lifetime, law schools could focus on better preparing students of all types to empathize more with future clients and others they will encounter in their professional careers. One professor ready to meet that challenge is Kristin B. Gerdy, director of the Advocacy Program at Brigham Young University. Professor Gerdy shares the belief of Karen J. Mathis, former president of the American Bar Association, who said in her inaugural address, "caring is as much a part of the legal profession as intelligence."[53] "True caring," in the view of Mathis, "cannot be reduced to problem solving." Rather, "an orientation to caring incorporates the attributes of attentiveness, honesty, patience, respect, compassion, trustworthiness, and sensitivity into all aspects of moral behavior."[54] "Thinking like a lawyer" is all well and good, but the real heart of law practice, Gerdy believes, is "understanding clients and exercising empathy and compassion."[55]

Gerdy's goal is to bring empathy instruction and practice into the first year of law school. She calls on schools to offer students a more client-centered education, an idea also put forward in the Carnegie Report's critique of legal education.[56] Too often, she believes, the focus in legal education is on appellate cases, edited in such a way as to emphasize legal doctrine and deemphasize those people affected by it. Students might easily forget that a court's decision has real consequences for real people. Every sterile appellate decision students read in law school courses is the story of people whose lives are changed in some way by their legal case. Gerdy offers several suggestions for making law school education more client-centered. She suggests small group discussions in classes, where students are asked to put themselves in a client's position. She advises ditching traditional casebooks in favor of books that offer clients' stories or personal reflections of lawyers. She proposes, as a way of increasing student sensitivity, assigning reading from novels such as Dickens's *Bleak House* or Kafka's *The Trial*. Reading fiction, as John Connolly suggested in *The Book of Lost Things*, "encourages us to view the world in new and challenging ways....It allows us to inhabit the consciousness of another, which is precursor to empathy."[57] The suggestion that reading a bit of Jane Austen or Anton Chekhov could substantially increase empathy might have its skeptics, but a 2013 study conducted by researchers Emanuele Castano and David Comer Kidd backs up the claim. The researchers found that after just three to five minutes of reading literary fiction—emotionally complex literature that encourages readers to draw inferences about character—subjects were able to much more accurately decode emotions from looking at thirty-six photographs of pairs of eyes. Subjects who read nothing, or read nonfiction or less nuanced popular fiction, showed no improvement in their empathetic recognition. Nicholas Humphrey, a Cambridge University psychologist, called the results "astonishing," especially the results that "separate off literary fiction, and demonstrate that it has different effects from other forms of reading."[58]

Near the top of any school's strategies for training students to interact in a more positive way with clients, Gerdy contends, should be providing opportunities for students to have client interaction, such as they might have by conducting interviews of people with real legal problems. Finally, she asks law professors to think about providing students opportunities for self-reflection, such as by assigning students the task of writing a personal narrative—"My Professional Journey" might be the title.[59] This is a pedagogical tool sometimes used in clinical education, where most of our authentic empathy education occurs. Expanding the scope of clinics and offering other opportunities for experiential learning provides possibly the best hope for students to cultivate—and practice—empathy and related virtues.

Ian Gallacher, a law professor at Syracuse University, warns that law schools must change if they hope to produce graduates who will demonstrate the care and compassion that their clients so want. "If we succeed in making students think like lawyers," he writes, "we make it difficult if not impossible for them to think like non-lawyers...[and] difficult to communicate with [their clients] as they must do much of the time."[60]

Gerry Spence wishes he could "unteach most of the things they learn in school." In his opinion, students "are trained to deny their emotions and humanness," yet they'll be "called upon to represent human beings who are emotional." Spence offers his own ideas for an innovative law school curriculum. "I would teach them to paint. And to dance, so they would learn about their bodies. I want them to experience poetry. Then I'd send them to prison so they'd see what it's like, what a terrible burden it is they really have. I would take them to see an autopsy and to watch a mortician prepare people for the grave—and thus have them realize what it is to be afraid and alone."[61] Art classes, freestyle dancing, prison camp-outs, and sessions in funeral homes would, to say the least, be an interesting departure from the monotony of Socratic classrooms, but don't expect any law school deans to jump up and say, "Amen!"

IS MORE EMPATHY ALWAYS BETTER?

If empathy is good—for lawyers and for people generally—is having more empathy always better? Not always, and the term "empathetic over-arousal" is used to describe people whose empathy is getting in the way of getting things done. One of the risks faced by highly empathetic lawyers is that they might choose to limit or avoid contact with clients who suffer from especially severe emotional pain, simply to avoid the distress caused by their own empathetic reactions. Another potential problem for lawyers with high empathy is the burnout that can come from repeatedly sharing the burden of their clients' pain. Finally, empathetic lawyers, out of a very natural strong desire to help clients whose pain they share, are at higher than average risk of cutting ethical corners. Just as too little empathy threatens the social fabric, too much empathy can be a problem as well.

Highly empathetic people tend to seek escape from situations that produce distressing empathetic reactions. They turn off the news when the story about the massacre in the Middle East comes on, and they stay away from violent movies. When work requires dealing with someone's serious pain, their empathy becomes a problem. Psychologist Nancy Eisenberg reports, for example, that "highly empathetic nurses tend to avoid terminally ill patients."[62] An intensely empathetic rescuer might be so overcome with distress while attempting to save victims of a mass disaster that he or she cannot finish the job.

In the practice of law, too much empathy can lead to problems for lawyers with death row clients, or clients who suffered serious permanent injuries as the result of an accident. To do their job effectively, lawyers must overcome their strong desire to avoid contact with those clients. Judges, too, sometimes report that feelings for defendants make their job painful. An empathetic judge, distressed by the task of criminal sentencing, may choose to resign rather than endure the pain any longer. Mandatory minimum sentences, which cause judges to sometimes impose long sentences on people convicted of rather minor offenses, led more than one federal judge to leave the bench. One federal district judge from California, hanging up his robe for the last time, told reporters: "I just can't do it anymore."[63]

In addition to being at a greater risk of a flight response, high-empathy lawyers also risk being led by their feelings for their clients to cut ethical corners. People are inclined to act dishonestly, but just enough to make it possible for them to continue to think of themselves as basically honest. Dan Ariely, in his book *The (Honest) Truth About Dishonesty*, discovered that a desire to help someone else we care about significantly increases our level of cheating. We're actually more likely to bend or break rules to help someone else than we are to help ourselves, apparently because it is easier to do so and still maintain our positive self-image. As Ariely observed, "Sadly, it seems that even altruism can have a dark side."[64] People with above average empathy levels also might have an above average tendency to cheat, and we all know the practice of law provides ample opportunities for that.

Occasionally, a lawyer will identify so completely with clients that he or she loses the perspective needed to argue a client's case effectively. That happened in the famous Chicago 8 trial, in which William Kunstler represented defendants accused of inciting riots at the 1968 Democratic National Convention. It's hard to read the transcript of that infamous trial before Judge Julius Hoffman without concluding that Kunstler felt his clients' pain almost as if it were his own. Time and time again, Kunstler responded to Judge Hoffman's adverse rulings by lashing back, earning a four-plus year contempt sentence (later overturned by the Seventh Circuit) as a result. For example, when Bobby Seale was ordered restrained because of repeated courtroom outbursts, Kunstler called the restraints "medieval torture" and blamed the judge: "Your Honor, this is an unholy disgrace to the law that is going on in this courtroom and I as an American lawyer feel a disgrace created by nothing other than what you have done to this man."[65] Later in the trial, when Judge Hoffman refused a defense request to call former Attorney General Ramsey Clark as a witness, Kunstler announced, "I am outraged to be in this court before you....I know that doesn't mean much in this court when the Attorney General of the United States walked out of here with his lips so tight he could hardly breathe, and if you could see the expression on his face, you would know, and his wife informed me he never felt such anger at the United States Government as at not being able to testify on that stand."[66] Kunstler ended his no-holds-barred speech (punctuated by voices in the courtroom crowd shouting, "Right on!") with the words, "I am going to turn back to my seat with the realization that everything I have learned throughout my life has come to naught, that there is no meaning in this court, and there is no law in this court, and these men are going to jail by virtue of a legal lynching, and that your Honor is wholly responsible for that, and if this is what your career is going to end on, if this is what your pride is going to be built on, I can only say to your Honor, 'Good luck to you.'"[67] Kunstler's strong identification with his clients stoked the fire in his belly and made for entertaining theater. Unfortunately, however, it also harmed his clients' case.

Empathize, yes, but regulate your emotions. As a lawyer, you need to have sufficient detachment to recognize that your clients usually benefit more from a respectful, reasoned response to a judge than an angry one. A good lawyer is empathetic but also understands his proper role. Being a good lawyer is not the same as being your client's closest friend. There will be times when it is necessary to step back and objectively evaluate the strengths and weaknesses of the case, unaffected by the stew of emotions your client might be experiencing. Stepping back from your client's situation allows you to be the critical eye that can provide a balanced assessment that the client needs. [68] However much you might see justice as on your client's side, you should remain cognizant of all of the obstacles that stand in the way of achieving a just result for her or him. Your client wants empathy, but also wants calmness and distance. As it was with the porridge in "Goldilocks," levels of empathy can be either too cold or too hot. Too little empathy leads to passivity or antisocial conduct. Too much empathy can either cause people to avoid addressing the dire needs of troubled people or to cross ethical boundaries in their zealous efforts to help. To reduce the likelihood of succumbing to the "flight response" triggered by distress over a client's pain, become conscious of your growing urge to avoid contact with a client, learn to pull back a bit and remind yourself that sometimes you have to turn off your empathy switch and get the job done.

THE EMPATHY DEBATE

Although there is general agreement that empathizing, at least to a degree, with clients is a good thing, that's about as far as agreement goes. The larger question of what is the proper role of empathy in the legal system turns out to be a surprisingly controversial subject.

In criminal trials, for example, it has been suggested that juror empathy sometimes subverts justice. Defendants who show sadness receive, on average, lighter sentences than defendants who demonstrate neutral emotion, even when their crimes are equally serious.[69] The empathy that jurors show for crime victims has been offered as an explanation for the high frequency of death verdicts returned when the victims share the race of the jurors, compared to cases in which the jurors and victim are of different races. Although the race of the defendant in a capital case is not predictive of whether a death penalty verdict is returned, the race of the victim is. Killing whites in America is far more likely to get you executed than killing blacks.[70] Why? Because, in general, jurors (who have until now been generally white) empathize most readily with persons with whom they share common characteristics, including race. Some writers have gone so far as to identify empathy as the "source of racism" because of the evidence suggesting that people have higher levels of empathy for others of the same race or ethnicity.[71]

Critics also complain that empathetic jurors are to blame for outrageously high awards in some personal injury lawsuits. They point fingers at plaintiffs' attorneys who tell moving stories that make tears flow and awards balloon beyond all reason, as emotionally overcome jurors ignore the law and dish out millions to sympathetic parties. Research by Jonathan Baron and Ilana Ritov suggests that stories that trigger empathy create a powerful desire to punish parties believed to be responsible for deaths or injuries. Subjects in their study were told that the defective vaccine of a drug manufacturer caused the death of a child and were asked what to do about it. Half the subjects were told that a heavy fine would encourage the manufacturer to develop safer vaccines, and half were told that the heavy fine would discourage the manufacturer from making the vaccine at all and, since no safer drugs were available, more deaths would result. For most subjects, the consequences of the hefty fine didn't affect their decisions. Fine the company heavily regardless of consequences was the call.[72] The debate over empathy in the jury room will never end.

However disputed the proper role of empathy in the jury room may be, it pales in comparison to the ongoing debate over the proper role, if any, of empathy in judging. Even if you are not a judge, understanding what role empathy plays in judging is important. Judges, after all, often will decide the fate of your clients, and you need to know what arguments are likely to move them and what arguments will instead strike them as irrelevant mush.

DO WE WANT JUDGES TO BE EMPATHETIC?

In April 2009, President Obama surprised reporters gathered for a routine press briefing by interrupting his press secretary, Robert Gibbs, to announce that Justice David Souter had just told him of his plans to retire at the end of the current term. The president offered a description of the type of person he hoped could be found to fill the vacancy. It included a lot of the expected stuff about high ethical standards, legal experience, and devotion to the rule of law. But the president added another qualification to the standard list. He said, "I will seek someone who understands that justice isn't about some abstract legal theory or footnote in a casebook; it's also about how our laws affect the daily reality of people's lives....I view that quality of empathy, of understanding and identifying with people's hopes and struggles, as an essential ingredient for arriving at just decisions and outcomes."[73]

Obama's use of the word "empathy" provoked a firestorm of criticism from conservatives. Wendy Long, legal counsel to the Judicial Confirmation Network and a former clerk for Justice Thomas, countered that the president should instead look for someone who has "empathy, if you will, for the law only" and who will "rule based on the law." Long said, "That's why Lady Justice is depicted as blind-folded. Lady Justice doesn't have empathy for anyone. She rules strictly based on the law."[74]

Republican senators warned that any judicial nominee predisposed to use empathy in deciding cases would be filibustered. Jon Kyl of Arizona, a member of the Senate Judiciary Committee, pledged to block any nominee who "takes into account human suffering and employs empathy from the bench."[75] Alabama Senator Jeff Sessions called the suggestion that judges use their capacity for empathy "deeply troubling." Sessions declared, "I fear this empathy standard is another step down the path to a more cynical, relativistic, results-oriented world where words and laws have no fixed meaning."[76]

The national debate that followed—*How much empathy do we want from our judges?*—reminded some legal scholars of debates that had erupted in the pages of U.S. Supreme Court opinions. One justice whom no one could accuse of lacking empathy was Harry Blackmun. To some critics, Blackmun's opinions were "personal statements" long on empathy and short on reasoned analysis. The justice—whom President Nixon referred to as one of his presidency's "biggest mistakes"—willingly conceded that the trajectory of jurisprudence interested him less than doing justice in the case before him. "I'm no jurisprude," Blackmun told one interviewer.[77] He added, "We're dealing with people—the life, liberty, and property of people. And because I grew up in poor surroundings, I know there's another world out there we sometimes forget about."[78]

Few cases better illustrate how Justice Blackmun's empathetic views differed from the views of many of his colleagues than the case of *DeShaney v. Winnebago County Department of Social Services*.[79] In 1989, the Supreme Court considered the claim of a boy, Joshua DeShaney, who had been beaten and permanently injured by his father. The beating occurred after local officials, who had received numerous credible complaints that Joshua was being abused by his father, allowed the boy to remain in his father's custody. The boy and his mother sued the department of human services, arguing that their failure to act deprived Joshua of his liberty in violation of the Due Process Clause of the Fourteenth Amendment. The Supreme Court held that the Constitution afforded no such protection.

Justice William H. Rehnquist, writing for the Court, conceded that "the facts of this case are undeniably tragic." County authorities first learned that Joshua might be a victim of child abuse when the second wife of his father, Randy, complained to the police that Randy had beaten Joshua and was "a prime case for child abuse."[80] A year later, Joshua was admitted to a local hospital with multiple bruises and abrasions. The examining physician suspected child abuse and notified the Department (DSS), but authorities returned Joshua to Randy's custody. A month later, emergency room personnel called the DSS caseworker handling Joshua's case to report that he had once again been treated for suspicious injuries. Still, the Department did nothing. For the next half year, the caseworker made monthly visits to the DeShaney home. She dutifully recorded in her files what she saw, including a number of new suspicious injuries on Joshua's head. But she did nothing more. A few months later, the emergency room notified DSS once again that Joshua had been treated for injuries most likely resulting from child abuse. Twice the caseworker visited the DeShaney home, but she was told that Joshua was too ill to see her. *Still* DSS took no action. Finally, Randy DeShaney pummeled his four-year-old son into a coma, causing brain damage so severe that Joshua is expected to spend the rest of his life confined to an institution for the profoundly retarded.

The majority of the Court saw it as their job to put aside feelings for Joshua and dispassionately determine whether the text of the Due Process Clause and existing case law supported the finding that DSS violated the Constitution. They concluded it did not. Justice Rehnquist wrote, "[N]othing in the language of the Due Process Clause itself requires the State to protect the life, liberty, and property of its citizens against invasion by private actors."[81] As the Court saw it, the Due Process Clause's purpose "was to protect the people from the State, not to ensure that the State protected them from each other." Cases suggesting otherwise, Justice Rehnquist wrote, are distinguishable and "afford petitioners no help."

Justice Rehnquist conceded that he felt sorry for Joshua and his mother, but emphasized that it was the Court's duty not to give into the impulse to allow compensation unless doing so found sufficient support in the law. "Judges and lawyers, like other humans, are moved by natural sympathy in a case like this to find a way for Joshua and his mother to receive adequate compensation for the grievous harm inflicted upon them," Rehnquist wrote. "But before yielding to that impulse, it is well to remember once again that the harm was inflicted not by the State of Wisconsin, but by Joshua's father. The most that can be said of the state functionaries in this case is that they stood by and did nothing when suspicious circumstances dictated a more active role for them."[82]

The dissenters in *DeShaney* included the Court's three most liberal members at the time, Justices Brennan, Marshall, and Blackmun. Justice Blackmun, in his dissent, accused the Court of lacking empathy. "Today," Blackmun wrote, "the Court purports to be the dispassionate oracle of the law, unmoved by 'natural sympathy.' [I]n this pretense, the Court itself retreats into a sterile formalism which prevents it from recognizing either the facts of the case before it or the legal norms that should apply to those facts." Blackmun called the Court's "sharp and rigid line between action and inaction" "formalistic reasoning" which "has no place in the interpretation of the broad and stirring Clauses of the Fourteenth Amendment. Indeed, I submit that these Clauses were designed, at least in part, to undo the formalistic legal reasoning that infected antebellum jurisprudence." Continuing his assault on the bloodless analysis of the majority, Blackmun wrote, "Like the antebellum judges who denied relief to fugitive slaves, the Court today claims that its decision, however harsh, is compelled by existing legal doctrine. On the contrary, the question presented by this case is an open one, and our Fourteenth Amendment precedents may be read more broadly or narrowly depending upon how one chooses to read them. Faced with the choice, I would adopt a 'sympathetic' reading, one which comports with dictates of fundamental justice and recognizes that compassion need not be exiled from the province of judging."[83]

Two simple words in Blackmun's dissent jump out at the reader: "Poor Joshua!" With those words, and that exclamation point, Justice Blackmun—for better or worse—clearly puts himself into the ranks of empathetic judges. Of course, that is not to say the six justices in the majority in *DeShaney* lacked empathy, only that they saw as their obligation to put aside their emotions and decide the case the best they could on the law and law alone. "We might like to decide for Joshua," the Court seemed to be saying, "but the law won't let us do it."

It is not the proper role of judges to rule in favor of the person they want to win. Judge Richard Posner is surely right when he contends that "unlike jurors [or] children," judges must "discipline themselves to respond to the problems before them with careful, linear rationality."[84] Posner warns that "a jurisprudence of empathy can foster short-sighted justice because the power to enter imaginatively into another person's outlook, emotions, and experiences diminishes with physical, social, and temporal distance."[85] But the law often is ambiguous, case law and text can point in opposite directions, and sometimes conscientious judges can plausibly find the basis for deciding cases either of two ways. When the balance is even, or nearly so, is it appropriate for a judge to allow his or her emotions to tip it one way or the other? Is there a better tiebreaker? That, ultimately, is the question that should be at the heart of the debate about empathy and judging.

We want our judges to understand their role, but we should also want them to feel. Yale law professor Charles A. Reich clerked for Supreme Court Justice Hugo Black. In a 2010 law review article, Professor Reich commended Justice Black for always being "acutely sensitive to the injury done to any individual" in any given case.[86] Reich recalled that when he and a fellow clerk discussed pending cases with Black, "I liked to sit back and watch the Judge's expressive face register his feelings. When we discussed a case where power had been abused and an individual had suffered harm, the Judge's face showed pain and anger." Reich lamented that in his own law experience as a law student, "My teachers made law seem like a game or even a joke, and any answer was just as acceptable as the opposite answer." This, he said, made him and his fellow students feel "cynical and disillusioned about the law as a profession." He wishes today that his own students "could have shared my experience in the Judge's study."[87] If they could, he suggested, their idealism might be renewed.

The takeaway from this debate for lawyers is that not all judges, whether serving on state trial courts or the U.S. Supreme Court, think alike, and it is important to know your judges, especially the ones whose votes are critical to a positive outcome for your client. Some judges can be moved by sympathy for your client and it's your job to try to move them. Other judges will resent what they consider to be emotional pitches for their votes and might punish you for making them. When you have judges of both stripes on the same court, it can be a delicate balancing act.

EMPATHY AND MORAL ACTION

While empathy orients us toward moral action, it alone is often insufficient to compel us to do the right thing, especially when there is a personal cost to be paid. Some Nazi prison guards shed tears as they executed Jewish women and children, but they did it nonetheless. Some judges of the Third Reich felt sad and remorseful as they ordered Jews to be sterilized or packed off to concentration camps. In Stanley Milgram's famous experiment, where subjects were told by a scientist in a lab coat to administer what they thought were electrical shocks, subjects anguished as they were told to keep pushing buttons with ever more dire warnings ("moderate shock," "intense shock," "XXX"), but still they kept following orders. When they heard screams or pleas for life coming from the next room, some subjects asked the scientist if they could stop, but when he replied with words like "the experiment must continue," most kept on going.[88] Being empathetic without the right emotions and without having the right moral codes in place won't get the job done.[89] Philosopher Jesse Prinz concludes that research shows empathy to be a thin reed that rarely stands up to personal concerns. "These studies," he says, "suggest that empathy is not a major player when it comes to moral motivation. Its contribution is negligible in children, modest in adults, and nonexistent when costs are significant."[90] A weak correlation with pro-social behavior appears only when the behavior comes with little personal cost.[91] Empathy won't produce courageous moral action unless it is accompanied by moral judgments—and moral judgments, according to Prinz, "contain emotions such as anger, disgust, guilt, and shame."[92] Empathy may be an important capacity for lawyers, but is not the solution to our moral problems.

At best, empathy makes us worry about the welfare of another, but when we act courageously, whether to prevent an injustice or save a child, we are propelled by emotions and, ultimately, a *sense of obligation*. In the next chapter, we consider what it takes to become a courageous lawyer. Law's heroes, we'll see, have life-structuring codes, not just feelings of empathy.

CHAPTER 2

The Good Lawyer Is Courageous

*In a lawyer, courage is a muscle. You develop courage by exercising it.
Sitting on the fence is not practice for standing up.*
—Professor Pamela S. Karlan

COURAGE IS A VIRTUE MORE OFTEN ASSOCIATED WITH, say, first responders and members of the military than it is with people who carry briefcases. Some people might even suggest that it isn't necessary to be courageous to be a good lawyer—and if courage meant physical courage only, they might well be right. Lawyers have been accused of battling windmills (and a few environmental lawyers representing wealthy seaside landowners in the Northeast have actually done so), but rarely in the practice of law—where words are the weapon of choice—is physical courage required. While some lawyers, such as prosecutors, accept some physical risks as part of their job, the greatest work-related risk most lawyers face is the drive to their offices.

But courage comes in different forms, and the courage most good lawyers have in abundance is of the moral, not physical, variety: they have the ability to do the right thing when doing the right thing isn't easy. In addition to physical and moral courage, there is a third form of courage, one that might be called "psychological courage," that good lawyers must call on from time to time. Psychological courage enables one to overcome personal fears (such as facing a jury trial for the first time) or a debilitating addiction. In this chapter, however, our primary focus is on moral courage—what it is and how we can get more of it.

Consider, for example, the sort of courage it takes to represent a hated criminal defendant. When John Adams agreed to represent eight British soldiers and their captain, who faced charges of murder for the deaths of five American civilians near the Custom House in downtown Boston in 1770, he understood he would pay a personal price for his decision. As a consequence of his spending nine months trying to save the lives of the British accused of "the massacre" in Boston, Adams saw his law practice shrink in half. Decades later, he observed that his legal work—for the modest sum of eighteen guineas—on behalf of the British soldiers made him, to many of his fellow citizens, "an enemy of my country." Despite the personal cost, Adams remained for the rest of his life fiercely proud of his efforts in representing Captain Preston and his soldiers. His diary and autobiography included this recollection of his work: "The part I took in defense of Captain Preston and the soldiers, procured me anxiety and obloquy enough. It was, however, one of the most gallant, generous, manly and disinterested actions of my whole life, and one of the best pieces of service I ever rendered my country."[1]

One of "the most gallant, generous, manly, and disinterested actions" in the life of John Adams? John Adams, who undertook a perilous sea voyage to France that likely meant the difference between winning and losing the Revolutionary War? And "one of the best pieces of service" he ever rendered his country by the man, who, as the second president of the United States, both steered a difficult course that kept us out of a potentially calamitous war with France and England and appointed the great John Marshall as Chief Justice of the United States? Well, yes—and here's why Adams is right. Adams believed in—and acted upon—a principle that all lawyers should hold dear: the principle that every person (citizen or noncitizen, popular or unpopular, hero or scumbag) is entitled to a defense. Unfortunately, it's not a principle widely accepted by nonlawyers, and therein is the source of Adams's gallantry. Knowing full well that his representation would come at a substantial personal cost, he did it anyway. Assuming that his recollection of events was correct, other Boston lawyers chose the easier path of just saying "no."

Moreover, Adams did not put in only a passable minimum effort; he represented his clients to the best of his considerable ability. Much of his satisfaction with his work came from the successful results he produced for his clients. He came to believe, as did twenty-four jurors of Boston, that what happened near the Custom House that March day in 1770 was not murder. "Judgment of death against those soldiers would have been as foul a stain upon this country as the executions of the Quakers or Witches, anciently," Adams wrote. "As the evidence was, the verdict of the jury (seven acquittals and, for two privates, convictions on the lesser charge of manslaughter) was exactly right."[2]

We can only speculate about what gave Adams the courage to represent the British soldiers when many other Boston lawyers said "no." Perhaps he felt outrage at what he sensed was a lynch mob mentality taking hold of the city. Perhaps he anticipated the shame and guilt he would feel if he declined to take the case. What we do know, from our modern understanding of moral action, is that emotion is at the bottom of courage—emotion that is strong enough to outbalance the personal costs that normally drive decision making.

The key role courage plays in producing good work or making a good life has been recognized by writers across many fields. The American poet and author, Maya Angelou, called courage "the most important of all the virtues, because without courage you can't practice any other virtue consistently."[3] Thomas Aquinas categorized courage, which he referred to as "fortitude," as one of the four cardinal virtues, although he put it in third place in terms of its importance, ranking it below "prudence" and "justice," but ahead of "temperance."[4] Psychologists Christopher Peterson and Martin Seligman, in *Character, Strengths, and Virtues*, a widely used handbook that proposes a uniform way of classifying positive traits, make no call as to whether courage deserves the gold or the bronze medal in the competition among virtues.[5] They do, however, identify courage as one of the six basic strengths of a thriving person. Peterson and Seligman broadly conceive of courage as including emotional strengths "that entail the exercise of the will to accomplish goals in the face of opposition, external or internal."[6]

As is the case with most virtues, courage is perceived best in the stories of those who have it in abundance. In the turbulent Deep South of the early 1960s, representing the federal government in civil rights cases required great courage, as the following story of one remarkable Justice Department attorney from that era makes clear.

A PROFILE IN COURAGE

In a windowless office in a sprawling building owned by the Ingersoll Machine Milling Company in Rockford, Illinois, I interviewed a lawyer who, at various times during his seven-year career at the Justice Department in the 1960s, stared down a segregationist governor, trekked across southern cornfields looking for blacks who had been denied their right to vote, singlehandedly prevented a confrontation between rioters and police officers just before it could have turned deadly, walked with demonstrators on a march from Montgomery to Selma, faced off with a racist federal judge who called black witnesses in his voter registration trial "a bunch of chimpanzees," guarded (as bullets and rocks flew through the nighttime air) James Meredith during his first night in a dormitory on the University of Mississippi campus, and shrugged off death threats to head the government's prosecution of eighteen

Ku Klux Klan members in the well-known "Mississippi Burning" trial. Surely, you'd think, a lawyer who had all those adventures would be a household name. But you'd be wrong. You probably never heard of John Michael Doar.

I first became curious about John Doar from teaching about his role as lead prosecutor in the "Mississippi Burning" trial in my Famous Trials seminar. A long FBI investigation into the deaths of three civil rights workers near Philadelphia, Mississippi, led to federal charges being filed against a sheriff, a deputy sheriff, and sixteen other white men. A newspaper account of the 1967 trial in Meridian, Mississippi, reported that when one of the defense attorneys, in his opening argument, told jurors that Doar was the same despised Justice Department lawyer who "forced the Negro James Meredith into the University of Mississippi," Doar nodded his head in agreement.[7] I needed to learn more about this guy.

INTO NO-MAN'S LAND

Doar turned out to be an even more courageous lawyer than I ever imagined. In a June 1963 edition of the *New York Times*, I found a front-page picture that blew me away.[8] Doar, dressed in a white shirt and tie, stood alone in a street between a crowd of black protesters and a line of helmeted Jackson, Mississippi, police officers, all white and all wielding batons. His arms are extended outward, palms out, in an obvious attempt to calm the protesters (Figure 2.1).

The demonstration in Jackson came three days after the assassination in that city of Medgar Evers, a national field secretary for the National Association for the Advancement of Colored People (NAACP), killed by a sniper in his driveway as he walked from his car to the front door of his house. A silent protest march followed Evers's funeral, and when the march ended, several hundred young blacks refused to disperse. They swept down Farish Street toward the main white business district singing "This Little

FIGURE 2.1. John Doar calms protesters in Jackson, Mississippi, June 1963. Credit: Associated Press Wirephoto.

Light of Mine" and clapping hands. A battalion of riot police in short-sleeved shirts and sunglasses formed a line to stop them. When a deputy police chief ordered the demonstrators to go home, some young demonstrators began throwing bricks, stones, and bottles in the direction of the police line. "We want the killer! We want the killer!" the crowd chanted. Demonstrators in the rear began stomping their feet and shouting "Freedom! Freedom! Freedom!" Police dogs went berserk and were yanked back by their leashes. Cursing police officers drew pistols or began swinging riot clubs. Merchants along Farish Street hurriedly bolted their doors.

Into the no-man's land between the police and the rioters walked John Doar. The crowd stopped for a moment, stunned as though they were watching a ghost. Then bottles, bricks, and other missiles began crashing around him. Doar called to the crowd. "You're not going to win anything with bottles and bricks," he said. He could hardly be heard above the roar of the crowd, which began to encircle him. A man with a tire iron lifted it and took aim at Doar's head. An angry black woman yelled in his face, "We get our rumps shot up!" She asked with sarcastic disgust, "Are we gonna wait for the Justice Department?" Doar shouted, "Hold it! Is there someone here who can speak for you people?" One black youth emerged from the demonstrators and joined Doar in the street. "This man is right," the youth said, pointing at Doar. Doar shouted, "My name is John Doar—D-O-A-R. I'm from the Justice Department, and anybody around here knows I stand for what is right." He walked toward the mob, calling—begging—for the crowd to disperse. "Medgar Evers wouldn't want it this way," he hollered. In an alley, a CORE worker grabbed a teenager with a rifle who was taking aim at Doar. "Hold hands with me and help us move these people along," Doar said to some nearby protest-ers. A few people linked hands and they slowly began to push the mob back from the police line. With the possible massacre averted, police began removing barricades and a motorized streetsweeper whisked up the broken glass and other hurled debris. The next day, President Kennedy called Doar to congratulate him on his defus-ing of the dangerous situation.[9] One observer, later a reporter for *Newsweek*, called Doar's actions in Jackson "the bravest thing I ever saw a human being do."[10] An account of the incident ran in the *New Orleans Times-Picayune* under the title, "The Day John Doar Saved Mississippi."[11]

Nearly forty years later, when I asked him about that frighten-ing day in Jackson, Doar broke into a still-youthful-looking smile. "I wasn't concerned about my safety—perhaps I should have been. I never was hit by any of the projectiles. They were sort of skipping in front of me."[12]

Trekking across Cornfields

Most of Doar's work at the Justice Department focused on voting rights cases. Within months of his arrival at the Department in 1960, Doar became impatient with standard bureaucratic responses to problems. Justice Department lawyers used what were called "coaching" or "box" memos to obtain from FBI agents the facts necessary to develop voting rights cases. Sometimes 200 pages in length, these memos dictated to agents the specific questions and follow-up questions they were to ask frustrated black voter applicants. Doar realized that it would be more efficient to do his own investigations.

His first trip took him to rural western Tennessee, where black sharecroppers had complained that farmers evicted them when they tried to register. The Justice Department needed to determine whether the complaints were justified and how many blacks were affected. Doar's first night in Tennessee was something of an epiphany. He walked into the dim light of a rural clapboard church filled with Negro sharecroppers and announced to the crowd that he was there to help. How many people, he asked, had received eviction notices? To his great surprise, virtually every hand went up. "I was the first Justice Department lawyer who went down South to see what the facts were for myself," he said.[13] He often traveled incognito so as not to alert local whites to the presence of an official from the hated Department of Justice. Wearing khaki pants, a work shirt, and old boots, he trekked across cornfields and knocked on doors in search of rejected black voters.

"I spent a great deal of each year on the road," Doar said in his plainspoken, understated way. In fact, his frenetic pace of traveling was legendary. "John Doar's in Birmingham," one reporter announced at dinner. "No, he's in New Orleans," another reporter said. "No," chimed in a third, "I saw him here in Jackson." "You're all right," said a fourth reporter. "He was in Birmingham this morning, argued a case in New Orleans this afternoon and arrived in Jackson tonight."[14]

Several voting rights cases brought Doar before federal judge William H. Cox, an ardent segregationist, who owed his position on the federal bench to his friend and Ole Miss Law School roommate, James Eastland, chair of the Senate Judiciary Committee. When President Kennedy wanted to nominate NAACP counsel

Thurgood Marshall for a position on the U.S. Court of Appeals for the Second Circuit, Eastland proposed a deal to Robert Kennedy: "Tell your brother that if he will give me Harold Cox I will give him the nigger."

Unsurprisingly, Judge Cox did not exactly welcome Doar into his courtroom with open arms. A 1963 letter from Cox to Doar, written in response to Doar's request to give the voting rights case of *United States v. Mississippi* immediate attention, is revealing of their relationship. Cox complained, "I spend most of my time in fooling with lousy cases brought before me by your department in the civil rights field, and I do not intend to turn my docket over to your department....I do not intend to be harassed by you or any of your underlings in this or any court where I sit and the sooner you get that through your head the better you will get along with me, if that is of any interest to you."[15]

Doar described Cox as "a piece of machinery" and remembered that the judge "would really lambast me when I came into his court with a motion."[16] Doar's efforts to have Cox censured by the Fifth Circuit for his lawless behavior on the bench added fuel to their already tense relationship. For the Justice Department, there was no greater obstacle in Mississippi than Judge William Harold Cox. In one voting rights suit brought by Doar, for example, Cox refused to let government lawyers inspect the public voting records of Clarke County. The Fifth Circuit Court of Appeals overruled that and many of Cox's other decisions, but his manipulations caused considerable delay in the progress of civil rights in Mississippi. Eventually, however, the volume of suits brought by Doar and other Justice Department attorneys began to limit Cox's ability to throw up major roadblocks. "We smothered them with paper," Doar later recalled. "We were really putting the bite on Judge Cox."[17]

John Doar saw Cox make the most serious mistake of his judicial career. "It was a Saturday morning in 1964," Doar recalled. "I was in his chambers on an application for a temporary injunction.

I said to Judge Cox, 'there's nothing un-American about blacks wanting to vote.'"[18] Cox responded to Doar's mild contention by describing Negro voter applicants as "a bunch of chimpanzees." Cox's offensive statement appeared the next day in a story in the *New York Times*.[19] The resulting controversy led to an impeachment attempt that nearly cost the chastened Cox his job.

IN A COURTROOM IN MERIDIAN

Judge Cox presided in the federal courtroom in Meridian on October 18, 1967, when John Doar delivered his summation in the "Mississippi Burning" trial. A reporter for the *Meridian Star* wrote that the local people in the audience sat in "rapt attention" as they listened to "Doar's crisp, unfamiliar accents."[20] Blacks in the audience occasionally dropped their heads into their hands when he graphically described the murder, during "Freedom Summer," of the three young civil rights workers on Rock Cut Road near Philadelphia, Mississippi. At one point in his summation, Doar pointed directly at defendant Deputy Sheriff Cecil Price and charged that the deputy had used "the machinery of his office, the badge, the car, the jail, the gun" to facilitate the murderous conspiracy that involved dozens of Klan members.[21] "Members of the Jury," he concluded, "this is an important case....What I say, what the other lawyers say here today, what the Court says about the law will soon be forgotten, but what you twelve people do here today will long be remembered."[22]

Most courtroom observers considered a guilty verdict to be impossible. William Bradford Huie, a native of the South covering the trial for the *New York Herald Tribune*, wrote of the jurors: "Those are little people. Some of them are quite poor. Some of them live out on the edges of small communities, far back in the piney woods. How can they afford to take the risks?"[23] After four days of deliberations, the jury returned with a verdict that appeared to be the result of a compromise. The jury convicted seven defendants, mostly those actually present at the scene of the murders, and acquitted seven others. For three other defendants, the jury failed to reach a verdict. The convictions were the first ever in Mississippi for the killing of a civil rights worker. The *New York Times* called the verdict "a measure of the quiet revolution that is taking place in southern attitudes."[24]

Forty days after the Mississippi jury returned its verdict, John Doar announced his retirement from the Justice Department. "I just felt it was the right time," he said.[25] Doar's departure from Justice caused dismay in the civil rights community. John Lewis, one of the civil rights' movement's most courageous figures and now a congressman, said of Doar: "His job was great, his will and talent even greater."[26] Columnist Jimmy Breslin wrote: "His life has been in those nothing motels on the highways or in the dirty-windowed hotels of small cities. It has been spent with people afraid to help him or with people who think about shooting him, in courtrooms where you can't win and with politicians who will not listen."[27]

"We Did Our Best"

John Doar had guts. His courage, both physical and moral, helped make him the remarkably effective lawyer that he was. But where does such courage come from: was it in his genes, or did it develop over his life? By high school, it seemed, Doar already had cemented a reputation for courage. In the final game of the 1939 football season, Doar's team from St. Paul's Academy in Minneapolis met its archrival, Blake. In the final quarter of a close game, Blake drove the ball deep into St. Paul's end of the field. Classmate Ted Brooks recalled, "Three times John Doar stood alone between the Blake ball carrier and the goal line. He nailed the guy. Three crunching tackles. We won 7–0. He was fearless."[28]

When I interviewed Doar in 2002, he really didn't have an explanation for the courage demonstrated throughout his career at Justice. He even denied that what he did was heroic. "I don't think it's quite the right word," he said. "We just knew viscerally that we were doing something that was awfully important. We weren't trying to be heroes."[29] Doar speculated that his work at Justice might have been aided by his strong sense of what is right and what is wrong, a view consistent with evidence suggesting that most acts of courage spring from emotions coupled with a sense of duty, not out of a desire to do something that people will call courageous.

With characteristic modesty, Doar summarized his career: "As a lawyer, no one could have a more fortunate career than I've had. It's been all luck and being at the right places at the right time."[30] He described himself not as a visionary legal thinker, but rather as a competent workhorse. "If someone says 'this is what the drill is,' I'll get it done."[31] He spoke reverently of "the spirit of Justice" during the sixties. It was, he said, a spirit shaped by a "philosophy grounded in hope." He and his colleagues persevered "because it made sense," not because they thought their work would succeed.[32] Failures and frustrations led to better approaches. "We learned," Doar says, "you just got to keep going back. We couldn't change Mississippi from a desk in Washington."[33] "All of us realized," Doar concluded, "that when our lives were almost over we wanted to be able to look back and say, 'we did our best: we worked as hard and as long as we could.'"[34]

What lessons can law students and lawyers today, a half-century after the civil rights battles in the South, derive from Doar's career?

PHYSICAL COURAGE

We can, as suggested earlier, divide courageous acts into three types: those that demonstrate physical courage, those that demonstrate moral courage, and those that demonstrate psychological courage.[35] Doar's career at Justice showed both physical and moral courage.

Walking into "no man's land" on Farish Street in downtown Jackson to head off a potentially deadly confrontation between police and demonstrators is obviously a brave thing to do. Putting your life on the line takes physical courage, and Doar apparently did so with little thought about his own safety. But what he did also showed moral courage because he acted out of concern for the welfare of others. Skydiving or swimming with sharks requires only a willingness to take physical risks, but exposing yourself to danger to protect others is a courage "two-fer." Doar stood alone in that tense street in Jackson in part because his position as a lawyer for the Justice Department heightened his sense of responsibility for the situation, but what he did was far outside of his, or any lawyer's, job description. Lawyers normally don't get paid to duck projectiles in street protests.

John Doar was on Farish Street that hot summer day because his job put him there. He took the extra step of moving into the street between the demonstrators and the police out of a deep belief in the importance of his work at Justice. If Doar had not worked where he did, if he had been merely a bystander strolling in downtown Jackson, would he have assumed the role of peacemaker? It's possible, but far less likely. Studies show that people who have jobs that carry a sense of moral responsibility are much more likely to step up and take action than are random bystanders.[36] It's not the actual duty to act that matters most; it's the set of beliefs that go along with the job that are critical. Take away a police officer's badge and uniform, put her into a dangerous situation, and you will likely see her respond in about the same manner as if the job required it. You accept a job and the job begins to shape your perception of your role in the world.

A sense of duty alone does not fully account for Doar's brave decision to play peacemaker. Emotions shape our moral judgments and propel our actions, even when we have a hard time articulating what they are. Sometimes it's a roiling stew of emotions—outrage, guilt, the anticipation of pride or of gratification—that sends us out into harm's way.

Given how Doar responded in Jackson, it is hard to imagine him not accepting the assignment to prosecute Klan members in the "Mississippi Burning" trial. Unlike his defusing tensions during the Jackson protest, prosecuting civil rights violators *was* part of his job description. He assumed, without giving the matter much thought, that ignoring intimidation and death threats to pursue cases was just part of the deal at Justice. It is unimaginable, having shown unbudgeable courage throughout his career, that Doar would have told superiors, "Prosecuting the Klan in Mississippi is just too dangerous. Find somebody else to do the job."

Few jobs in law pose the physical risks of Doar's position at Justice in the 1960s. Being a lawyer generally carries far less physical risk than many other jobs. (If you crave risk, become a soldier, lumberjack, crew member on a fishing boat, or a NASCAR driver.) It is worth noting, however, that some law jobs do require facing down reasonable fears for one's safety on a regular basis. Federal and state prosecutors know that the criminals they prosecute (and the criminals' friends) sometimes do crazy things. Criminal defense attorneys, not always working with the sorts of people inclined to peaceful resolution of disputes, also accept a degree of risk with their jobs. One of the defense attorneys in the Charles Manson trial, for example, met an untimely end after pursuing a defense strategy that aggravated Charlie.[37] Even lawyers involved in civil litigation occasionally are not immune from threats. Family law lawyers, key players in sometimes intense emotional dramas, know they might have nights when they sleep with one eye open.

MORAL COURAGE

For most lawyers, thankfully, the only on-the-job courage needed on a regular basis is moral courage. It takes moral courage to represent an unpopular client. It takes moral courage for a prosecutor to turn exculpatory evidence over to a defense attorney, knowing it will hurt her own case. It takes moral courage to tell a client, who might be paying your firm big bucks, something that client doesn't want to hear. There are, in fact, a nearly limitless number of situations that lawyers face in a career that require moral courage. All that will be different about them, as they say about Olympic gymnastics events, is the degree of difficulty.

Moral courage can be sliced into two subcategories. First, there are the *socially oriented acts of courage*, such as those demonstrated in Doar's career, that include standing up against unjust practices (such as racial bigotry), and doing one's duty even when it imposes significant personal hardship. *Maintaining focus under pressure*—Ernest Hemingway said courage was "grace under pressure"—is the other type of moral courage.[38] Pressure, by definition, is not easy to withstand. We talk of a witness "standing up to a withering cross-examination" or a principled juror "refusing to cave in." When holdout Juror Number 8 (played by Henry Fonda) in the film *Twelve Angry Men* resisted pressure to cast his vote for conviction so his fellow jurors could escape that cramped, stuffy jury room, he showed moral courage—and that would be true even if it turned out that he was flat out wrong and the defendant really was guilty as charged. There will be times in your legal career when the pressure to go along (close the deal, drop the appeal) will be great, and you will need moral courage to maintain your focus on your goal of serving the true interests of your client as well as you possibly can.

Courage (both of the moral and physical variety) is a virtue that is best thought of as a mean between the extremes of timidity and recklessness. If John Doar had rushed on to Farish Street in Jackson in an attempt to stop on ongoing exchange of gunfire, we'd be more accurate to call him reckless (and dead) than courageous. Filing a motion for disqualification of a judge for bias, especially when you expect to appear against that same judge in the future, might be courageous—or it could be rash, depending upon the motion's likelihood of success and the consequences for your client. Courage often entails deliberative thinking about the costs and benefits of possible actions.

PSYCHOLOGICAL COURAGE

Both physical and moral forms of courage have received recognition and praise since the days of Ancient Greece, but Peterson and Seligman, in their *Character, Strengths, and Virtues*, identify a third form of courage that has gained recognition in the academic literature over the past few decades: *psychological* bravery.[39] When people triumph over their own anxieties or addictions, in the new view, they act courageously even if they are the only ones to benefit. Finally saying goodbye to Joe Camel forever, or overcoming public speaking fears and knocking out of the park an address to a bar convention, does take a form of courage, though we typically don't think of those acts as being courageous. Good lawyers take care not only of their clients but of themselves as well. When heavy drinking, excessive gambling, or any other devil starts taking a toll on a career, it's time to address the problem—and that takes psychological courage.

CAN WE LEARN COURAGE?

Courage is found and valued in all cultures. Virtually all religious traditions, including Buddhism, Judeo-Christianity, Islam, and Hinduism, sing its praises. Studies show that people across the American political spectrum view courage as a positive virtue and see it in essentially the same way. One researcher found that female students at Yale and males at the U.S. Air Force Academy, when presented with short stories involving acts that might be called courageous, fixed on the same elements of the stories as key to their definitions of courage.[40] Courage, it is generally agreed, is voluntary, requires judgment, and involves acts undertaken in the presence of some form of danger, risk, loss, or personal cost.[41]

Given its long history as an important virtue, it is a bit surprising how little is known about whether courage is a product primarily of nature or of nurture, whether it can be taught or learned through interventions, and to what degree various environmental conditions make acts of courage more or less likely. As Seligman and Peterson note, research on courage is "one of psychology's open frontiers."[42]

In a better world, there would be more John Doars. There would be more lawyers acting with courage to serve the interests of society, or at least of their clients. Is there anything law schools can do to produce more courageous lawyers? Is there anything you (whether you are a law student or a practicing lawyer) can do yourself to make it more likely you will do the right thing, even when the going gets tough?

Research suggests that courage has both genetic and developmental roots, and that training or the establishment of proper conditions can increase the likelihood of courageous acts. Peterson and Seligman conclude from the psychological data that courage is enabled by contextual messages expressing support for pro-social values, strong leadership, trust, clear expectations for pro-social behavior, and strong community ties. A study of Korean War veterans who were decorated for bravery suggested that more socially mature, more intelligent, and more emotionally stable soldiers were more likely to perform valorous acts than those without those traits. Other studies suggested that soldiers who witnessed acts of valor became more likely to perform valorous acts themselves, and that pro-social role models inspire acts of courage. [43] Simply telling stories about courage seems to increase courage in listeners.[44] (We confess to having included the story about John Doar not just to illustrate what courage is but also to inspire you.) Psychologist Jonathan Haidt proposes that there should be an emotion called "elevation" for the feeling of awe and inspiration that comes over us when we witness or learn about a moral act.[45]

A variety of groups have tried to cultivate courage, but there is little objective data measuring their success in doing so. The Tonglen Buddhist practice, for example, attempts to increase bravery by using breathing techniques to "breathe in fear and breathe out bravery and kindness." Through active meditation, Tonglen instructors believe, the student becomes more aware of thought patterns and can better regulate emotions to respond appropriately in situations triggering fear or other courage-blocking emotions.[46] As you might expect, Navy Seal and Outward Bound instructors have other ideas for increasing bravery, including exposing trainees to difficult challenges, presenting courageous role models, and building fraternity based on shared goals and mutual respect. Creating a sense of shared values is probably the approach to courage-building most suitable for adoption in the practice of law. It's likely that the civil rights lawyers of the 1960s accomplished what they did in no small part because of the fraternity and mutual respect felt within the Department—what John Doar called "the spirit of Justice."

Among the thousands of self-help books that have flooded the market in recent years, at least a few have offered help for those feeling in need of more courage. Suggestions for increasing courage generally center on two approaches: reducing fear and—when the fear remains—increasing one's determination to act. In *The Courage Quotient: How Science Can Make You Braver*, Robert Biswas-Diener defines "the courage quotient" as a ratio: one's willingness to act (say, to tell the truth or to persist in a difficult task) divided by one's fears (say, fear of embarrassment or fear of failure).[47] He encourages his readers to try strategies to decrease the denominator or increase the numerator. Specifically, he proposes two strategies for reducing fear and three strategies for increasing a willingness to act.

His first suggested strategy for reducing fear is to "visualize the future." For example, the natural fear that might precede a big trial could be reduced a bit by visiting the courtroom before the trial and becoming familiar with the space—the location of the witness stand, the bench, the jury box. Visualizing yourself examining witnesses or making your final pitch to the jury will give you a sense of greater "control over the ambiguousness of the situation."[48] His second (and probably less helpful) strategy for controlling fear is to engage in "magical thinking"—that is, convince yourself that the rabbit foot in your pocket really does have the power to improve your upcoming oral argument. Convincing yourself you are lucky, Biswas-Diener contends, both reduces fear and gives you the self-confidence to act more courageously.[49] He admits the idea is little more than "psychological trickery," but swears that it works.[50]

To boost your willingness to act, Biswas-Diener suggests putting yourself in a situation where courageous action becomes more likely. For example, simply holding a job that carries a sense of responsibility to others, such as representing the state or federal government, makes it more likely that you will act when action is called for. Second, he advises resisting "the crushing power of social influence" that "extinguishes" our "best impulses" and causes us to simply go along with the crowd.[51] If you are in a firm where corruption is rampant, get the hell out. Finally, he urges focusing attention on progress, not peril. Meaningful goals and a healthy sense of optimism will give you the necessary "energy" needed "to face danger."[52] Embrace the view of Winston Churchill who said, "Success consists of going from failure to failure without loss of enthusiasm." Norman Vincent Peale preached much the same message in his classic *The Power of Positive Thinking*.[53]

COURAGE IN LAW SCHOOLS

When it comes to teaching courage, law schools have punted. Courage either is of little interest to those in the law teaching game or they assume (perhaps rightly) that it is difficult to teach well and they won't be able to do it. This should change; courage is too important for law schools to ignore. Simply encouraging students to become aware of how their own language (e.g., "I just can't do it") limits their ability to act courageously would be a step in the right direction. Going further along the Courage Track, students might read stories about heroic lawyers (*To Kill a Mockingbird* and *Gideon's Trumpet* undoubtedly have inspired at least a few people over the last half century to become lawyers of courage). Studies show that courage can be conditioned, and expressions of outrage at injustice, whether coming from an author's pen, a pulpit, or a lectern, might cause readers and listeners to feel—and potentially act upon—a similar sense of outrage. Students in a course on courage also could be asked to engage in exercises in which they visualize themselves acting courageously on behalf of their clients.

Unfortunately, at present, law schools are ill-equipped to offer courage training. In American law schools you can find hundreds of torts and contracts professors, dozens of admiralty and aviation law professors, but you'll never find a professor who specializes in teaching courage. Faculty at law schools are neither selected for their own courage nor their ability to teach it. That fact, coupled with the rather scant evidence concerning the effectiveness of programs designed to increase courage (you have to have such programs before you can evaluate them) makes it unlikely we'll see "Courage for Lawyers" courses added to law school curricula anytime soon. Even if no one could predict with absolute confidence that such a course would succeed in actually producing more courageous lawyers, isn't the possible prize worth the try?

The fact is, given the incentives in legal academia, it takes courage to teach courage. Imagine the objections that a proposal to teach courage or (fill in your favorite virtue here) would prompt from faculty members. They will harrumph about courage not being teachable, complain that the subject is hopelessly squishy and belongs in the Philosophy Department, question its relation to the practice, and worry about how the decision to offer such a course would be viewed by alumni or colleagues in other law schools. Then there's the personal cost to the teacher. Teaching about courage hardly seems to be the first rung on the ladder to a tenured position at Harvard.

CODES AND COURAGE: TWO STORIES

If some of the suggestions for increasing courage seem a bit unsatisfying, it might be because they tend to focus on just one of the two keys to courage. For the most part, courage researchers tell us how we might build the personal codes that create predispositions to act morally. When you reflect on whether to take an action, you should ask "whether acting (or not acting) is consistent with the type of person"[54] you want to be. Strive to create a vision of yourself that makes moral actions more likely. But a predisposition to act is not the same as action. Courage ultimately depends as much on having the emotional states that trigger emotional judgments. Jesse Prinz argues that anger is a "very important" trigger of moral action.[55] Studies using various economic games have shown that angry subjects are likely to punish non-cooperators even at substantial personal costs to themselves.[56] Guilt also triggers moral action, according to studies showing that subjects who had been asked to administer shocks to innocent persons later made three times as many fundraising calls as did subjects who did no shocking of the innocent.[57] "Why does an attorney work tirelessly for modest pay to free a wrongfully convicted prisoner? The answer might be born in anger: a burning desire to punish an unethical prosecutor, for example. Why does an attorney tell the developer who wants to cover up an asbestos problem to go find a less scrupulous lawyer? The real reason might be the guilt and shame that he or she anticipates would come from doing what the client wants.

Courage is a virtue best understood in the context of stories, and so we consider the stories of two courageous men, one a judge and one a lawyer, who both found, in part because of their life-structuring codes, the courage to act when those around them could not.

ONE BRAVE JUDGE

Dr. Lothar Kreyssig served as a judge at the Court of Guardianship in the town of Brandenburg during the Third Reich. Almost alone among the judges of Germany under Hitler, he clung stubbornly to the notion that justice mattered more than career advancement. Since his appointment in 1928, Kreyssig's superiors had considered him to be a good judge—that is, until he began a series of minor insubordinations such as slipping out of a ceremony in his court when a bust of Hitler was unveiled, publicly protesting the suspension of three judges who failed to follow the interpretation of "Aryan laws" favored by Nazi authorities, and referring to Nazi church policies as "injustice masquerading in the form of law."[58]

Reassigned to the Petty Court in Brandenburg, Kreyssig continued to be a thorn in the Nazi side. When the judge discovered that inmates at a local mental hospital were secretly being removed and killed, Kreyssig sent a letter of complaint to the president of the Prussian Supreme Court in which he denounced the "terrible doctrine" that placed people "beyond the reach of law" in concentration camps and mental institutions.[59]

Officials at the Reich Ministry of Justice summoned Kreyssig in an effort to straighten out his thinking on matters of civil liberties, but it didn't work. Kreyssig returned to Brandenburg and issued injunctions prohibiting several hospitals from transferring wards of his court without his permission. The final straw for the Reich Ministry came when Kreyssig brought criminal charges before the public prosecutor against a Nazi party leader who headed the regime's euthanasia program, "T4." When efforts failed to persuade Kreyssig that the euthanasia program was "the will of the Fuhrer" and that the Fuhrer was "the fount of law" in the Third Reich, Justice Minister Franz Gurtner demanded that Kreyssig withdraw his injunctions against the hospitals. Kreyssig refused. Gurtner accepted instead Kreyssig's early retirement and a criminal investigation opened against him, but the investigation closed without prosecution. Kreyssig retired to his farm where, it turned out, he hid Jews until war's end.

In his book, *Hitler's Justice: The Courts of the Third Reich*, Ingo Müller writes of the courageous judge of Brandenburg: "No matter how hard one searches for stout-hearted men among the judges of the Third Reich, for judges who refused to serve the regime from the bench, there remains a grand total of one: Dr. Lothar Kreyssig."[60] Understanding what gave Kreyssig his courage begins with understanding a second role the brave judge had. Kreyssig served as a leader of "Bekennende Kirche" (Confessing Church), which fought hard to resist the determined efforts of the Reich to "Nazify" it and other Protestant denominations. Kreyssig saw in the Reich's policies not just the individual injustices that many other judges presumably saw in their courtrooms. He also saw them trample the religious beliefs of a church he cared about deeply—and with that seeing came outrage.

There Should Be a Statue in Chattanooga

Our last profile in courage is of Noah Parden, an attorney who practiced law in Chattanooga. One day, in February 1906, Parden answered the knock on the door of his small wood-frame office, and looked into the face of a black man known around town as

Skinbone Johnson. Over a cup of tea, Johnson told Parden that his son, Ed, faced execution within days, but that he had no money to pay a lawyer. Parden already knew, as did everyone in the city, that days before a jury had convicted Ed Johnson of raping a twenty-one-year-old white woman named Nevada Taylor as she walked near a cemetery gate on her way home from work. He also knew about some serious concerns with the verdict in the trial: Johnson's arrest was based on the statement of a discredited witness, Taylor's identification of Johnson as her attacker was hesitant and uncertain, and alibi witnesses had placed Johnson in a saloon more than a mile away from the crime scene at the time of the rape. Today we'd call this a classic recipe for a wrongful conviction; in 1906, before an all-white southern jury, it was an open-and-shut case. So slim did Johnson's appointed lawyers think his chances were for a successful appeal that they chose not to appeal Johnson's conviction, telling the judge that they would acquiesce in the finding of the jury.[61]

Parden listened to Skinbone's story knowing full well that he was Ed Johnson's last hope. If he turned down the case, Johnson certainly would be hanged. On the other hand, if he took the case, Johnson would most likely be hanged anyway. Moreover, Parden understood that by standing between Johnson and his date with the hangman, he jeopardized the stream of civil cases that was his bread and butter. Over the years, Parden and his partner, Style Hutchins, had become the two most successful African American lawyers in Chattanooga. Parden's practice consisted mainly in representing black families and businesses that had been denied claims by insurance companies as part of a cynical strategy that assumed black claimants would lack either the knowledge or resources to sue them for wrongful denials. He took the cases on a contingency fee and won them by convincing white jurors that if insurance companies got away with cheating black policyholders, the jurors could be their next victims. Compensation from the insurance cases financed his criminal practice, which was almost entirely pro bono. All this could end with Parden's acceptance of Johnson's case. The legal establishment and the white citizens of the city were unanimously hot for a speedy execution and would not look kindly on anyone who stood in their way. And once word got out that the county's judge hated him, as he surely soon would, what client would want to hire him?

After listening to the appeal of Skinbone Johnson, Parden and his partner, Hutchins, sat down to talk. They talked about how taking the case would adversely affect their practice and reputations. They talked about the possibility of a lynch mob coming after them. And then they agreed to take the case. It came down to one basic principle, really. As lawyers, they felt bound to defend a man who almost certainly was innocent. Hutchins, an ordained minister, used scripture to make his points: "Much has been given to us by God and man. Now much is expected."[62] That night, after breaking the news about the case to his wife, Parden sat down and read all forty-two chapters of the Book of Job. He said it gave him the inspiration to take the case.

Parden encountered roadblock after roadblock. Townspeople shunned and threatened him. The black preachers of Chattanooga, concerned about the possible consequences of an appeal for their community, opposed his efforts. Parden found this opposition from church leaders to be the hardest blow of all. But Parden knew his client was indeed an innocent man—not that innocence meant much when it came to a black man charged with such a crime in such a place at such a time. When the Tennessee courts rejected Pardon's appeal, he did not give up. Despite long odds, he turned to the federal courts. As of 1906, not a single state court criminal conviction ever had been reversed by federal courts on due process grounds, and only one conviction ever had been overturned on equal protection grounds. The district judge in Tennessee, as expected, denied Parden's habeas corpus petition.

When Parden announced he would take Johnson's case to the U.S. Supreme Court, townspeople reacted angrily. Tennesseans expected lawyers for defendants to play by their rules, not Washington's. On the day Noah Parden was to board a train for the nation's capital, someone set fire to his law office. He got on the train anyway.

Once in Washington, Parden entered the waiting room of the Supreme Court. It was the morning of March 17, 1906, three days before the date set for Ed Johnson's execution. The wait seemed interminable, lasting for hours. Parden later wrote: "As the day expired, I prepared my soul for failure. Then I convinced myself this effort required nothing short of a miracle. It was late in the evening and I had all but given up. I folded my hands and asked God for guidance on how to tell Ed Johnson's family that I had failed."[63]

Finally, however, the Court's receptionist stood in the doorway and announced, "He will see you now." The "he" turned out to be Justice John Harlan, the same justice who famously dissented in the landmark case of *Plessy v. Ferguson*. Seated at the end of a long oak table in the Court's conference room, Harlan asked, "Mr. Parden...tell me why the United States Supreme Court should care about this case?" The lawyer proceeded to do so. As he finished his account of the case, the elderly justice nodded without giving a word of encouragement.[64]

Parden called the trip back to Chattanooga "the longest train ride of my life. I relived every word spoken in my meeting with Justice Harlan." When he arrived at the Chattanooga train station, his overjoyed partner rushed to greet him. Hutchins waved a piece of paper in the air. It was a telegram from Washington signed by Justice Harlan that read: "Have allowed appeal to accused in habeas corpus case of Ed Johnson."[65]

Parden's joy proved short-lived. About 8 o'clock the next night a mob carrying guns descended on the Hamilton County Jail where Johnson was being held. Only a single guard was at the jail. Sheriff Joseph Shipp had told his other deputies that they might want to take the night off. Ed Johnson, on the third floor, looked out the window of his cell to see the crowd of nearly 200 men and women in the courtyard below. Mob members tied Johnson with rope and dragged him from his cell. Someone yelled, "To the county bridge!" The crowd marched for six blocks to the Walnut Street Bridge. "Do you have anything to say?" a man holding a noose asked Johnson. With the noose around his neck and blood dripping from his mouth, the prisoner remained calm. Ed Johnson spoke for the last time: "God bless you all. I am innocent." Ed Johnson's body "jerked with life" as it swayed high above the Tennessee River, then it stopped. A leader of the mob pinned a sheet of paper to Johnson's body. The note read: "To Justice Harlan. Come and get your nigger now."[66]

Word of Johnson's lynching led to a call for a response in Washington. Justice Harlan and Justice Oliver Wendell Holmes insisted on an urgent meeting with Chief Justice Fuller and expressed their outrage to the press. President Theodore Roosevelt ordered an investigation that could aid the Supreme Court if it chose to bring criminal contempt charges against the lynchers of Ed Johnson. Federal agents soon discovered that on the matter of the lynching, most lips in Tennessee were firmly sealed. Noah Parden, however, provided Secret Service agents with valuable background information. He led agents to witnesses who might help build a prosecution case against the conspirators—and then helped convince them to talk. After the investigation wrapped up, Parden traveled to Washington to advise the attorney general on how to proceed with what would be the first and only criminal trial ever to take place before our nation's highest court.

In Chattanooga, you don't get popular helping the federal government prosecute Tennesseans. Life became even more difficult for Noah Parden. Death threats came. No one wanted to hire a lawyer hated by the local judge. They stoned his office and they stoned his home, but no deputies investigated the crimes. Like Job, Parden endured his trials.

In the end, the nine justices found Chattanooga's sheriff, a jailer, and four members of the lynch mob guilty of criminal contempt of the Supreme Court of the United States—they became the first and only people in our nation's history directly sentenced and imprisoned by the U.S. Supreme Court.[67] Noah Parden praised the Court's decision: "The very rule of law upon which this country was founded and on which the future of this nation rests has been enforced with the might of our highest tribunal."[68]

As far as anyone can tell, Parden never practiced law again. He never returned to Chattanooga either. Instead, he moved to the Oklahoma Territory, where he started a small newspaper. There is no statue in Chattanooga honoring Noah Parden. There is, however, a statue in Chattanooga honoring Sheriff Shipp.

PARDEN'S LIFE-STRUCTURING CODE

We admire Noah Parden for his dogged, even heroic pursuit of justice, first for Ed Johnson and then for those who lynched him. Few, if any, lawyers, in two cases arising from the same incident, ever have fought both to save the innocent and to punish the guilty—and each time at such a high personal cost. What gave Parden the courage to do what no other lawyer would do? His genes might have played a role (a subject to which we turn in a future chapter), but there was clearly something else at work. Parden's motivation came in large part from his deep Christian faith. Turning to the Book of Job gave Parden the will to take on Johnson's defense and weather the troubles that followed.

Although not a lot is known about the life of Noah Parden (early black lawyers have rarely captured the attention of biographers), we do know one thing: he was a very religious guy. Faith came early to Parden, when, at age six, his mother died, and authorities handed him off to missionaries who ran a nearby orphanage. The missionaries taught him to kneel by his bedside for several minutes of prayer each evening, a practice he continued into adulthood. Throughout his life, he refused alcohol or tobacco products, or even to eat pork, explaining that the body was "the temple of the Holy Spirit."[69] Even in the dark days following Ed Johnson's lynching, religion was his source of comfort. Speaking at Johnson's funeral, Parden expressed joy that he had helped Johnson find the Lord in the days before his death.

Religious faith seemed to give Parden the strength to fight relentlessly for justice. While there may be no study that specifically links religious beliefs to courage, there is considerable evidence that religious folk in general devote more time and energy to working for the needy and the afflicted than do their secular neighbors. Robert Putnam and David Campbell, both political scientists, summarize the findings this way in their book *American Grace: How Religion Unites and Divides Us*: "By many different measures religiously observant Americans are better neighbors and better citizens than secular Americans—they are more generous with their time and money, especially in helping the needy, and they are more active in community life."[70] Interestingly, it is not the specific religious beliefs or practices that seem to be the motivating source for this good work. Jews, Mormons, Catholics, and Protestants are all about equally generous in serving their communities. Rather, what matters is the sense of belonging to a religious community. Putnam and Campbell conclude: "It is religious belongingness that matters for neighborliness, not religious believing."[71]

A sense of being a part of a moral project or tradition greater than oneself undergirded the courage of John Adams, John Doar, Lothar Kreyssig, and Noah Parden. For Adams, it might have been his commitment to helping build an America founded on notions of justice. Doar spoke of "the spirit of Justice" that supported his work in southern fields, mean streets, and courthouses. Nazi attacks on his beloved Confessing Church helped give Kreyssig the backbone to resist the Reich's injustices. And for Parden, his deep and abiding Christian faith lifted him onto the train to

Washington, comforted him through fires and threats, and led him to undertake the fight to bring the lynchers of Ed Johnson to justice.

COURAGE AND JUSTICE

Your own practice may seem far removed from those of the lawyers profiled in this chapter. We can't all fight Nazis and bigots. Your fights might be with amoral clients or senior partners, bored judges, abusive opposing counsel, or lying witnesses. The one thing for certain is that every lawyer will need courage from time to time.

Good lawyers are courageous (though, like all such qualities, courage comes and it goes). If you feel you lack courage, here are two reasons for hope. One reason is that people tend to become more courageous as they age, most likely because fears tend to lessen over time. The second reason is that "the capacity for courage lies within us all"[72] and can, to a significant degree, be strengthened with effort. Lao-Tzu said, "From caring comes courage." Courage, ultimately, allows us to protect and defend what we value, whether it is a principle or a person. Care enough and you can overcome your fears and do the right thing.

Courage, involving the exercise of will in the face of challenges, is closely related to the more general subject of willpower. All your legal insights, all your great ideas and clever strategies get you nowhere without the ability to follow through and use them in what are often trying situations. It is to the subject of willpower—what it is and how we can conserve or build it—that we next turn.

CHAPTER 3

The Good Lawyer Has Ample Willpower

Self-control is really about making the future bigger.
—George Ainslie

LAWYERS WORK IN A HIGH-STRESS PROFESSION THAT requires lots of effortful thinking. Recent research establishes that willpower is something like a muscle in that it becomes fatigued by overuse but also can be strengthened with the right form of exercise. Conscious decision making, a staple of most lawyers' days, depletes our supplies of willpower and makes us more vulnerable to temptations that can distract us from doing what needs to be done for our clients. This chapter considers the new science of willpower, what it means for lawyers, and what steps lawyers can take to keep their supply of willpower adequate for the tasks at hand.

Building up our finite stores of willpower is no small thing. Self-control, along with intelligence, turns out to be one of the two best predictors of a successful career and a successful life.[1] And, unlike the case with intelligence, we actually can do things that will increase our self-control. The importance of willpower, however, escapes most people. Researchers who surveyed more than one million people around the world found that self-control was ranked dead last in perceived importance among more than twenty listed "character strengths," trailing such virtues as humor, modesty, and creativity. Interestingly, however, when these same million people were asked to rank their failings, lack of self-control came out at the very top of the list.[2] Clearly, there's some muddled thinking going on about the value of willpower.

Willpower, psychologists have noted, has two distinct, but related, aspects. On the one hand, there is the "I will power" that enables us to see ourselves through difficult and meaningful tasks.[3] A lawyer with a plentiful supply of "I will power" is persistent. "I will power," of course, is critical for the lawyer who puts in hundreds of demanding hours preparing for trial, writing an appellate brief, or helping a client complete a complex transaction. Robert Pirsig, in *Zen and the Art of Motorcycle Maintenance*, used the word "gumption" to describe the feeling of initiative that makes persistence, or sustained action in the face of challenges, possible.[4] Gumption does for a person what Powdermilk Biscuits, Prairie Home Companion's long-time imaginary sponsor, promises: "it gives a person the strength to get up and do what needs to be done." We all have emotions and urges from time to time that threaten to drain our gumption and derail our important efforts. Pirsig called these internal states "emotional traps" and offered his readers tips on how they might be avoided.

There is also, however, the "I won't power" that enables us to avoid the temptations exacerbated by the stressful work lawyers must do, temptations that range from alcohol and drugs to excessive Internet surfing or e-mail checking. This temptation-avoidance aspect of willpower we more typically refer to as self-control (though it also—of course—requires control of the self to persist at challenging tasks). Self-control makes workdays more productive and keeps us from falling into the trap of addiction, with all of its adverse consequences. The good lawyer needs both sufficient "I will" and "I won't" willpower. Without willpower, nothing hard gets done—and most things that are important come only with hard work.

ONE PERSISTENT LAWYER

It can take a lot of willpower to see a case through to conclusion when a well-funded defendant has attorneys who are tossing every roadblock they can think of in your way. No one knows that better than Marc Z. Edell, the lawyer who won the first ever judgment—though a disappointingly modest one—against a tobacco company for smoking-related lung cancer. Before a New Jersey jury awarded $400,000 to Tony Cipollone, the husband of Rose Cipollone who had died after decades of cigarette smoking, Edell had put in thousands of hours of work over more than four years, exhausted millions of dollars that his firm advanced on the case, watched his client die from cancer during the course of the litigation, and overcame the best efforts of dozens of tobacco companies' attorneys to get him to drop his lawsuit. How did he have the stamina to do it?

The goal of the tobacco companies in the 1980s was, simply, to destroy the will of plaintiffs and their attorneys to continue to pursue lawsuits. With over 350,000 tobacco-related deaths a year, settling each case that might be brought for, say, $100,000, would put a serious dent into company profits. As a result, according to Richard Dent, director of the Tobacco Products Liability Project, companies would spend "literally billions of dollars in defense. They will do anything they can to discourage plaintiffs' attorneys."[5] Lawyers representing tobacco companies adopted what was called "a strategy of intimidation."[6] They brought out their heavy ammunition to defend even the most trivial cases. They bombarded plaintiffs' attorneys with a never-ending procession of pretrial motions. When company officials were deposed, they consistently denied knowledge of any link between cigarette smoking and cancer. Defense attorneys required plaintiffs to endure what were called "lifestyle depositions," days-long exhausting and intimate interrogations designed in part to identify any and all alternative explanations for a cancer, but just as importantly, to serve as a warning to other possible plaintiffs of the heavy costs of bringing suit. Edell told his client, Rose Cipollone, "You're gonna be dissected. Chopped apart. Nothing is going to be sacred."[7]

Against long odds, Edell persisted in his suit in the hope that it might lead to the birth of a new litigation industry, built around claims against tobacco companies. Millions of people, including yet unborn generations of potential tobacco addicts, might benefit from his efforts. Of course, he also hoped—as do most personal injury attorneys—that he might make a bundle and, in the process, help a deserving client. Mostly, though, Edell took the long view. Explaining his willingness to work countless hours and advance more than $2 million of his firm's money, he said the case was "one of those rare instances where a lawyer can accomplish something for a client and also, at the same time, have a substantial positive impact on our society. Those chances come around once in a lifetime."[8] Also, Edell noted, competition appealed to him: "I like it; I thrive on it," he said.[9]

Edell and his associates needed all the willpower they could muster to plow their way through hundreds of thousands of subpoenaed documents looking for the smoking gun they needed to win their case. Specifically, they looked for research that might reveal that executives of the tobacco companies knew of the dangers posed by their product, but ignored or suppressed research and continue to peddle their cigarettes. Pushing the case to trial proved harder than Edell ever imagined. "The main defense strategy was a war of attrition," he said. "They hire very, very good lawyers and they divert your attention from the main issues. You end up in the Third Circuit on writs of mandamus and disqualification motions." Edell found that he could not win the war of attrition: "It's impossible. We can only survive."[10]

By the time the Cipollone trial finally opened in 1987, Edell could deliver a memorized two-hour opening statement without notes. He could produce and explain through testimony the significance of previously secret company documents, showing that tobacco executives knew far more about the cancer-causing effects of their product than they ever let on. Document by document, Edell patiently presented a timeline that compared the growing scientific consensus about tobacco dangers with the profit-motivated words and actions of tobacco companies. The hard, day-after-day work of trial preparation was driven by emotion. "Thank God for adrenal glands," Edell said.[11] But trials (especially trials in which your side is outnumbered by lawyers on the other side, thirty-two to three) take their toll in lost time with family, in lost sleep, in lost weight. In the first month of the trial, Edell lost ten pounds.

Apart from whatever help his adrenal glands provided, Edell claimed that fear kept him pushing forward. "I look at each witness as the most important witness," he said. "If I don't *get* that witness, I'll *lose* my case."[12] He dealt as well as he could with the frustration that came from bench rulings on points of law going against him. Edell compared his four-and-a-half year fight against the tobacco companies to a long race. "When you start the case you're like a trained marathon runner. But you get to the start and they take away your shoes. Then you start running and they break your arm. You keep going and they cut off one of your legs. Still, you keep running."[13]

After four months of trial, the jury began deliberations that culminated in a $400,000 jury award based on Cipollone's breach-of-warranty claim against Liggett & Myers. Writing about the trial in his book *The Litigators*, John A. Jenkins called the small judgment "still sweet revenge" for Edell and Tony Cipollone, "who'd stuck with the case for their own private reasons."[14] Where there's the will, there's the way.

WILLPOWER IN A STRESS-FILLED PROFESSION

As jobs go, law practice is particularly mentally demanding, though few lawyers go through the stress-ringer that Edell did in the Cipollone case. Kelly McGonigal, author of *The Willpower Instinct: How Self-Control Works, Why It Matters, and What You Can Do to Get More of It*, notes, "In the long term, nothing drains will-power faster than stress."[15] Lawyers typically do not have to deal with the physical stress faced by marathoners, Navy Seals, or long-shoremen, but instead must deal with a steady stream of mental stress caused by filing deadlines and demanding clients and senior partners. Moreover, more than most jobs, lawyers make a lot of decisions requiring conscious and sustained thought. Rarely can lawyers go long on autopilot and follow whatever impulses their fast-thinking systems come up with. Writing a brief, for example, demands constant attention as to which of various points to include or exclude, how various options for phrasing might influence a judge, and whether the style matches the expectations of review-ing partners. In mediations and arbitrations, lawyers are asked to quickly size up options and make highly consequential judg-ments, all the while making sure clients are on board. Preparing for trial is even more stressful, demanding long hours and usually requiring a number of last-minute adjustments. In the trial itself, attorneys might worry about whether a witness will perform up to expectations, how to handle a difficult cross-examination, whether to object or not to potentially excludable testimony, or what to do about the juror in the jury box with his arms crossed and a sour look on his face. Transactional lawyers have different sources of stress, wondering whether they've really covered all the bases in the proposed contract or whether a future change in the law might destroy their best-laid legal plans. Sources of stress are never far from a lawyer, it seems. All of this cognitive busyness has its costs.

No work a lawyer does is more stressful than a major trial, especially if you are, like Marc Edell, a small-firm David fighting corporate Goliaths. Marc Edell managed to see the Cipollone case through to a jury verdict by using some of the techniques proven to be associated with producing willpower benefits. First, Edell had clear goals in mind, which included helping a deserving client, sending a message to tobacco companies, and making a name for himself as a legal champion of lung cancer victims. Roy Baumeister and John Tierney, co-authors of *Willpower: Rediscovering the Greatest Human Strength*, call setting a clear goal "the first step in self-control."[16] While goal setting is more associated with the "I won't" form of willpower ("I won't smoke another cigarette"; "I won't waste so much time surfing the Net"), it also is critical to "I will" willpower as well. The clearer a goal, the more importance we attach to a goal, and the more committed we are to a goal, the more likely we are to achieve it. It's also helpful not to set too many goals, as multiple goals can be distracting and stressful. For lawyers, willpower-depleting decisions are unavoidable and come in many forms. Figure out what's really important, what's not so important, and what's not important at all. Focus on the important, delegate what's less important, and ignore the rest. Benjamin Franklin learned from experience that setting too many goals can prevent any from being reached. He concluded: "I judg'd it would be well not to distract my attention by attempting the whole at once, but to fix it on one of them at a time."[17] In general, while it is necessary to maintain some long-term goals, it is specific proximal goals ("Today I will draft the Jones contract") that are more likely to be achieved and have the additional benefit—at least when they are met— of building a habit of goal achievement that brings confidence and efficiency to our work. A clear goal keeps us from developing what David Allen, author of *Getting Things Done: The Art of Stress-Free Productivity*, calls a "monkey mind," a mind constantly leaping from thought tree to thought tree.[18]

As helpful as a clear goal is in seeing a project through to completion, giving yourself a pep talk along the way is often necessary. Reminding yourself of why what you're doing is worthwhile is perhaps the most common way of enhancing motivation. Fear, however, is another powerful motivator. Rick Morris, an avid marathoner, suggests that fellow marathoners will themselves through "the wall" and across the finish line by "imagining a rhino chasing you."[19] Marc Edell had his own charging rhinos to keep him running. His fear of losing millions of the firm's money, his fear of not doing all he could for a client he cared about, and his fear of embarrassing himself in court all helped him to do what needed to be done in the Cipollone case.

Lawyers who wish to develop more willpower should consider that willpower, like so many other traits, is contagious. Simply hanging around people you like who have lots of willpower gives you a boost of willpower. Kelly McGonigal notes that "both bad habits and positive change can spread from person to person like germs, and nobody is completely immune."[20] If your friends are successful in kicking the cigarette habit, you are more likely to be successful as well—and if they give up and start lighting up again, you are too. For lawyers, the takeaway from the evidence about willpower's infectiousness is that if the lawyers you spend your time with share your goals or have the sorts of work habits you admire, you are more likely to develop good habits yourself and are more likely to achieve your goals. You choose your tribe, and then your tribe shapes you. "When the rest of our tribe does something," McGonigal says, "we tend to think it's a smart thing to do."[21]

THE IMPORTANCE OF WILLPOWER

In the late 1960s, Stanford psychologist Walter Mischel conducted "the marshmallow study," the study that first suggested willpower might be the most important measure of a successful life or a successful career. Mischel rounded up a bunch of four-year-olds and presented them with two marshmallows and a choice: they could eat one marshmallow now after ringing a nearby bell, or wait fifteen minutes and eat both marshmallows. Then Mischel left the room to take his place behind a one-way mirror and watch what would happen. Videos taken of the experiment show the children adopting a variety of strategies. Some kids covered their faces to avoid looking at the marshmallow, others rang the bell in a matter of seconds, and still others licked (but did not eat) the tempting treat. Years later, Mischel tracked down hundreds of the subjects in the marshmallow study to see how they fared in school and in life. Remarkably, the four-year-olds who managed to resist the marshmallows for the full fifteen minutes went on to score an average of "210 points higher on SAT tests than those who caved" in the first thirty seconds.[22] In general, the kids who showed the most willpower at age four went on to achieve higher grades, became more popular with peers and teachers, were less likely to be obese, had lower rates of drug abuse, and earned higher salaries than the less self-controlled subjects in the marshmallow experiment. In short, the study suggested, willpower is the key to a successful life.

Confirmation of Mischel's discovery of the importance of willpower came in later experiments. When researchers in one study compared students' grades with almost three dozen personality traits, they concluded that self-control was the only one of all the traits that was a better-than-chance predictor of grades. Willpower also turned out to predict grades even better than the predictor generally used most by elite college admissions offices, the SAT.[23] According to the study, self-control mattered because it got students reliably to classes and helped them start their homework early and complete assignments on time. Willpower is no less important in the workplace, studies show. Workers with above average self-control tend to be better empathizers, are thought of more highly by fellow employees, and lose their temper less than workers with below average self-control.

Willpower has been called "a uniquely human strength."[24] With rare exceptions, animals will give a task at the most twenty minutes before they are ready to give up and move on. A lawyer such as Marc Edell, on the other hand, can persist in seeking justice for a client for more than four years, undaunted by obstructionist opposing counsel and a court system whose pace of movement can sometimes generously be described as glacial.

Our willpower is centered in the prefrontal cortex, with the right side controlling our impulses (our "I won't power") and the left side regulating our persistence, or "I will power." As long as you have a prefrontal cortex, you have willpower, but persistence and self-control come easily to some and hardly at all to others. Social science research suggests that willpower might well have— and, in fact, probably does have—a genetic component. The differences in behavior revealed in the marshmallow study cannot be accounted for entirely by the early childhood experiences of the participating four-year-olds. Of course, if genes explained all the differences, as they largely do for IQ, we might as well say to law students with below-average willpower, as Professor Kingsfield famously did in *The Paper Chase*, "Here's a dime. Go call your mother and tell her you'll never be a (good) lawyer."[25] As we've noted, however, we do have the ability to strengthen our willpower.

Certain personality traits and experiences are associated with higher levels of willpower. Research has shown that optimistic people—people inclined to expect that they will succeed at a task—are more persistent than pessimistic people.[26] Research also suggests that people who experience "near wins" (or "close losses") tend to be more persistent, presumably because coming so close to victory left them feeling that next time victory could be theirs.[27] Most importantly for our purposes, perhaps, research has shown that people who interpret failures and other negative events as the result of their genes or some dark cloud hovering over them are less likely to persist at tasks than people who don't have that response of "learned helplessness."[28]

Finally, and perhaps most provocatively, studies show gender differences in both self-control and persistence. Females, it seems, generally have more self-control than males. Males, on the other hand, are somewhat more likely to attribute failure to lack of personal effort and less to lack of ability, and so they persist longer on skill-related tasks than do females.[29] These studies suggest, for example, that female lawyers would be less likely to rise to the bait dangled by opposing counsel, whereas male lawyers would be more likely to keep at it until they finally punch their way through that tax loophole and save a bundle for a client. Overall, however, gender differences are small—they offer neither you nor sexist hiring committees any excuses. We all can be good lawyers.

MINDSETS AND WILLPOWER

A route to avoiding the feelings of helplessness that are so destructive of willpower is to adopt what Stanford psychologist Carol Dweck has dubbed "the growth mindset," her term for a belief or habit that has been proven to contribute both to better learning and success on the job.

In her book *Mindset: The New Psychology of Success*, Dweck tells the story of a lawyer who spent seven years of his career battling the biggest bank in his state on behalf of clients whom he believed it had cheated. In the end, he lost. But rather than mope about countless hours of his life going down the drain, the lawyer said: "Who am I to say that just because I spent seven years on something I am entitled to success? Did I do it for the success or because I thought the effort itself was valid? I do not regret it. I had to do it. I would not do it differently."[30]

Dweck describes the lawyer who represented the bank's customers as having "a growth mindset." A person with a growth mindset values his experience regardless of the outcome. Life is not primarily about winning or losing; it is about working on things that matter. Satisfaction comes from charting paths, working hard, and feeling you've done your best. Recent research in education has demonstrated persuasively that having a growth mindset contributes to success in school, in a career, and in life.

While people with growth mindsets believe that their basic qualities are things they cultivate through their own efforts, people with the opposite mindset—which Dweck and others call "a fixed mindset"—believe their abilities are inherent and can't be changed.[31] They face a future of self-doubt, anxiety, and limited achievement. A person with a fixed mindset believes his or her God-given (or God-denied) intellectual abilities are set in stone.

For students, that means letting their test scores define them. They begin to think of themselves as an "A student" or a "B student" or a "C student" or, if the grades are really bad, as "a failure." A fixed mindset student will consider a good exam grade more as confirmation of his or her intelligence than as a reflection of the effort put into learning the material. For persons with fixed mindsets, each exam presents the need to demonstrate natural abilities, and when a score is disappointing, they worry that they have been exposed as deficient. Fixed mindset people are "endlessly trying to prove themselves"—a sure recipe for stress. (The increased stress probably contributes to the much higher levels of depression found among people with fixed mindsets.)[32] In their eyes, tests are all about getting answers right or wrong, not about learning material.

Having a growth mindset, on the other hand, allows students to focus on learning, not on grades. Rather than fretting that an exam will prove them a failure, they are inclined to view it as an indicator of whether their learning strategy paid off. If the test score is not what they hoped, it means that they'll have to revise their study approach or work harder. They don't let test scores define them as failures; instead they rise to the challenge, try to figure out what went wrong, and promise that they'll do better next time. Eventually, growth mindset students learn to discover themes across lectures and master underlying principles. They maintain interest in a course even when the teacher is boring because they enjoy digging for answers—even when the teacher appears to be hiding them.[33] Unlike the fixed mindset students, they welcome criticism as a tool for improvement.

As law professors, we see lots of students with each kind of mindset. The growth mindset student who received a "C" shows up in our offices, trying to figure out what went wrong and asking how she might do better. She might request that we provide her with another sample problem for her to work through or per-haps an example of an "A paper" to use for comparison. The "C" student with the fixed mindset we never see again. He makes it a point to take future courses from other professors. He hopes that another professor might better reward his innate abilities and that he'll get a better grade as a result. Usually, the student will find that using his tried-and-failed approach of reading and rereading class notes will produce grades on future exams that are pretty much like the ones he got in the past.

What's true for law students is also true for young lawyers. The mindset lawyers have when leaving law school often shapes how they approach the challenges of a new career. The budding associ-ate with a growth mindset understands that becoming a successful attorney will require a lot of adjustment and learning. She doesn't hesitate to ask more experienced attorneys questions about how they do their work or how they managed to overcome early dif-ficulties. She observes other attorneys closely, always trying to identify techniques and approaches that might help in her own work. This approach offers a nice side benefit. Simply by asking questions and paying close attention, she becomes more quickly accepted as a full team member of the firm.[34] Armed with a bag full of strategies, she then makes an all-out effort to solve what-ever problems come her way.

Compare the approach of the growth mindset attorney with how the fixed mindset associate might go about his work. Each assignment is viewed as a test, both of his worth as a lawyer and the wisdom of the firm's decision to hire him. Gripped by fear of failure, he plugs ahead alone because asking questions of other attorneys in the firm could be seen as an admission of deficiency. When things go sour and the case is lost, or the contract is exposed as poorly drafted, or the client complains to a senior partner about his work, he concludes that he just wasn't cut out to be a great lawyer. He feels powerless. Lacking the focus that comes with a growth mindset, he is easily distracted and may begin to wallow in self-pity.

Every lawyer will lose some cases. What matters is what a lawyer takes away from those experiences. When a good lawyer loses a case, it becomes an opportunity to learn from mistakes. When a trial ends the wrong way, the good lawyer is likely to replay parts of the trial over and over in his or her head. The lawyer asks whether a different strategy might have produced a better result. Perhaps there's a pretrial motion that should have been made that wasn't? Perhaps too much reliance was placed on hunches during jury selection? Perhaps a witness could have been better prepared for cross-examination? Or the lawyer's thoughts might turn to whether the case was misjudged from the start. Perhaps the facts or the law made the result all but inevitable? Perhaps a new approach to evaluating case prospects is in order? Obsession might not be too strong a word for the hold that a disappointing loss might have on the losing lawyer's mind—for a while. But then, as they say in sports, the good lawyer shakes it off and gets back into the game, better prepared for the next challenge.

On the other hand, some lawyers view lost cases not as opportunities to learn but as a reflection of their fixed abilities. For lawyers whose takeaway from a disappointment is "I'm a failure"—well, they probably are. Or at least they are unlikely to improve as they could if they determined instead to learn what it takes to do better next time. A trial outcome shouldn't define you. Rather, it should be seen as a source of clues for achieving future success.

CHANGING YOUR MINDSET

Fortunately, Dweck says, it is possible to change mindsets—mindsets, after all, are just beliefs. No one is born with a "fixed mindset gene." Because a mindset is a set of beliefs, it—like the neural networks whose growth they influence—can change. In fact, research has shown that workshops aimed at turning fixed mindsets into growth mindsets have been successful. In one controlled experiment, students who attended a growth mindset workshop showed much more improvement in grades than those who attended a workshop that emphasized other learning strategies.[35] Encouraged by results like these, researchers at Stanford have devised computer modules (one program is called "Brainology") to help students develop growth mindsets.

Dweck contends that for a person with a fixed mindset, simply knowing about the growth mindset can be the first step toward change. Recognizing the existence of an alternative mindset can offer hope that the shackles of the fixed mindset might be lifted. Of course, mindset change won't happen without dedication and clear focus on your goal. Casting off a fixed mindset requires changing the internal monologue that is running in your head and viewing learning as a challenge that involves bringing your sharpest tools and best strategies to bear on the problem. Dweck warns that mindset change "is not about picking up a few pointers here and there." Rather, she says, "It's about seeing things in a new way."[36] Embracing criticism and welcoming suggestions don't come easily for some, and until they become a habit, learning potential will be limited.

A good first step toward becoming a better lawyer is to assess your own strengths and weaknesses. In fact, the ability to perform an accurate assessment of one's abilities correlates highly with professional success. According to Howard Gardner, author of *Extraordinary Minds*, people who excel at what they do generally have "a special talent for identifying their own strengths and weaknesses."[37] Interestingly, people with a growth mindset are substantially better able to identify both their strengths and weaknesses than are people with fixed mindsets. This might be because fixed mindset people, believing that there is little that could be done about their weaknesses, are less likely to admit to having them.

Needless to say, it is your weaknesses that will require your attention. For some, that means developing better strategies for moving information from short-term memory storage into long-term storage so that you might improve your pattern recognition. For others, the focus will be on learning to see the legal forest and not just its trees in order to present arguments in a more compelling way. There are dozens of techniques for improving information retention and analytical flexibility, and one of them might be just right for you.[38]

Finally, if you are serious about becoming a more effective lawyer, enlist allies. You might find that a friend or colleague can help you identify weaknesses to which you are blind. Seek out people whom you respect and who might be willing to offer constructive criticism. Ask them to critique your memo or draft contract or opening statement—and try not to be overly defensive when you get what you ask for. Even if your allies do nothing more than offer moral support for your self-improvement program, they'll be providing a valuable service. We all can use a few good cheerleaders.

Thus far we've suggested that there are just two possible mindsets when, of course, mindsets actually occupy a continuum. Many people might believe, for example, that they are capable of cultivating their abilities to a more modest extent than is really the case. They have what might be called "a limited growth mindset." They underestimate the degree of change that is possible and fail to appreciate the improvement that increased effort might bring about. Most likely, you are somewhere between the two poles of the continuum. Despite the fact that the two-mindset model is an oversimplification, it provides a useful way of thinking about how to become a more effective lawyer. There's not much downside in moving more toward the full growth mindset, even if your mindset already leans in that direction.

The Danger of Fixed Mindset Perfectionism

Lawyers, for the most part, are smart people. It has taken a lot of academic success to get where they are. For lawyers with a fixed mindset, success after success has likely been the result of their deep need for perfection. At the same time that perfectionism explains success, however, it risks ultimately sabotaging it.

Lawyers with a need for perfection run the risk of failing to meet deadlines because their work product does not yet satisfy their own extremely high standards. They have difficulty deciding what has to be done immediately and what can be placed on the back burner. They fail to advance creative arguments or propose creative solutions to a client's problem because creativity almost always means making a few mistakes. They fail to seek out potentially valuable feedback from colleagues because they are reluctant to admit their mistakes when they do occur. A study comparing the writing quality of undergraduates high in perfectionist tendencies with that of other undergraduates found that the perfectionists' writing was actually "significantly lower in quality" than the writing of the nonperfectionists. The researcher, Smith psychology professor Randy Frost, theorized that perfectionists avoid writing tasks. "The result may be that those perfectionists don't practice writing in any consistent way and don't benefit from feedback on their work," he said. He added that perfectionists "seem to be motivated by a fear of failure and…new tasks are viewed as opportunities for failure rather than as accomplishments."[39] All of this, unsurprisingly, comes at a high psychological cost. Achieving anything short of perfection is a cause of agony.

In her book *Better by Mistake*, Alina Tugend suggests that the problem with perfectionists comes from having unrealistic goals that "inevitably lead to a sense of failure."[40] Tugend makes a distinction between striving for excellence and obsessing about perfection: "Excellence involves enjoying what you're doing, feeling good about what you've learned, and developing confidence. Perfection involves feeling bad about a 98 (out of 100) and always finding mistakes no matter how well you're doing."[41]

WILLPOWER LESSONS

Researchers say that people persist at attempting to solve problems longer when they are told the problems are difficult than when they are told the problems are easy.[42] This result, at first blush, appears paradoxical. Why would people work longer when a problem is less likely to be solved? The answer seems to be related to self-esteem. When we are told a task is difficult, we feel we can keep at it longer without being thought of as untalented or stupid. There is a lesson here for lawyers, or at least for senior partners. When you assign a project to an associate, be sure to describe the project as challenging, one that will test the person's abilities as a lawyer.

Moreover, research demonstrates that "people persist longer when they feel personally responsible for choosing the task." The reason, it seems, is that choosing a task makes it seem "more relevant to the self."[43] This finding underscores the importance to lawyers, whenever possible, of having work that aligns with their own values. When you work on something that matters to you, you'll keep working longer.

Surprisingly, researchers also discovered that simply by changing one habitual behavior, people can increase self-control over other, unrelated habitual behaviors. For example, right-handed people who practice performing daily tasks, such as lifting a cup or brushing their teeth, with their left rather than right hands might suddenly find themselves with more stamina for confronting bad habits, such as smoking or excessive Net surfing at the office. Apparently, the effort required for the hand-changing exercise strengthens willpower overall. As Baumeister and Tierney note, "Exercising control in one area seemed to improve all areas of life."[44]

Researchers also have uncovered three circumstances in which our self-control is especially challenged. One situation arises the moment after we first cave in to a temptation. That is the time when you find yourself vulnerable to what researchers call the "what-the-hell effect."[45] You've already broken your diet by ordering the milkshake, so you might as well have the fries and cheeseburger too. You've been unfaithful once in your marriage, so what's the big deal about a second time? You've misrepresented facts once in a brief, so you might as well do the same again. The second situation that presents a special challenge to self-control arises in almost the exact opposite circumstance—when you've been unusually good. You've made it to the gym and put in a good workout, so you reward yourself with a pizza. You've gotten that Shmutz contract off your desk, so you deserve an hour of surfing a few of your favorite websites. Willpower researchers call this "licensing."[46] Of course, there's nothing necessarily wrong with allowing yourself a reward for a job well done—and, in fact, holding out to yourself the promise of reward for completion of an onerous task has been shown to increase the likelihood you'll actually get the job done. The third situation in which willpower is tested is when you feel sad or depressed and, not without reason, believe that giving in to temptation is necessary because it can give you a temporary mood boost. Unhappy lawyers tend not to be very productive lawyers. All three of these proclivities— "what-the-hell," licensing, and mood boosting—will lead you into the valley of temptation from time to time (and if it's just from time to time, that's okay).

OUR FINITE SUPPLY OF WILLPOWER

None of the stress associated with law practice would matter so much if our supplies of willpower were unlimited, but they're not. Each of us starts our day with a finite supply of willpower, and stress during the day constantly depletes that supply. Willpower is almost always higher in the morning and lower at the end of the day. Our finite willpower supply has been likened to a muscle that becomes fatigued through overuse and to a gas tank being drawn down as we travel through our day. Sybil Dunlop, a litigator in a Minnesota firm, writes that she thinks "of my willpower store like a videogame. I imagine the little bar in my head depleting as I focus on an issue."[47] At day's end, research shows, we're less able to make decisions and the decisions we do make tend to be poorer. When our willpower is depleted, we look for ways to conserve energy such as avoiding or postponing decisions. Baumeister and Tierney point to "abundant research showing that people have a hard time giving up options, even when the options aren't doing them any good. This reluctance to give up options becomes more pronounced when willpower is low."[48] The result, researchers suggest, is that we gravitate to safe decisions such as sticking with the status quo.

The tendency to pick safe options when willpower levels are depleted explains the results of the study of more than 1,000 decisions made by the parole boards of four major prisons in Israel. Researchers compared the decisions made by the board when willpower supplies could be expected to be high, such as early in the morning or just after a snack break, to those made just before the break or late in the afternoon. The results were striking. Prisoners who appeared before the board early in the morning found their parole requests granted 70% of the time, while those unfortunate enough to face the board late in the day received favorable results less than 10% of the time. Prisoners who appeared right after a replenishing late-morning break during which the judges ate sandwiches and fruit won parole requests 65% of the time, compared to prisoners who appeared just before the break and had parole requests granted less than 20% of the time. After a one-hour lunch break, the same thing happened: grants of parole requests shot up to over 60%, only to fall back at the end of the day to below 10%[49] (Figure 3.1). The researchers, after exhaustively considering other possible explanations for the disparity, concluded that as mental energy levels dropped before meals and late in the day, the parole board members usually fell back to their default position, which was to deny parole requests. Judging, like practicing law, is mentally stressful work. Granting parole is, for a parole board, the riskier choice, because board members are likely to be criticized when a paroled prisoner later commits a serious crime. The safe option is to keep a prisoner in jail for now and let him try again next time. As willpower supplies of the board members depleted, they became biased toward the safer option: letting

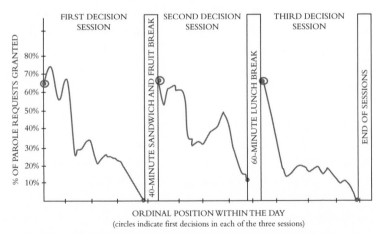

FIGURE 3.1. Graph showing grants of parole requests during course of day.

the prisoner linger in jail. The lesson here is if you want a bold ruling from a judge, make sure he or she is operating on a full stomach. (The same lesson applies, by the way, for scheduling your medical procedures. A study of colonoscopy results showed that with each passing hour, gastroenterologists became 4.6% less likely to detect a colon polyp,[50] while a second study showed that problems related to anesthesia increased from 1 percent for surgeries at 9 A.M. to a high of 4.2% for surgeries beginning at 4 P.M.)[51]

Why, you might ask, did the parole board grant more parole requests after snack breaks and lunches? The rather surprising answer is that willpower supplies are replenished by glucose. Willpower is not just a matter of psychology; it is equally a matter of physiology.[52] An impressive collection of studies makes clear, as Baumeister and Tierney put it, "No glucose, no willpower."[53] Brain imaging shows that glucose ingestion causes dramatic shifts of activity within various regions of the brain. Unlike a computer, which ceases to function at all without a source of energy, the brain instead "stops doing some things and starts doing others."[54] Low on glucose, you are, for example, more likely to lash out inappropriately at a secretary. Impaired glucose tolerance, which leads to bad decision making of many kinds, has even been identified in two recent studies as a substantial risk factor for criminal recidivism and juvenile delinquency.[55]

CAN WILLPOWER BE STRENGTHENED?

Glucose, of course, is found not just in simple sugar but in many kinds of foods. Sugar can give us the fastest boost, so you might consider gulping down a soda (but not a diet soda) or a chocolate bar before an oral argument, important meeting, or trial summation. In the long run, however, foods with a low glycemic index are better for producing steady self-control. Foods such as nuts, vegetables, fish, olive oil, and raw fruits are converted into glucose by the body, just at a much slower rate than simple sugars and starchy foods, which produce "boom or bust" cycles within our bodies. Prisons that shifted from sugary foods to more vegetables, fruits, and whole grains report decreases in violence and other problems involving prisoners.[56]

The evidence is really beyond dispute and your mother was right. Have a good breakfast and eat those vegetables—and other wholesome foods. Both your life and your law practice will benefit. You'll have better focus, make better decisions, and be a whole lot more pleasant in the office.

There is also ample research showing the willpower benefits of a good night's sleep. Sleep deprivation increases the body's demand for glucose and impairs our ability to make use of glucose in the bloodstream. Studies show that people deprived of sleep make poorer decisions and are more likely to cheat and engage in other forms of unethical conduct.[57] Catching up on sleep can make a world of difference. Brain scans taken after a good night's sleep show increased levels of activity in the prefrontal cortex, the energy-hungry region of the brain and the area associated with maintaining self-control.[58] As much as you might feel the need to pull an all-nighter before trial or an important meeting, resist the temptation and you're likely to perform better.

Physical exercise is another means by which lawyers, and anyone else, can improve willpower. McGonigal calls exercise "the closest thing to a wonder drug that self-control scientists have discovered."[59] Even as little as fifteen minutes on a treadmill has been shown to reduce temptations, such as cravings for cigarettes or chocolate. Longer term exercise produces greater benefits, relieving stress while increasing the ability of brain cells to efficiently and quickly communicate with each other, allowing better decision making. Studies show that butt-busting hour-long sessions aren't needed to produce significant improvements in willpower; even five-minute sessions can make a difference. And when workouts in the gym aren't possible, walks, gardening, or just playing with the kids might be enough. In short, if you are one of the 89% of Americans who don't meet the recommended guidelines for physical exercise,[60] remember that any exercise is better than none.

Finally, willpower can be enhanced by a little head-clearing or, more precisely, "mindfulness." The best means available appears to be meditation. In researching our book, *The Happy Lawyer*, we were astonished by the powerful evidence linking meditation (as well as sleep and exercise, by the way) to increased happiness. The research showing the benefits of meditation for self-control is at least as compelling. Neuroscientists who observe brain scans of persons meditating (or praying) see increased activity in the brain regions most associated with self-control.[61] Meditation seems to increase blood flow to the brain much like pumping iron increases blood flow to muscles. University of Miami psychologist Michael McCullough calls meditation "a kind of anaerobic workout for self-control."[62] Kelly McGonigal says that the brains of regular meditators become "finely tuned willpower machines," and in her Stanford University course on willpower she advises students to engage in frequent five-minute breath focusing exercises, gradually increasing to fifteen minutes a day.[63] Of course, some lawyers—especially older lawyers—are convinced that meditation is too "New-Agey" for their serious selves. Mindfulness experts advise that head-clearing benefits can be derived in more conventional ways, such as listening to calming music, taking a stroll in a park, socializing with close friends, or simply savoring a cup of tea in a sunny spot.

EMOTIONAL TRAPS THAT DRAIN WILLPOWER AND HARM DECISION MAKING

Anxiety, boredom, impatience, and addiction are among the emotional traps that can sap willpower and prevent lawyers from seeing problems with fresh, open eyes. Fortunately, each of these traps is avoidable.

THE ANXIETY TRAP

Evolution has made us anxious. From an evolutionary standpoint, being in a persistent state of contentment would not be a recipe for reproductive success. Survival depends more on having a brain that sends out the message "Danger!" when we are threatened than one that is constantly telling us "Be happy" when we are not threatened. Early humans who ignored poisonous snakes and saber-toothed tigers weren't around long enough to pass their genes on to future generations. Nature has programmed us to notice better the negative than the positive. Psychologists call this our "negativity bias" (not to be confused with our "optimism bias," which relates to predictions about the future, not perceptions).

When you become stressed or anxious, your pituitary gland signals to your adrenal gland that it is time to release the "stress hormones," cortisol and epinephrine. The epinephrine increases your heart rate to enable you to pump more blood while the cortisol causes the brain's emotional center, the amygdala, to ramp up, increasing further the intensity of your reaction to negative information. Under the influence of stress hormones, you are more likely to read other people's intentions as sinister.

Anxiety has several adverse effects on our decision making. First, it harms the formation of our explicit memories. We are less likely to remember what happened in a meeting, a deposition, a hearing, or a trial if we are anxious. Second, longer-term anxiety tends to weaken our existing neural networks, causing us difficulty in recalling information that was once easily within our grasp. Additionally, frequent bouts of anxiety or stress tend to reduce our powers of concentration and can eventually lead to depression. Depression, with its attendant lack of motivation, often leads to a sort of decision paralysis, hardly a condition conducive to wise lawyering.

Anxiety also tends to suppress our production of serotonin, the brain's neurotransmitter most responsible for good moods. As you fall into a blue mood, your openness to people and awareness of your environment both suffer. If you are feeling anxious and stressed out, you'll have a much more difficult time picking up subtle signals from your client, a witness, a judge, or anyone else you encounter on your job.

When anxiety is specifically focused on job performance, one danger is paralysis: fear of doing something wrong prevents doing much of anything at all. Worry about whether you'll meet your own high expectations (recall our discussion of "the fixed mindset") locks you in position, as your mind bounces around like a pool ball. Anxiety might also cause you to become excessively fussy. If you are worried about an important brief with a fast-approaching deadline, you might engage in a disorganized round of heavy tinkering on the project, resulting in a brief that is less coherent than it was before you started the revising. You might turn almost wildly from one source to another, looking for the magic bullet that will convince the judges to go your way. Instead of being the steady but sure tortoise that wins the race, you become a hopped-up hare zig-zagging off course.

Discipline and organization can give you a sense that you control your future and help you proceed in the face of anxiety. If you are anxious about that oral argument coming up in the court of appeals, spend some time reading everything you can about the issues in your case, outline your arguments, do a moot court run of the argument by a trusted colleague. You can also feel more in control by imagining in advance the event that is making you anxious. Visiting the courtroom where you will soon make your big argument, for example, allows you to have a clearer picture of the future and eliminates the "finding-the-courthouse" worry. Research shows that when people visualize themselves successfully completing actions, they tend to get better results.[64] No one's perfect, so don't try to be. If you can convince yourself that perfection is an unrealistic goal, you'll feel better when you make your (with luck, minor) screwups. Mistakes are part of life and accepting that fact reduces anxiety.

The Boredom Trap

The Anxiety Trap's opposite is the Boredom Trap. Almost every lawyer, at some time in his or her career, will not want to do the work required for a client because the work is, well, boring. Experienced attorneys, more so than younger attorneys, are likely to become ensnared in the Boredom Trap. Boredom is a problem associated with not seeing things freshly. When we are bored we close ourselves to inputs and our ability to empathize drops. If we continue to work while bored, we are likely to make mistakes. Or, if boredom gets the better of us, we simply postpone the boring task and pick up something else. Procrastination in the practice of law, with its many non-negotiable deadlines, can be a dangerous thing.

Challenges that seem beyond our ability tend to cause anxiety; work that is routine causes boredom. Not all legal work can be in the sweet spot where the work tests our abilities to the fullest but is still within our ability to complete competently. (In the happiness literature, work in this sweet zone is associated with "flow," which produces a sense of time flying by.)[65] Some work of lawyers will be boring, but still it must be done. If we can't change our work, it is our minds that must change. How do we push through the boredom and argue that same motion for the twentieth time? How do we will ourselves through hundreds of hours of document review?

A simple solution is to stop and do something else until the boredom passes. Take a walk, get a cup of coffee, walk down the hall and chat with a colleague. If you have other, less tedious, work on your desk, turn to it. Another approach is to view boring work as a ritual, or perhaps penance. You do your morning pushups to keep your muscles strong; you draft your operating agreements to keep your legal skills sharp. It's all part of life's experience—it's your chopping of wood to keep the home fire glowing.

Harvey Mackay, a columnist who writes frequently on leadership, offered a set of suggestions for avoiding the boredom trap. His recommendations included making changes in your work habits or work environment. These changes—some substantial, some more trivial—might include taking on some pro bono work to add variety to your workday, making new friends in the firm, or redecorating your office.[66] Novelty gives us a dopamine rush and pushes boredom out the door.

Kevin Houchin, writing in *Lawyering Skills*, came up with another list; his focused on tips for fighting the procrastination often associated with boring tasks. Houchin's tips range from the materialistic ("Think: '$250/hour. $250/hour. $250/hour' or whatever your billing rate is") to the altruistic (Think: "Drafting this contract will really help this client, and this client is doing great things. I'm contributing to making the world a better place by doing my part in this project") to the pragmatic (Think: "I'll get grieved or fired if I don't do this RIGHT NOW!") to the "athletic" (Think: "Just Do It").[67]

The Impatience Trap

Much of the work lawyers do requires close attention to detail. It's not work that mixes well with impatience. Impatience leads to mistakes, sometimes big and sometimes small, but most avoidable if you can just keep the right attitude.

The problem with impatience is that it triggers a strong desire to make up for the time you unexpectedly lose. Having finally made their way through a traffic jam, drivers tend to speed up "to make up for lost time." The same thing happens when we hit work jams. We try to make up time by cutting corners; we fail to double-check information; we "go with instincts" to spare the trouble of additional research or reflection. And, as a result, we screw up. In addition, impatience can quickly turn to anger, leading to ill-chosen words that we soon regret.

Remaining patient is a worthy goal but sometimes difficult in practice. As anyone who has ever sat through an especially long red light or bided time in a long airport security line knows, patience is easier to lose than to keep. Whenever the time it takes to complete a task exceeds our expectations, our impatience begins to grow.

One of our goals as lawyers, then, should be to minimize the number of tasks whose completion time becomes unexpectedly long. One way of doing this is by being well-organized. A frequent source of impatience for many lawyers is the time it takes to find a key source or document that is needed right away. Simply keeping sources and documents in a good, logical order can help you avoid the impatience trap. Another common source of impatience for lawyers comes from underestimating the time it takes to complete a job (especially one of a type you haven't done before), which can lead to cutting corners and generally shoddy work. Most jobs, frankly, take longer than you think they will. If you can find a way to allot more time than you think you will need for a project, impatience is much less likely to be a problem. Alternatively, you might consider scaling down the size of the project, if that is possible, to allow some extra time for completion. Or perhaps you can scale down work on other cases or projects to allow more time for your more important work.

The Addiction Trap

I can resist everything but temptation.

—Oscar Wilde

The addiction trap catches those who routinely sacrifice their long-term goals for short-term pleasures. Who among us has not

on occasion made such a choice? Whether the short-term pleasure came from alcohol, drugs, or excessive gambling or partying,
we've almost all, at times, chosen immediate pleasure over other
personal goals. And if the times are relatively few and far between,
little harm is likely to come from those choices.

The pressures of law practice, however, seem to incline lawyers
toward more risky choices than is the case for many other professions. Lawyers, for example, suffer from exceptionally high rates
of drug abuse and alcoholism, compared to those in other professions. A study of lawyers in the state of Washington, for example,
estimated that one in five lawyers suffered substance abuse problems, a rate almost twice the national average.[68]

It almost goes without saying that substance abuse issues can
adversely affect a lawyer's management of his or her clients' cases.
In the practice of law, deadlines matter, and anything that stands in
the way of meeting them is a serious problem. Moreover, lawyers
more than most people need to operate at something close to
their maximum mental abilities to do the best for their client—and
hangovers and drug-induced fogs clearly can impair thinking skills.

Self-control, our power to resist temptation and addiction, as
we indicated earlier, has both genetic and environmental roots.
Peterson and Seligman conclude that self-control is "thwarted in
people who live (or have grown up) under chaotic and unpre-
dictable conditions in which the future seems so uncertain and
remote that long-term planning is pointless."[69] If you grow up in a
murder-ravaged neighborhood or a war zone, you might very well
engage in risky behavior based on your prediction that your life is
likely to be short in any event. Research also shows that prudence
is thwarted when autonomy is denied and personal control is limited—in cults, for example. It's also true that who you spend your
time with can greatly influence your willingness to engage in risky
behavior—just look at rock stars if you have any doubts about that.

Simply believing that you have the ability to resist impulses
is a start. Getting exercise, plenty of sleep, good nutrition, and

building a solid support network all can help make smart choices more likely in both your life and your practice. Despite the lack of established programs for increasing self-control, Kelly McGonigal contends that people do have within themselves the ability to better resist temptations. "There's very little evidence this stuff is fixed," McGonigal says. "The brain is relatively plastic and the most plastic regions tend to be most related to stress and self-control."[70]

One promising strategy for avoiding temptations is to burn your bridges—that is, the bridges that lead to your temptation. When best-selling author Jonathan Franzen decided he was spending too much time surfing the Net and playing videogames instead of writing, he destroyed his computer's Ethernet port. "What you have to do," Franzen explained in an interview, "is plug in an Ethernet cable with superglue, and then you saw the little head off it."[71] In the past, one of this book's authors polished off entire bags of potato chips while cruising down interstates. Then he discovered that he could keep his chip eating to a more reasonable level by, after stuffing a handful of them into his mouth, heaving the bag into the back seat and safely out of reach. You probably can come up with a few "bridge burning" tactics of your own that might make your days at the office more productive.

Each of us has different traps that we need to worry about most. Some of us struggle with impatience, others with our ego, and others of us yet with anxieties or boredom or substance abuse issues. What is important is that we have the psychological courage to be honest with ourselves and identify our weaknesses—the traps most likely to ensnare us—and then to address those weaknesses the best way we can.

MAKING THE FUTURE BIGGER

George Ainslie, author of *Breakdown of Will*, makes the point that "self-control is really the art of making the future bigger."[72]

He argues that to build a successful career or successful life one must first imagine the type of career you want to have, or type of person you want to be. Then pay attention to that idea of a career for your future self. Ainslie says that "wisdom as it applies to self-control is really the awareness that what you do now predicts your future."[73]

Most people overweight the present and apply a steep discount to their future. We choose not to exercise today because we fully weight its costs ("It will cause pain," "I'll miss my favorite television show") but give only half as much weight to its future benefits ("I'll be healthier," "I'll lose weight and feel better"). And a similar analysis keeps us from getting tedious but necessary work done around the office until it's almost too late and the costs of further procrastination become painfully evident. In short, most people suffer from a nearsightedness that allows them to see their present selves clearly but their future selves only as a blur, almost as another person. We thus are inclined to follow our ever-changing wants, running on autopilot, and deny ourselves the bigger future we all deserve.

Simply by understanding our own nearsightedness, we can—if we try hard enough—correct our vision. Kelly McGonigal observes, "We are born to be tempted, and born to resist."[74] We have the ability to train our minds to recognize when we are making choices that will cost us in the long run. McGonigal calls this "getting to know [our] future selves."[75] We can pause, think clearly about our tendency to discount the future, and make the better choice. If we are self-aware, if we develop our ability to turn off autopilot, we can have the type of career, and be the type of person, we imagine.

Psychologists Philip Zimbardo (best known for his Stanford prison guard experiment) and John Boyd also link willpower to time orientation. Zimbardo calls time perspective "one of the most powerful influences on human thought, feeling, and action."[76] As Zimbardo and Boyd see it, every person overuses a particular time perspective—focusing mostly on the future, the past, or the present. People with predominantly future perspectives—constantly imagining achieving a better future life through their own planning and efforts—are vastly overrepresented at highly selective schools and in professions like law and medicine. They are the competitive go-getters who push aside the pleasures of the present (sex, alcohol, drugs, rock and roll) and "consider work a source of special pleasure."[77] "Futures," their research shows, tend to be more successful than present- and past-oriented people in negotiating deals and arguing. Just as importantly, people having a future orientation "will be the first to cooperate with others for a common win-win" by avoiding "the social traps that ensnare present-oriented competitors."[78]

So hurray for your future orientation, if you are one of the many lawyers who share that time perspective. It will serve you well in the practice of law. But Zimbardo and Boyd remind us that too much of anything, including too much focus on the future, has its costs. Futures tend to work long hours and live long lives, but their constant attention to the future takes spontaneity and joy out of relationships and reduces the opportunities for happiness that come from savoring the simple pleasures of life. They advise people with a heavy future orientation to do *less*, not more, to learn to put unimportant things on the back burner, and to give others the *gift of time*.[79]

Our focus in the next chapter is on our relationships with others. More specifically, we consider relationships between lawyers and other members within the legal community. Keeping those relationships healthy and productive is, as you might easily imagine, one of the keys to a successful and satisfying career in law.

CHAPTER 4

The Good Lawyer Values Others in the Legal Community

Every action done in company ought to be with some sign of respect to those that are present.

—George Washington

LAWYERS WORK IN AN ADVERSARIAL PROFESSION WHERE emotions run high and politics rarely seems far from the surface. Lawyers can, and sometimes do, argue about anything. It is well to remember, as Stephen Easton, dean of the Wyoming Law School, observed, "Most issues that you could fight about are not worth fighting about."[1] In this chapter, with the goal of increasing civility and perhaps even fraternity in the practice of law, we suggest ways of behaving and ways of thinking that might minimize fights and bridge the divides that can separate lawyers into warring camps.

In the first section of this chapter we consider the importance of emotional balance, the quality that saves lawyers from being thrown off their game by negative events. To turn a bad event into a disastrous one, there's nothing like blowing your top in a negotiation or telling a judge exactly what you think of an unhelpful ruling, then stewing and making excuses for your bad behavior.

Lawyers, like most people, often rationalize rude words to opposing counsel or a judge with the excuse that "it had to be said." Professor Steven Lubet, director of Northwestern University's Center for Trial Strategy, wisely reminds us, however, "It almost certainly did *not* have to be said."[2] Good lawyers cope well. They tend to have humility and an inner quietness that leads to careful decisions and trusting clients, and they look for reasonable ways to believe the best about other lawyers. They don't suspend their powers of critical thinking or hold their tongues when the facts reveal other lawyers to be guilty of serious transgressions, but they do give them the benefit of the doubt. Believing that the legal system functions best when an atmosphere of mutual respect among lawyers prevails, they try to see the words and actions of others in a favorable light.

In the second section of this chapter, we turn our attention to the political and value-based divisions among lawyers that have weakened ties that traditionally have bound lawyers together. Psychologists and neuroscientists exploring the sources of our political differences have discovered that our differences run deep, being rooted in our intuitions and, perhaps surprisingly, even in the structure of our brains. Although it would be inaccurate to say we are born into this world as either conservatives or liberals, we have genetic predispositions that point us in one political direction or the other. There is no gene, of course, that determines political attitudes, but collectively a set of genes influence personality traits, such as openness to novelty or reactivity to threats—traits that correlate with political attitudes. As this new understanding of our political differences spreads, there is hope that there might be less shouting across the political divide and a bit more acceptance: "Joe can't help holding his benighted view; he is wired that way." The better understanding people have of the different moral foundations that separate us, the less inclined they will be to think of their political opponents as evil or deranged, and the more likely they will be to find points of commonality and establish trust.

A HUMBLE (BUT VERY FAMOUS) ATTORNEY

In 1854, Philadelphia and Washington, DC attorneys were defending an Illinois man accused of violating Cyrus McCormick's patent for the reaper; they asked Abraham Lincoln to serve as local counsel, and Lincoln took his assignment seriously. According to William Lee Miller, in his book *Lincoln's Virtues*, Lincoln traveled to Rockford to inspect his client's reaper, researched patent law, and wrote out a long legal argument.[3]

Later, however, the eastern attorneys decided they would prefer as local counsel Edwin Stanton, a more formally educated lawyer from Ohio. They neglected to inform Lincoln of their decision, even after they had the case transferred to federal court in Cincinnati. They ignored his letters and didn't bother to send him pleadings connected with the litigation. Nonetheless, Lincoln learned through direct communication with his client that the case had a new venue, and on the date set for trial Lincoln showed up in Cincinnati ready to help—he thought—with his client's defense. Surprised to see Lincoln at the Cincinnati railway station, the eastern attorney and Stanton refused to walk with him to their hotel; "refused to let him sit with them at counsel table; refused to invite him to dinner during the trial; and refused even to look at the written argument Lincoln had prepared for the case."[4] Despite this series of insults, Lincoln sat without complaint throughout the multiday trial, paying close attention to the arguments in the hope of learning a thing or two. When a check arrived from Washington for his promised fee, Lincoln mailed the check back with a note explaining that he provided no actual services at the trial and thus felt unable to accept the money.

Remarkably, seven years later, as president of the United States, Lincoln invited Edwin Stanton—the same Ohio lawyer who had treated him so rudely in the patent case—to become his new secretary of war. In Lincoln's view, Stanton was the best man for the job, and the nation's interests had to trump any bruises to his ego that Stanton might have inflicted. If he thought Stanton required forgiveness for his insensitive behavior, he forgave.

Being humble means being secure in yourself, and Lincoln demonstrated the virtue of humility as well as anyone. He never imagined himself as the center of the universe—even when, because of his position, there were plenty of people ready to tell him that he was. In the words of C. S. Lewis, "Humility is not thinking less of yourself, it's thinking of yourself less."

Humility reduces friction and enhances cooperation. Stephen Hall describes it as "a social lubricant, greasing the wheels of group interaction."[5] It's maybe not surprising, then, that humility is associated with strong leadership potential. A study in the *Harvard Business Review* concluded that "extreme personal humility" (along with "intense professional will") was one of the two characteristics that best defined successful business leaders.[6] Humility certainly served the sixteenth president well.

REMEMBERING WHAT MATTERS

When it's all about you, then it's necessarily not about the client—and it really is all about the client. That's your job: to do right by your client regardless of whether it wins you fortune or acclaim. Of course, it is only natural to want to look good. You want to present yourself as smart and savvy, and it is tempting to opt for approaches that make your abilities more apparent to clients and colleagues alike. You might think that the facts of your case create the perfect opportunity to showcase your many God-given talents and so might be tempted to recommend that a client reject a fairly generous settlement offer that it is probably in the client's interest to take, or to litigate when litigation will likely impose more costs than bring benefits. Resist these temptations! Follow the advice of Lincoln, who never felt compelled to display his courtroom prowess unless doing so served the best interests of his client. "Discourage litigation," Abe advised. "Persuade your neighbors to compromise whenever you can....As a peace maker, the lawyer has a superior opportunity of being a good [person]. There will still be business enough."[7]

Lawyers with inflated views of themselves tend to have little interest in the advice, opinions, or feelings of others. Care, commitment, and concern for others are not qualities associated with narcissistic personalities. Unsurprisingly, then, lawyers who overvalue themselves tend to be viewed negatively by clients and are less likely to produce satisfactory results for them in negotiations. Ego can also lead you not to admit mistakes. You worry that conceding error will make you look bad. Despite growing doubts about your chosen path, you continue to plunge ahead, often with disastrous consequences.

Humility doesn't come naturally to everyone. Women, according to social science research, are somewhat more likely to have this virtue than men. Also, some cultures value humility more than others. Japanese culture, for example, emphasizes the virtue of humility more than American culture does.[8] Whether humility can be taught to a fully grown adult is not entirely clear. Positive psychologists Christopher Peterson and Martin Seligman speculate that "any technique, resource, or relationship that provides a person with an alternative means of feeling safe" might help.[9] As they see it, having an inflated sense of self provides for some people a sense of security, and before it can be taken away, it has to be replaced by something than can fill that same need. Susan Cain, author of a best-selling book about the power of introverts called *Quiet*, suggests that if you're not naturally unassuming, "try faking it."[10] Little harm can come from deliberately assuming you're not particularly good at something. If events prove you wrong, all to the good. And if events prove you right—well, at least you were right.

THE POWER OF HUMILITY: ONE LAWYER'S APPROACH TO NEGOTIATIONS

When a senior lawyer at her Wall Street firm left on vacation, junior associate Susan Cain took charge of a negotiation involving the restructuring of loan terms for an about-to-default South American manufacturing company. It was the most important assignment she had ever had at the firm and by her own admission she was worried about her ability to go toe-to-toe with a seasoned negotiator and a whole stable full of disgruntled investment bankers.

In her account of the negotiation, Cain writes that things got off to an unpromising start when the investment bankers' lawyer "launched into an impressive speech" on how Cain's "clients would be lucky simply to accept the bankers' terms." Cain responded to the speech by using her ability, facilitated by her mild-mannered and patient nature, to "take strong, even aggressive positions while coming across as perfectly reasonable." She did what came most naturally to her; she began asking questions:

"Let's go back a step. What are your numbers based on?"
"What if we structured the loan this way; do you think that might work?"
"That way?"
"Some other way?"

As the negotiation went on, Cain's questions became less tentative. Having prepared well for the session, she never was forced to concede facts or pound the table. She met every seemingly "unbudgeable" assertion with a constructive response: "Are you saying that's the only way to go? What if we took a different approach?" In the end, by staying true to her style and keeping her emotions regulated, Cain struck a favorable deal for her clients. She was able to stop the "speech-ifying" and start "an actual conversation." When, at one point, a banker threw down a bunch of papers and "stormed out of the room," Cain simply ignored the display. The next day, Cain reported, she received a phone call from one of the bankers offering her a job. "I've never seen anyone so nice and so tough at the same time," the banker said.[11]

Cain even writes nice. As she tells her negotiation story, there's no suggestion that the Harvard-educated lawyer is doing so to toot her own horn. Cain is, however, on a crusade. She's an introvert and she wants other introverts to know that with their quiet, unassuming manners, they have a lot to offer in a world that often favors and rewards extroverts.

MELLOW BEATS BELLOW

It is human nature to believe you are right and want to seek confirmation for that belief, and that goes double if you have an over-sized ego. You've probably observed that Republicans watch Fox News, read *Wall Street Journal* editorials, and listen to conservative talk show hosts, while liberals tune into MNBC and NPR, and read the *New York Times*. When we hear facts that support our existing beliefs, they are likely to be robustly encoded and go into our long-term storage, while we soon forget facts that raise questions about our beliefs.[12] The risk, of course, is that when you seek out only persons and information that reinforce your ideas, you are left open to being blind-sided when your idea turns out not to be as brilliant or airtight as you thought. The larger your ego, the more difficult it becomes to be receptive to ideas and information that challenge your own (supremely well-thought-out) view of the universe and how it operates—and get ready to be blind-sided. Humility begins with not being so sure that you are right.

Our egos work hard to convince us that any significant achievement is our own doing, and any failure the fault of others. As a result, it is easy to convince yourself you did a great job on a case when the fact is you didn't. Ego also naturally leads you to want to share your assessment with a client. Justice Antonin Scalia notes that advocates before the Supreme Court sometimes do "terrible jobs" but win their case anyway because decisions aren't based on the quality of advocacy but on the merits of the case. He feels certain that some of these advocates, despite doing a lousy job, go back and tell their clients, "We won another one for you!"[13] For better or worse, lawyers are not graded on the quality of their work. Compare the work of lawyers to that of the mechanics that Robert Pirsig wrote about in *Zen and the Art of Motorcycle Maintenance*: "There's no way to bullshit your way into looking good on a mechanical repair job."[14] Although an ego-driven lawyer might succeed for a while in convincing himself he's doing a terrific job when he isn't, the quality of your work reflects your actual efforts, not whatever conjured self-assessments your ego produces. Over the long run, your track record will be hard to ignore. You won't always be playing hands that any lawyer can win. Lawyers who consistently fail to recognize the vulnerabilities of their arguments or who time and again fly into tilt mode are headed for a fall.

Perhaps we can all draw some encouragement from knowing that age appears to play a role in our emotional balance, and that studies show older adults take themselves less seriously and more readily let go of negative emotions than do younger people—perhaps accounting for some of the greater wisdom generally attributed to persons who have reached midlife. Laura Carstensen, a researcher at the Stanford Center on Longevity, notes that the "mixed emotions" more commonly held by older persons "regulate emotional states better than the extremes of emotion" more common among younger people. Carstensen says, "There's a lot of loss associated with aging, and to the extent that you use these losses as a motivation to savor the day-to-day experiences you have, it allows you to be more positive."[15] Neuroscientific research supports the conclusion that negative emotions are more intense in the young. When confronted with the prospect of monetary loss, young subjects in an experiment showed more activity in their brains' emotional center, the amygdala, than did older subjects.[16] Emotional equilibrium, a state allowing focus and most associated with older persons, proves in studies to produce better (we could also say "wiser") solutions to problems involving interpersonal relations. When life is screwed up, go see someone playing life's back nine.

WHAT TO DO ABOUT INCIVILITY

Civility is a low hurdle. It only demands that we recognize the right of others to hold and act on positions that differ from our own and that may be adverse to our own interests. We don't have to try to understand anyone—we just have to put up with them. Even this low bar, however, frequently is not cleared. There is general agreement that there has been a decline in civility in the legal profession over the last generation or two.

Erik Kimball, a bankruptcy judge in Florida, offered an assessment that is echoed in many fields of law. When he started work as a young bankruptcy attorney in Boston, Kimball writes, the bankruptcy bar was characterized by "a great sense of collegiality, of belonging to an exclusive group whose members respected and trusted each other." Kimball says he "does not remember a single discovery dispute that required court intervention" or even one instance of a refusal to extend a deadline. "Our word was literally our bond" when it came to settlement negotiations. Now, as Kimball sees the practice, things have "changed dramatically." Discord among bankruptcy lawyers is commonplace, a fact the judge attributes to a fractured practice in which lawyers have lost "a sense of belonging to a legal community."[17] When practices evolve from local to national, when firms grow ever larger, and when lawyers no longer work with each other on a regular basis, civility suffers.

The degree of decline in civility is hard to measure, and it varies with geography and area of practice. Mostly, when lawyers complain of declining civility they offer anecdotes that support their case. One example is the frequently recounted story of incivility involving a deposition conducted by the highly successful Texas plaintiffs' lawyer, Joseph Jamail. During the deposition, Jamail attempted to block opposing counsel's questions of his client with a stream of obscenities and personal insults directed at opposing counsel. In one particularly shocking outburst, Jamail warned the lawyer who was questioning his client, "You can ask some questions, but get off of that. I'm tired of you. You could gag a maggot off a meat wagon."[18] Despite Jamail's nearly unsurpassed incivility, the University of Texas Law School, Jamail's alma mater, honored him with an alumni award and large statue of himself. One statue of Jamail proved not enough, however, and the following year a second statue was erected on campus, making him the only person honored with two statues on the entire University of Texas campus.

While few lawyers, it is hoped, would defend Jamail's behavior, some lawyers remain unconvinced that civility is a worthy goal. Yale Law School professor Stephen L. Carter, in his book *Civility: Manners, Morals, and the Etiquette of Democracy*, cites the response of a prominent divorce attorney to a proposal by the chief judge of New York to adopt new rules aimed at increasing civility. Writing in the *New York Times*, lawyer Raoul Felder wrote, "If lawyers truly care about the causes they represent, they should on occasion, get hot under the collar, raise their voices, get pugnacious." Civility, Felder contended, "may not always be the right reaction in the adversarial courtroom." In his own experience, he said, "I have never heard a client complain that his or her lawyer was rude."[19] Carter observes that the views of the New York divorce lawyer, if accepted, would mean that the practice of law is essentially an immoral endeavor. By making "the principal ethic merely one of victory," lawyers cede the field to those with the least concern that "we are, all of us, not lone drivers but fellow passengers."[20] Our moral standing, God forbid, would be no higher than that of political consultants, for whom nastiness is considered a virtue.

As we suggested, the reasons for decline in civility among lawyers are numerous and complex. A flood of new lawyers in recent decades has resulted in increased competition in the legal marketplace and reduced prestige and self-esteem. More important, larger bar membership and the increasingly national and international nature of law practice means that lawyers are less likely to have "repeat dealings" with opposing counsel. When a lawyer expects to face another lawyer again in a future case, there is good reason to try to maintain a civil relationship. When they meet in the next case, a more cooperative approach could better serve a client's interests, so lawyers think twice about bridge burning. Marvin Aspen puts the problem this way: "Today's metropolitan lawyer may deal with a particular opponent lawyer, law firm, or judge only once in her career. Thus, the incentive to retain cordial relationships often dies because the relationship will not likely become an ongoing one."[21] Moreover, uncivil lawyers are less likely than in earlier times to be stigmatized for their misbehavior. As the number of lawyers has increased, the effectiveness of professional ostracism as a tool for keeping would-be violators of common decency in line has diminished: informal sanctions are losing their bite. Lawyers today are getting away with behavior that, a generation ago, would have irrevocably damaged their standing in the legal community.

At the same time, lack of repeat dealing means there are few opportunities for respect and trust to build between lawyers. In the past, young lawyers might learn lessons in civility from repeated dealings with respected older lawyers who cared about preserving time-honored traditions. These mutually beneficial encounters occur much more rarely in the modern practice of law.

In many quarters of the legal profession, the conception of litigation itself has evolved in a way that condones incivility. While it was at one time common to think of litigation more as a debate among experts, now it is far more likely to be compared to a battle, where the spoils go to the fighter with the fewest scruples. Today, Jonathan Macey argues, "Antiquated notions...of professional courtesy and civility are at best character flaws and at worst signs of incompetence or sloth."[22]

What can be done about this depressing state of affairs? One possibility is to set our goals high and aspire to create a sense of fraternity among lawyers. We are likely to fall short, but our efforts might at least lead to increased civility. We might also learn from social scientists who tell us we care more about looking good than we do about truly being good. If more of a stigma attached to incivility, fewer people would engage in it. (Perhaps putting an egregious offender or two in stocks at an annual bar gathering might work?) Ignoring—or worse yet, applauding—lawyers who behave badly only encourages more such behavior.

Of course, when *you* are the bad actor, you hold the power to do something about it—and an apology is a good way to begin repairing the damage. San Diego lawyer Heather Rosing, who represents lawyers in fraud and malpractice cases, says "I have seen apologies being used more and more frequently in order to maintain good relationships. Good lawyers are pretty willing to apologize to their opposing counsel. I'm certainly not afraid to do it. And when people do it to me, I respect it."[23]

The good news about civility, according to Jonathan Smaby, executive director for the Texas Center for Legal Ethics in Austin, is that there are plenty of lawyers, including many just entering practice, who would like "to do the right thing, but don't know what the right thing is." Smaby says these young lawyers "are hungry for information on the proper balance between advocacy and civility."[24] He thinks part of the problem has been the "mixed messages" lawyers are getting from movies, television, and elsewhere that typically present legal practice as "much more cutthroat" than it really is. Recognizing a problem and a thirst for information, law schools and professional organizations have begun to respond by offering civility training programs.

Civility in the end, however, is less about being properly trained than it is about becoming a decent person. As you age, you come to appreciate how much work that is.

ONE LAWYER'S PATH TO CIVILITY

John W. Davis had a career in law and politics that most people can only dream about. His 140 arguments before the U.S. Supreme Court is a number bested by only a couple of nineteenth-century advocates (one of whom was Daniel Webster). His skills as an oral advocate were legendary. Chief Justice Edward White once quipped, "Of course, no one has due process of law when Mr. Davis is on the other side."[25] Great judges, including Oliver Wendell Holmes and Learned Hand, called Davis one of the most persuasive advocates they ever heard. Of his oral argument for Youngstown Steel, in a landmark case challenging the seizure of steel mills by President Truman, the *Washington Post* reported that rarely "has a courtroom sat in such silent admiration for a lawyer at the bar."[26] Davis served for three years as solicitor general under President Wilson and built the New York City firm of Davis Polk, which today continues to bear his name. (Also of note, but hardly a source for modern-day admiration, Davis defended South Carolina's policy of segregated public schools in one of the companion cases to *Brown v. Board of Education*.) In addition to his stellar legal career, Davis had a notable career in politics and diplomacy. He represented West Virginia in Congress, served as ambassador to the United Kingdom, and ran as the Democratic nominee for president in 1924, when he was defeated by Calvin Coolidge in a landslide.

Few might have guessed, watching the performances of Davis as his legal career began in the rough and tumble mountain town of Clarksburg, West Virginia, that he might one day become one of the most admired lawyers of all time. He lost his first three cases. More disturbingly, his courtroom conduct was dreadful. In one case, young Davis struck opposing counsel, earning him a contempt citation. In another courtroom, he hurled an inkwell at a lawyer.[27] Success came to Davis only when he learned to master his emotions. The inkwells stopped flying; no more fisticuffs broke out. Over time, he developed a reputation for personal charm, emotional balance, and dispassionate focus. When lawyers all about him seemed to be losing their heads, Davis remained calm. One biographical sketch of Davis notes that he could "dispel the hard emotions in a room with a gentle word. He became the master of his age."[28] Davis did all this without entering an "anger management" program. He simply saw how his greatest weakness, his temper, was keeping him from achieving his goals, and then mustered the strength to control his emotions. Personal change is possible.

THE IDEA OF POLITICAL FRATERNITY

Increasing civility in the practice of law is a good start, but former Yale Law School dean Anthony Kronman envisioned doing more. He advocated creating "political fraternity" within the legal profession to restore its ideals of old.[29] In *The Lost Lawyer: Failing Ideals of the Legal Profession*, Kronman bemoaned changes that threatened what he called "lawyer-statesmen" with virtual extinction. He found depressing trends everywhere he looked—law schools, law firms, bar associations—but held out a glimmer of hope that commitment to his idea of political fraternity might yet save the profession.

Political fraternity, according to Kronman, is a condition in which "the members of the community are joined by bonds of sympathy despite the differences of opinion that set them apart" on questions concerning the direction of their community. In terms of cohesiveness, he placed political fraternities about halfway between tightly knit religious communities and communities that operate on the principle of mere tolerance for views they oppose. A member of a political fraternity accepts the fact that he or she will have deep disagreements with other members and recognizes that those differences might never be resolved; nonetheless, he or she commits to giving the views of others serious consideration and seeing them in "the best possible light."[30] Treating the claims of opponents with generosity, in Kronman's view, reduces strain in the community and ultimately is the best safeguard against its disintegration.

Unfortunately, the legal profession today falls far short of Kronman's ideal. Little effort is made to understand different moral views and, lacking understanding, "winners gloat" and "losers sulk." Lawyers whose views prevail make few conciliatory gestures to losers. Simple courtesies that could avoid resentment are ignored. And so, in the increasingly competitive arena, opponents are "forever on the lookout for opportunities to turn the tables and to do to their opponents what has been done to them."[31]

Not every lawyer aspires to be the "lawyer-statesman" who Kronman worried was rapidly vanishing from the legal profession. For those who do, however, Kronman warned that treating opponents' arguments with generosity requires great effort, and that only when the practice becomes habitual does it become easier. By supporting the ideal of political fraternity, where true "deliberation and the pleasure it affords" becomes possible, lawyers reap the reward of increased satisfaction with their careers. As guardians of the fraternity and the satisfactions it brings its members, lawyer-statesmen spread the message that political fraternity is a precious thing and honor its values through their actions. The very best of the bunch, as Kronman sees it, are the lawyers who "enter the embattled precincts and work to arouse in others a similar, if less intense, devotion to political fraternity."[32]

You might find Kronman's notion of political fraternity abstract. A vision of the lawyer-statesmen might come naturally to someone in the position of dean of a law school that sends more than its share of graduates on to careers where high-profile conflicts are commonplace, including many with strong political overtones. Some lawyers have a hard time relating to that type of practice. Political fraternities can exist, however, in the bar of any city. Whenever lawyers meet in a courtroom, conference room, or meeting hall, political differences can surface. All lawyers—whether they fight in the trenches of municipal court, perform due diligence, work to reduce clients' payments to taxing authorities, or perform any of the countless other tasks that remain far from the limelight—benefit themselves and their communities when they engage in the "sympathetic fellow-feeling" Kronman preached.

Sympathetic fellow-feeling might become a bit more widespread if there were a better understanding of the source of our different political and moral intuitions, the topic to which we turn next.

OUR POLITICAL DIFFERENCES: WHOSE SIDE ARE YOU ON?

Until late in his career, Theodore B. Olson held rock star status in conservative legal circles. As head of the Office of Legal Counsel in the Reagan administration, Olson led drives to ease government regulation and to end race-based busing and affirmative action programs. As solicitor general in the George W. Bush administration, Olson defended the government's anti-terrorism policies. When attorneys for Paula Jones took their case alleging sexual harassment by Bill Clinton to the Supreme Court, Olson was the lawyer they turned to for help in preparing their argument. Conservatives most revered Olson, however, for arguing the 2000 election case of *Bush v. Gore* before the Supreme Court. A white quill commemorating his argument in that case, along with fifty-six other quills marking each of his Supreme Court appearances, is displayed in his office near a framed photograph of Ronald Reagan, inscribed with "heartfelt thanks."

In 2008, the voters of California narrowly passed Proposition 8, which amended the California Constitution to prohibit gay marriage and effectively nullified recent legislation enacted by the California legislature authorizing such marriages. In a meeting of a small group of persons seeking to mount a constitutional challenge to Prop 8, the name of Ted Olson came up. One member of the group, Hollywood director Rob Reiner, recalled that the suggestion gave him pause, especially given Reiner's close friendship with Al Gore. He remembered thinking, "My God, Ted Olson, that's a remarkable thing." More because of Olson's strong conservative credentials than in spite of them, the decision was made to call Olson to see if he would lead the challenge against Prop 8. Olson said, "I really did not need to give it a great deal of thought." He accepted the offer.[33]

After Olson agreed to take on the gay marriage case, he worried that many supporters of gay marriage would raise hell about "this right-winger" having control of a case so close to their hearts. Olson expressed concern that when news of his representation got out, "It would be more about me than about the case."[34] So he called an old friend and biking trip companion that he had opposed in a courtroom in Tallahassee in the weeks following the 2000 election, David Boies. Would Boies, he wondered, join forces to challenge the constitutionality of California's Prop 8? Boies, the champion of many liberal causes, jumped at the chance. The press quickly labeled the two lawyers "the Odd Couple," as if there were something distinctly unusual about a Democratic lawyer and a Republican lawyer working together on a case.

For Olson, and for Boies, there was nothing odd about their partnership. Olson described Boies as "one of the most remarkable, skilled, talented lawyers that I've ever known....He's a marvel to watch in the courtroom. He's been an absolute, unmitigated pleasure every step of the way. He's a wonderful colleague and a very, very dear friend." Don't think, however, the two men now see eye-to-eye on *Bush v. Gore*. They kid each other about the case and Olson praises the work Boies did on the Florida recount case. "I tell him now that he almost persuaded me, but not quite," Olson said.[35] Despite their political differences, each lawyer expresses respect for the views of the other (Figure 4.1).

"The intellectual challenge of looking at different points of view," according to Olson, was why he went to law school. It's a decision he never regretted: "My first day of law school I thought,

FIGURE 4.1. David Boies, on the left, with Ted Olson. Credit: Photographer Kevork Djansezian, Collection Getty Images News, Getty Images.

'My God, I'm finally here; this is so incredible.' I've loved every minute of [my career]."[36]

Olson's decision to represent plaintiffs challenging the constitutionality of Prop 8 came easily to him, but it shocked many of his conservative friends and allies. Chuck Cooper, the lawyer representing proponents of the marriage ban, said, "I never expected him to take this case, or at least not this side of it." Former judge Robert Bork, a close friend of Olson, also reacted with surprise. The former judge whose nomination for the Supreme Court failed in the Senate, called same-sex marriage a "judicial sin" and said, "I'd like to know why" Olson agreed to take the case.[37] Ed Whelan, president of a conservative think tank, claimed Olson had "abandoned the legal principles that he had previously professed to hold" and, as a result, "burned a lot of bridges with folks."[38] Olson's e-mail inbox flooded with angry messages, including one who called his representation of the Prop 8 challengers "a disgraceful betrayal of the legal principles you purported to stand for."[39] While some on the right saw Olson as betraying conservative principles, at least a few liberals expressed suspicions that Olson took the case to sabotage it.

For his part, Olson knew his decision to take the case was the right one. He called it "the most compelling, emotionally moving, important case that I have been involved in in my entire life."[40] Olson saw no inconsistency with his conservatism: "If you are a conservative, how could you be against a relationship in which people who love one another want to publicly state their vows...and engage in a household in which they are committed to one another and become part of the community?"[41] He expressed frustration with both liberals and conservatives who assumed that his decision must have something to do with having a gay family member, which he does not. "It's frustrating that people won't take it on face value," he said.

Those who really knew Ted Olson understood. Olson's wife, Lady Booth Olson, confided that her husband tears up when he recalls an incident during a restaurant stop on a college debate trip in Texas. According to the debate team's coach, when the owner of the restaurant in Amarillo refused to serve Olson's black team-mate, Olson "tore into" him and insisted "the team would not eat unless everyone was served. If he sees something that is wrong in his mind, he goes after it." Olson's own clients also have no doubt where he stands. Paul Katami, one of the plaintiffs in the Prop 8 case, recalled that Olson "put his arm around me and said, 'We're going to plan your wedding in a couple of years—this is going to happen.'"[42] It did happen—live on MSNBC's the *Rachel Maddow Show*, on June 28, 2013, exactly two days after the Supreme Court ruled in the case.[43]

CAN LIBERALS AND CONSERVATIVES BE FRIENDS?

In the view of many conservatives, Ted Olson was a good lawyer until 2009, when he went over to the dark side. In the views of some liberals, exactly the opposite is true. If the measure of lawyer's worth is whether he is championing a cause you agree with, then it is all about whose side he's on today. This, of course, is no way to judge a lawyer's career. Fair or not, though, it is how the public judges lawyers. As Harvard professor Alan Dershowitz notes, "The public will love you when your client is popular and hate you when your client is unpopular."[44] Dershowitz knows personally the criticism that comes from representing unpopular clients, having defended accused wife murderers, porn stars, and spies.

The particular ring of hell a lawyer is presumed to deserve depends, of course, on whom you ask. If you question liberals, they might reserve their greatest scorn for defenders of "Big Tobacco" or "Big Oil," or perhaps for administration lawyers who write legal memos justifying the use of torture in terrorism cases. On the other hand, conservatives deride plaintiffs' personal injury lawyers, or lawyers who defend clients who they think do despicable things, such as provide abortion services or burn flags.

The close friendship between Olson and Boies puzzles strong partisans, who view friendship between a conservative and a liberal as about as surprising as one between "the farmer and the cowman" in the musical *Oklahoma!* There are, of course, reasons why deep friendships blossom more frequently between persons with similar political outlooks. Humans feel most at home in familiar groups and we have long used politics and religion as bases for our grouping. We empathize more readily with members of our group and feel a sense of loyalty to members in our group that makes us react to perceived threats from persons outside our group.

Yet there is much more to life than politics, and lawyers can build friendships that cross political divides. Judges can, too. In an interview on CNN, Justice Scalia revealed, "My best buddy on the Court is Ruth Bader Ginsburg, has always been." The bonding between one of the Court's most conservative and one of its most liberal members surprised CNN's Piers Morgan, who pointed out to Scalia that "you disagree with her about almost everything." Scalia agreed, repeating, "Just about everything."[45]

ROOTS OF OUR POLITICAL DIFFERENCES

If psychologist Jonathan Haidt had his way, there would be a lot more friendships like that of Ted Olson and David Boies that cross political divides. Haidt contends that our minds have evolved for "groupish righteousness." Because "intuitions rule" and, for the most part, drive our reasoning, we find it difficult to connect with people who have moral foundations—or what Haidt calls "moral matrices"—that differ substantially from our own. Difficult, but it is not impossible.[46]

Our political differences may, in part, be rooted in biological differences. Studies comparing identical twins and fraternal twins raised in separate households because of adoptions suggest that genes are a significant predictor of political attitudes, accounting for between one-third and one-half of the observed variability. Researchers at the University College London announced in 2011 that they had discovered a link between brain structure and political orientation. Conservatives, they said, showed "increased volume in the right amygdala," the section of the brain that processes fear and disgust. Liberals, on the other hand, had "increased gray matter volume in the anterior cingulate cortex (ACC)," the brain portion most associated with understanding complexity. University College's Ryota Kanai speculated that people with larger ACC volumes "have a higher capacity to tolerate uncertainty and conflicts, allowing them to accept more liberal views."[47] (The correlation between brain structure and political views is not especially high, however. Looking at brain structures, the researchers predicted the political views of the brain's owner correctly just 75% of the time.[48] Researchers also cautioned, "It remains unclear whether the structural differences cause the divergence in political views, or are the effect of them.")[49] The London findings are consistent with the results of earlier studies at Cornell, Yale, and the University of Nebraska, which indicated that disgusting images, such as maggots on a wound or a spider on a frightened face, caused a significantly stronger fear reaction in conservatives than in liberals.[50] Libertarians, interestingly, score more like liberals than conservatives on most measures of personalities, which might account for why conservative but libertarian-leaning Ted Olson and liberal David Boies hit it off so well.

Genes are not destiny, however. We may come prewired to be conservatives or liberals, but we can be rewired, especially by our childhood experiences. You might be inclined at birth to flow toward the Republican Party, but the actions of your parents, teachers, and friends can redirect you. What you read, where you travel, who you spend your time with, and what memorable experiences you have can all lead you to a political place that could not have been predicted at birth. In short, genes push you toward liberalism or conservatism, but you might not fall that way.

The significant contribution genes make to our political attitudes suggests there are evolutionary advantages to having both liberal and conservative perspectives represented in a community. As silly as it might be to speak of "conservatives" and "liberals" sharing our ancestral savannah, there are adaptive advantages both to the personality suite that is associated with liberal attitudes (including openness to new experiences, more rebelliousness) and to the personality suite associated with conservative attitudes (including increased wariness of threats, greater respect for authority). Haidt argues that we should think of liberals and conservatives not as political enemies but rather as yin and yang—contrasting forces that help keep society in balance. For millennia, societies have witnessed tugs of war between teams that are pulling for more or less cohesion. A society in balance will have liberals to remind it of the renewing energy that comes from loosening bonds as well as conservatives to remind it of the risk of dissolution such loosening carries with it. If we accept that both the liberal and conservative perspectives have real social benefits, it becomes hard to continue to think that the politics of our next-door neighbor, or opposing counsel, make him a lunkhead.

THE SIX FOUNDATIONS FOR MORAL JUDGMENTS

The neuroscience findings based on brain scans of conservative subjects being shown revolting or disgusting images are consistent with other social science research that shows conservatives, unlike liberals, sometimes see immorality even where there is no harm to anyone. Haidt asked subjects how they felt about a woman cleaning her closet who "finds her old American flag. She doesn't want the flag anymore, so she cuts it into pieces and uses the rags to clean her bathroom."[51] While social conservatives called the woman's actions morally wrong, liberals typically ran a "no harm" check and gave the woman the green light for bathroom cleaning. Haidt concludes from this and other research that conservatives have a moral foundation that liberals do not have, one he calls the "purity/degradation foundation." As it turns out, the purity/degradation foundation is just one of three foundations that conservatives generally have, and liberals generally lack.

In all, Haidt identified six basic foundations for moral judgments. Not everyone, however, has a value matrix that includes all six foundations. Haidt discovered that liberals share a "three-foundation morality," while social conservatives base their decisions on the full "six-foundation morality." Liberals, essentially, do not recognize (or at least give very little weight to) three of the foundations of morality that conservatives use for making a moral decisions. Haidt compares the six foundations to the different taste receptors found in each taste bud of the human tongue. (Separate receptors exist to detect sweet, salt, sour, bitter, and savory.) It's as if, Haidt says, liberals were born missing certain taste receptors—they simply lack the ability to be moved by concerns that can be very important to conservatives.

The three moral foundations shared by liberals and conservatives are what Haidt calls the care/harm foundation, the liberty/oppression foundation, and the fairness/cheating foundation. In addition to the purity/degradation foundation, the three moral foundations found in the value matrices of social conservatives but largely missing from the value matrices of liberals include the loyalty/betrayal foundation and the authority/subversion foundation.[52]

Taking the "sanctity foundation" as an example, Haidt says the differences between liberals and conservatives are often obvious. With a single piece of data or two, one can quickly categorize a person as a liberal or as a social conservative. For example, if you spot a bumper sticker that reads, YOUR BODY MAY BE A TEMPLE, BUT MINE IS AN AMUSEMENT PARK, you know you are not looking at a car owned by a social conservative. Social conservatives tend to treat certain objects as having infinite values while liberals typically weigh the value of objects against other values. The result is that when disagreements turn, for example, on a whether a flag should ever be a dish rag, or whether the Bible holds all the answers, or whether Originalism is the best guide to constitutional interpretation, debates can turn heated.

In addition to the different numbers of foundations for liberals and conservatives, the fairness/cheating foundation has a significantly different spin for liberals and conservatives. Fairness for liberals is all about equality while for conservatives it tends to be more about proportionality—people deserve rewards that are based on what they contribute, even if that means uneven outcomes. (Libertarians, by the way, use only a two-foundation matrix, one based only on the liberty/oppression and fairness/cheating foundations.)

There's a lesson in these two contrasting notions of fairness for law students and lawyers. Below-average law students might want to avoid, whenever possible, taking courses from conservative professors. Conservative professors, according to one study, have a broader grade range than liberal professors and are far more likely to give out very low grades to poorly performing students.[53] Presumably, the greater weighting liberal professors place on care and preventing harm and their tendency to think of fairness more in terms of equality cause them to use a narrower grade range. Extrapolating, one might also expect conservative judges to impose harsher sentences on convicted criminals than liberal judges—and this, too, is borne out by the data.

A few things should be made clear about our moral foundations. First, Haidt is by no means suggesting that social conservatives are twice as moral as liberals, or three times more moral than libertarians, because they use a six-foundation morality scheme compared to three- or two-foundation moralities. Liberals draw more heavily from the three moral foundations that they share with conservatives because they do not also draw from the other three moral concerns of social conservatives. For liberals, preventing harm really matters a lot, and they give more weight to this concern than do social conservatives because they are not balancing their harm concern against, for example, obedience to authority or concerns related to sanctity. Second, Haidt does not suggest one value matrix is better than the other, although he does note that the moral matrix of social conservatives is more prevalent among world cultures than the liberal morality, which is—for the most part—confined to North America and Western Europe. The highly individualistic moral order of the West is the exception, not the rule. Third, he observes that moral matrices in the population form a continuum and don't just clump around two poles. Yes, there are extreme liberals and extreme conservatives, but there are also moderates, and liberals and conservatives of all stripes.[54]

You can get a sense of your own moral matrix by visiting Yourmorals.org and answering the questions on the Moral Foundations Questionnaire. Based on how much or how little you agree with statements such as "I think it's morally wrong that rich children inherit a lot of money while poor children inherit nothing," "I am proud of my country's history," "I would call some acts wrong on the grounds that they are unnatural," and "One of the worst things a person could do is hurt a defenseless animal," you will be assigned a ranking on a one-to-five scale for your concerns about harm, fairness, authority, loyalty, and purity. You can also see how your ranking compares to that of the average liberal or conservative. Taking the test with a spouse or a friend, based on personal experience, can be a good conversation starter.

Whether your politics leans left or right, if you're like most lawyers, your circle of lawyer-friends generally shares your political values. It is no secret that the plaintiffs' bar tilts to the left, and the corporate defense bar tilts to the right. Most criminal defense lawyers consider themselves liberals, and most state and local prosecutors consider themselves conservatives. Overall, however, lawyers have more liberal views than the general population. In each election cycle in recent history, lawyers contributed more money to Democratic candidates than Republican candidates. In 2008, for example, 76% of lawyers' campaign contributions went to Democrats.[55] Again in both 2010 and 2012, Democratic candidates enjoyed a better than 2 to 1 margin of support among lawyers.[56]

In Haidt's characterization, most lawyers share the "three-foundation morality" of liberals rather than the more common "six-foundation morality" of conservatives. This puts liberal lawyers at a distinct disadvantage when it comes to understanding why conservatives reach different decisions than they would make. Lacking understanding of conservatives' intuitions, they are poorly equipped to change the minds of judges or jurors holding conservative values. Like everyone else, lawyers have a hard time looking for evidence that contradicts previously held views. Instead, they are more likely to do the easy thing and generate more reasons that are consistent with their own moral intuitions. Being, for the most part, smart people, they are very good at doing just that. Law schools are often full of relatively like-minded people expert at making clever justifications for intuitively generated positions. Lawyers have learned how to spin out rationalizations that support positions that align with their gut feelings, but they have much greater difficulty making arguments for causes or persons they detest.

When lawyers cluster by politics, political views are rarely challenged. Hanging out with like-minded folk results in reinforcement of political views and makes positions even more resistant to change. This unfortunate fact also undermines good lawyering by leaving lawyers unprepared to make the arguments that can best move their political opposites. In these partisan times (and most times are), lawyers need the courage to reach across the political divide.

"FOLLOW THE SACREDNESS" AND SEEK DIVERSITY

To better understand our political opposites, Haidt advises that we "follow the sacredness."[57] By that he means when you are ensnared in a controversy with political overtones, the best course lies in trying to figure out which of the moral foundations support the position of those with whom you find yourself in disagreement. When interaction is based on a respectful understanding of differences, the disagreement usually will not disappear, but it is far less likely to be destructive.

Haidt's second suggestion is to rethink and expand our definition of "diversity" to include political diversity.[58] If law school faculties, student bodies, law firms, and bar organizations were more evenly divided along political lines, and respectful dialogue among political opposites was encouraged, the green shoots of trust might poke their way through our hyper-partisan landscape.

Friendships like that between Ted Olson and David Boies give us hope that the political differences that separate us can be overcome. Partisanship will never disappear, but as we come to better understand the sources of our moral intuitions, we might begin to see our political differences in much the same way we have come to see differences, say, of race or sexual orientation. When we understand that liberals and conservatives were, to an extent, "born that way," it is harder to view the positions taken by our opponents as the product of ignorance or malignant calculation. Instead of thinking of lawyers as the enemy if they pursue a vision of justice that differs from ours, we begin to think of our real enemies as those who don't care about justice at all. We stop "talking past each other" and begin talking to each other. We gain the ability to step across a moral divide and empathize with a client who doesn't share our moral foundation. Finally, we can refocus our goals, should we wish, to align with that of the famously gloomy Clarence Darrow who wrote, "The best that we can do is to be kindly and helpful toward our friends and fellow passengers who are clinging to the same speck of dirt while we are drifting side by side to our common doom."[59]

CHAPTER 5

The Good Lawyer Uses Both Intuition and Deliberative Thinking

As we know, there are known knowns; there are things that we know. We also know there are known unknowns; that is to say there are things we know we do not know. But there are also unknown unknowns—the ones we don't know we don't know.

—Defense Secretary Donald Rumsfeld

Intuitions come first, strategic reasoning second.

—Jonathan Haidt

ACCURATE INTUITIVE JUDGMENTS ARE OFTEN SEEN AS akin to magic. There's nothing magic about them. Accurate intuitive judgments are hard earned, coming from a well-developed ability to almost instantly recognize patterns. The influential social scientist Herbert A. Simon studied the work of chess masters to understand how they came to play the game so well. His conclusion? The success of chess masters came from practice, practice, practice. Thousands of hours spent poring over chess boards gave the experts the ability to see the pieces on the board in a different way from other chess players. They saw patterns where most players saw individual pieces. Simon writes: "The situation (on the chess board) has provided a cue; this cue has given the expert access to information stored in memory, and the information provides the answer. Intuition is nothing more and nothing less than recognition."[1]

Good lawyers, like good chess players, earn their stripes primarily through practice. Years of work in a practice area provide a lawyer with the ability to see patterns in facts and in cases that other lawyers miss. Years of jury practice give a trial lawyer the ability to spot inadmissible testimony almost as soon as it is uttered or to sense when a jury is growing impatient with a witness's testimony. As much as we might wish it otherwise, there really is no substitute for experience.

We come equipped with brains that allow us to engage in two distinct modes of thinking, one fast and one slow.[2] Intuition is a form of fast thinking. Over the past three decades psychologists have come to appreciate that intuition plays a far bigger role in our decision making than the slow, effortful thinking we more often associate with the task. Our brains are constantly producing feelings and impressions that form the main basis for our beliefs and choices. Sometimes, however, our deliberate thinking system kicks into gear and overrules the impulses generated by our intuitions. Each of our two thinking systems, fast and slow, has its advantages and limitations. The trick is to know, in a particular situation, which of the systems to trust.

Our automatic, quick-thinking system is forever spinning out suggestions—and, unfortunately, not every one of these suggestions is sound. Psychologist Daniel Kahneman calls our fast mode of thinking "a machine for jumping to conclusions."[3] In a well-oiled system, most of those conclusions find support in reality, but sometimes they don't. Knowing when our intuition is most likely to lead us astray, and when we therefore need to check our automatically generated suggestions with effortful thinking, is a quality shared by good lawyers. Better decisions can be made by becoming aware of the cognitive traps that our fast-thinking, automatic, intuitive system is prone to lead us into.

Psychologist Jonathan Haidt compares the relationship that exists between the two thinking systems to "a lawyer serving a client." Our intuition, as he sees it, is the client and our effortful thinking system is the lawyer. Lawyers, he notes, generally try to serve their client's interests. Our reasoning systems have evolved primarily to serve as "an apologist" for the decisions that are really made by intuition.[4] The usual role of our controlled reasoning process, writes Kahneman, is as "an endorser rather than an enforcer." Only rarely does our slow-thinking system assume the role of critic of the steady stream of requests and demands generated by our fast-thinking system. Still it is possible, in these relatively rare cases, for our deliberative thinking systems to step up and "refuse to go along with requests" they determine to be unethical or self-destructive.[5]

In law school, it's mostly about exercising and developing the skills of deliberative thinking, and precious little attention is paid to the real mover and shaker in the world, our intuition. There's a reason for that—the practice of law requires more effortful reasoning than most other occupations. But neglecting the role that automatic processes play in our decision making has too often left lawyers unprepared to serve their client's true interests. Law schools were built largely on the faith that they can teach people to reason more thoroughly, but that faith can count Jonathan Haidt among its skeptics. In his view, schools simply "select the applicants with the higher IQs, and people with higher IQs are able to generate more reasons."[6] Law schools pick students who can snow people with *more* reasons, not *better* reasons.

In this chapter, we examine the critical role intuition plays in our decision making as well as ways in which we might learn when and how to review our intuition in situations where it is likely to point us in the wrong direction.

THE MEDICAL INSTRUMENT THAT WASN'T

One of the most controversial murder trials of the mid-twentieth century turned on a few key pieces of evidence. In the bedroom where in 1954 police found the dead body of Marilyn Sheppard, wife of Sam Sheppard, a handsome, young Ohio surgeon, they noticed a pillow with a large, irregular bloodstain. Testing of the blood showed that it matched that of Marilyn. Close observation of the stain itself revealed the imprint of two lobster-like claws, widely theorized to be the telltale signature of the missing murder weapon (Figure 5.1).

Dr. Sheppard told investigators that he fought with the murderer, who he described as "a bushy-haired biped," in the bedroom just after his wife's killing. Coroner Sam Gerber, who headed the investigation, didn't believe him. Gerber thought the case to be a domestic homicide, most likely connected to Sheppard's ongoing affair with a lab technician named Susan Hayes.

Guessing what caused the lobster-claw imprint on the bloodstain became a sort of Rorschach test. From the standpoint of the prosecution, the best of all weapons was a surgical instrument, one that would neatly tie the doctor to the wife's murder. And so, for the coroner and for prosecutor John Mahon, that is exactly what it became. On the witness stand in a Cleveland courtroom, Gerber offered two color slides of the bloodstained pillow. Using a pointer to direct the jury's attention to the claw-like imprint, he told the jury, "In this bloodstain I could make out the impression of a surgical instrument." Under questioning from Mahon, the coroner didn't stop there. He testified the murder weapon used to kill Marilyn was a heavy two-bladed surgical instrument about three inches long with teeth on the end of each blade. It was, Gerber told jurors, an unmistakable "blood signature."[7] Some reporters called the blood imprint the most damning evidence presented by the prosecution. Jurors interviewed after the trial indicated that Gerber's testimony concerning the

FIGURE 5.1. The bloodstained pillow found in the Sheppard bedroom. Credit: Bay Village, Ohio, Police Department.

bloodstain helped lead to their decision to convict Sheppard of second-degree murder. One Cleveland newspaper, to highlight Gerber's testimony, ran a front page photo of the pillow, with the imprint doctored to make it look much more like a surgical instrument than it actually did.

Twelve years later, after the U.S. Supreme Court overturned Sheppard's conviction because the excessive publicity surrounding the trial might have prejudiced jurors, Sam Sheppard faced a second trial.[8] This time, when Gerber took the stand he faced a much rougher cross-examination, by a young lawyer named F. Lee Bailey, whose later high-profile clients would include Patty Hearst, My Lai massacre defendant Captain Ernest Medina, and O. J. Simpson. On Gerber's claim that the imprint was caused by a surgical instrument, Bailey let him have it:

> BAILEY: Well, now, Dr. Gerber, just what kind of surgical
> instrument do you see here?
> GERBER: I'm not sure.

BAILEY: Would it be an instrument you yourself have handled?

GERBER: I don't know if I've handled one or not...

BAILEY: Do you have such an instrument back at your office?

GERBER: [Shakes head to indicate no.]

BAILEY: Have you seen such an instrument in any hospital, or medical supply catalogue, or anywhere else, Dr. Gerber?

GERBER: No, not that I can remember.

BAILEY: Tell the jury, doctor, where you have searched for the instrument during the last twelve years.

GERBER: Oh, I have looked all over the United States.

BAILEY: And you didn't describe this phantom impression as a surgical instrument just to hurt Sam Sheppard's case, did you doctor? You wouldn't do that, would you?

GERBER: Oh no. Oh no.[9]

The jury in Sheppard's second trial acquitted him. Freed from prison, Sheppard lived only four troubled years—years that included heavy drinking and an unlikely stint as a professional wrestler under the name "Killer Sheppard," but litigation was not quite over.

Sheppard's son, Sam Reese Sheppard, brought a civil suit for the wrongful imprisonment of his father against Cuyahoga County. In the 2000 civil trial, Sheppard's legal team argued that Richard Eberling, Sheppard's window washer, killed Marilyn after an attempted sexual assault. They pointed out that police found a cocktail ring of Marilyn's in Eberling's possession, and that Eberling, after being convicted for the murder of another woman, confessed to killing Marilyn in a jailhouse interview. Authorities still insisted Sam did it. In the decades since the last criminal trial, authorities developed a new theory for what caused the claw-like imprint in the bloodstain. Lawyers for the County contended that the imprint resulted from a lamp missing from a table near Marilyn's bed, and which Sam used in a fit of passion to kill his wife. The U-shaped bow that surrounded the lamp's bulb would leave just such an impression, they argued. For its part, the defense resisted the temptation to argue that the impression resulted from "a window washing instrument." In this third, and presumably final, trial, jurors sided with the county on the liability question, although they said in interviews that they were split on the question of whether Sam killed Marilyn.[10] The mystery endures.

Coroner Gerber and Prosecutor John Mahon probably believed that the imprint in the bloodstain on Marilyn's pillow was caused by a surgical instrument. People are very good at believing what they want to believe. Both probably felt certain Sheppard murdered his wife and a surgical instrument could well have done the job. Yet if you had asked either man if they'd be willing to stake their life on a surgical instrument being the murder weapon, you can bet they'd back off.

When he testified at the first trial, Gerber did not say "I think it probable that the impression is of a surgical instrument." He did not even say, "I think it is extremely likely that the impression is of a surgical instrument." He said, "I could make out the impression of a surgical instrument."[11] Gerber made a statement of fact, not of probability, and he even repeated his assertion when asked a second time by the trial judge, Edward Blythin. "Did I understand you to testify the imprint on the pillow was made by a surgical instrument?" the judge asked. "Yes," Gerber replied.[12]

Were Gerber and the prosecutor being intentionally misleading or just careless about words? The fact is that humans experience feelings of knowing and feelings of doubt, but they don't *experience* probabilities. We know we have two hands. We doubt we can make it down the ski hill without falling. Probabilities are consciously assigned, in those rare times when they are assigned at all, only *after* we have experiences of knowing or of doubt. Given all we know about the case now, we'd think much better of Gerber and Mahon if the testimony about the cause of the impression had been couched in probabilities rather than as a certainty. You might say that Gerber, and Mahon for allowing him to testify as he did, lacked the proper mental disposition toward knowledge. Gerber and Mahon did nothing more than what we all are inclined to do: they jumped to a conclusion.

EXPERT INTUITION IS SIMPLY GOOD PATTERN RECOGNITION

Our fast-thinking system is the seat of emotions, prejudices, and intuitions, but that doesn't mean that it is incapable of making good decisions. Malcolm Gladwell's best-selling book *Blink* popularized the notion that our automatic, intuitive mode of thinking often can do amazing things, all in the blink of an eye. Gladwell recounted a story about an art expert who knew in seconds that a statue was a fake after a Getty Museum team had spent months convincing itself the work was an authentic Ancient Greek kouros. To the expert, it just didn't look right.[13] Gladwell might have also, had he chosen to do so, found experienced lawyers who could quickly digest a complex set of facts and tell you what the major legal issues will be and how the case will eventually be decided.

To the lay person, the ability of experts to quickly size up a situation can seem like an almost supernatural power. However, the feats of experts that impressed Gladwell, and undoubtedly most readers of his book, actually are nothing more than a two-step cognitive process that used both the experts' fast-thinking and controlled-thinking systems. First, the expert sees cues in the situation that trigger access to information stored in memory—specifically, memory built only through thousands of hours of experience. The memory might have been created by studying countless ancient statues or by litigating hundreds of patent disputes. Intuition is simply a form of rapid accessing of information called pattern recognition. With enough experience, it becomes possible to see patterns that cannot even be articulated. The second step in the process, the step that uses effortful concentration, is the mental check to determine whether the decision or plan stimulated by the pattern recognition applies in the present situation. By seeing patterns where others don't, the expert is able to evaluate a problem by thinking *less* than the nonexpert, not more.

You've heard (too often, probably) that the goal of legal education is to make students "think like lawyers." What legal educators mean by that statement is that they aim to train students to be able to examine a complex collection of facts and, out of those facts, sort the legally relevant from the irrelevant. From one set of facts different cases can be constructed, some more favorable to a client than others. When done right, the mental processes involved include both intuition and effortful thinking. The well-trained lawyer develops the ability to quickly spot patterns of facts that might be used to construct a persuasive argument. This is intuition in action. But the good lawyer doesn't stop there. He or she tests, through slow or deliberative thinking, the strength and possible consequences for clients of using various imagined arguments. There is a sense in which merely by entering the practice we begin to think like lawyers, whether we try to or not. We eventually begin to recognize patterns that relate to whatever type of legal issues we encounter. David Brooks put it this way in *The Social Animal*: "You decide to enter a field and the field enters you."[14]

The validity of expert intuition depends upon an environment in which predictions are made; unless reliable patterns are encountered with some frequency, there is every reason to be skeptical of predictions. In the Sheppard case, it is highly doubtful that Coroner Gerber had sufficient experience examining bloodstain imprints, or surgical instruments, to spot a surgical instrument's bloodstain when he saw one. A coroner might well develop expert intuitions about crime scene patterns, perhaps allowing the coroner to make valid judgments as to whether a murder was committed by an angry spouse or by a professional killer. However, bloodstain imprints of murder weapons aren't discovered very often; there probably is no such thing as a "bloodstain weapon imprint expert." Gerber's guess was as good as yours or mine—probably worse, actually, because he saw what he wanted to see.

What about the field of law in general? Are legal outcomes sufficiently predictable to allow experts to recognize patterns that can be the basis for solid judgments? To outsiders (and even some insiders), law seems like a crapshoot that depends on the luck of the jury pool, what your judge had for breakfast, the whims of a regulator, or the personality quirks of your legal adversary. Most of us who have spent decades in law have a different take, however. Although legal outcomes do often depend on many variables outside of a lawyer's control, there is at least a distribution of probable outcomes for different situations that one can begin to recognize with enough time and practice. Expert lawyers often—but not always—can see the familiar in a new situation and react appropriately. A couple of decades in traffic court or drafting real estate contracts will give you an edge in heading off potential problems in those fields. The skilled trial lawyer doesn't stop to do the careful analysis that a student in Evidence class might do when she hears hearsay coming out of a witness's mouth; the veteran litigator knows it is hearsay almost as soon as it is uttered. The experienced family law lawyer draws on patterns built over hundreds of hours with clients to intuitively respond appropriately to a client's deep concerns—she knows when to soothe, when to warn, and when to focus attention on the problem at hand. Law does not have the regular environment of a chess game, but neither is it as random as the world of stock picking. If all else is equal, put your money on the experienced lawyer.

Experience is the one big thing we have going for us as we age. In our twenties, our brain cells started dying off, our short-term memory began to worsen, and our mental processing began to slow. But as the years pass, our experience helps us become better at recognizing patterns. As Elkhonon Goldberg observes in *The Wisdom Paradox*, "What I have lost with age in my capacity for hard mental work, I seemed to have gained in my capacity for instantaneous, almost unfairly easy insight."[15] Of course, what brings wisdom is having the right types of experiences, not just getting older. Tom Wilson notes, "Wisdom doesn't necessarily come with age. Sometimes old age shows up all by itself."[16] But if we play our cards right, according to Goldberg, we accumulate "numerous and generic" patterns that "facilitate an effortless and instantaneous solution of a wide range of important problems."[17] Expert pattern recognition, a product of ever-growing chunks of networked information stored in memory, is not an entitlement for getting older, but rather has "to be earned."[18]

Research by Goldberg and others has shown that the right hemisphere of the brain, the center for creative thinking and novel solutions, degrades earlier and more rapidly in life than the left hemisphere, where most of our pattern recognition takes place. Youth is the period for novelty, daring, and overflowing creativity. It is the right brain's time. Gradually, as we age, the period of right brain dominance ends and the period of left brain dominance begins—or, as Goldberg describes the trend, our "center of mental gravity shifts" to the left, and less-impaired, hemisphere.[19] Neuroimaging allows us to peer into brains and see neural firing patterns that confirm that a novice, when asked to perform a task, will show primarily right-brain activations while a skilled professional, when asked to do the same task, will show primarily left-brain activation.[20] None of this may compensate for hair loss, declining virility, and reduced ability to speed around a tennis court, but it's what we've got to look forward to.

Pattern recognition allows us to learn from our personal experiences and, over time, to navigate our complex environment more efficiently. Properly tuned over the years, it provides the mechanism for making us more effective professionals. Pattern recognition—the identification of relevant similarities and differences between a present pattern of inputs and past patterns of inputs—allows the human brain to accomplish feats not yet within the capability even of advanced computers. All things are alike and all things are different. Well-tuned perceptual machinery not only recognizes similarities and differences it also tells you when the similarities are most important and when the differences are most important. It allows you to predict with some confidence, for example, whether a judge will rely on a prior case because "fact A" in that case is similar to yours or whether the judge will instead discount the importance of the prior case because "fact B" in that case is different from yours.

THE COSTS AND BENEFITS OF INTUITION

Our automatic system of thinking does often serve us well, and not just by allowing us to impress our clients with our quick diagnosis of their problems. Pattern recognition keeps us alive, just as it did for our ancestors on the savannah for whom the fundamental question of life was "Approach or avoid?" We see movement in the grass and we instantly stop, before we even have time to consciously say, "Danger, snake!" We see a red octagonal sign beside the road and we automatically touch our brake pedal, without bothering to analyze the message the sign contains. We detect an inflection in a judge's tone of voice and know that he is skeptical of our argument. Pattern recognition not only helps us serve our clients; it also gets us through our days.

The mechanisms of our unconscious brains "deliver answers to questions we don't even know we're asking."[21] When we consciously weigh our decisions, we often produce worse answers than when we trust our snap judgments. When subjects in an experiment were asked to rank the quality of a variety of jams, their answers correlated much more closely with the judgments of jam experts—yes, there are jam experts—when they simply reported which ones they liked best. When the subjects were asked to explain why certain jams were better than others—causing them to rely on words such as "color" or "texture" or "sweetness" or "consistency"—their choices diverged dramatically from those of the experts. The features of jam that subjects found easiest to critique turned out not to be the features most closely linked to taste quality. The world is so complex that conscious thought about options is often unproductive and we are better off going with what we often call "our gut instincts," but which are really our emotional brains trained through pattern recognition. Weighing the costs and benefits—and there might be thousands of each, and how do we know when to stop?—gets us nowhere in many situations. Without our emotional brains pushing us onward, we are nearly paralyzed and unable to make almost any decisions of consequence. It is our emotional brain that gets us out of park and into gear—and once moving forward, helps convince us that we are going in the right direction. Even if we aren't, it turns out.

Unfortunately, our very useful automatic system can sometimes cause us to head off into the woods. Because it is the source of our belief system that is always seeking reinforcement, it can cause us to mistakenly think a surgical instrument caused an imprint, that a legal argument is more compelling than it really is, or that a witness is telling the truth when he really isn't. Our intuition might cause us to think we will win a case we will likely lose, that we should accept a settlement offer we should reject, or that we should seat a juror we should excuse. Knowing when those mistakes are most likely to be made—knowing when we are about to fall into a cognitive trap—is one of the things that separates good lawyers from bad lawyers.

Our fast-thinking system sometimes lets us down because it neglects ambiguity, has a bias toward confirmation rather than skepticism, causes us to plunge ahead without considering options, assumes it has enough information for a decision when in fact it doesn't, invents causes when none exist, frames problems too narrowly to supply good answers, is generally terrible at weighing probabilities and making risk calculations, and leads us to make very bad predictions about the future.[22] Apart from that, the system works great. The list of cognitive traps that our auto-matic thinking system can cause us to fall into is too long for us to be able to consider them all in this chapter. But let's examine some of the traps most likely to catch the unwary lawyer—and consider how to get around them.

CONFIRMATION BIAS

Confronted by evidence bearing on a question of importance to us, we instinctively attempt to interpret the evidence in such a way as to confirm our prior beliefs. Opposing attorneys often look at the same evidence and draw two starkly different con-clusions. Note that we're not suggesting bad motives here—no allegation that anyone's trying to pull the wool over jurors' eyes. Psychologist Tom Gilovich came up with a simple formula-tion to describe how we come to believe what we do. Gilovich says that when we want to believe something, we ask ourselves "Can I believe it?" On the other hand, when we don't want to believe something, we ask ourselves "Must I believe it?"[23] Our effortful thinking system—our apologist—is remarkably good at coming up with reasons to support conclusions we've already jumped to.

In the Sam Sheppard case, coroner Gerber and prosecutor Mahon, feeling certain that Sam was the murderer, answered the question about what caused the bloody imprint on the pillow with another question, "Can I believe it was a surgical instru-ment?" Yes, they could. There was nothing about the shape of the imprint that would foreclose belief that it was left by a bloody surgical instrument. Of course, one could also believe it was a lot of other things, including the bow from a lamp or the claw of a lobster. So long as we assume Sheppard did not confess to his lawyer that he did indeed batter his wife with an instrument pulled out of his surgical bag, F. Lee Bailey asked a very different question about the evidence: "Must I believe it was a surgical instrument?" Quite obviously, the answer to that question was "No, not by a long shot."

Of course, when the evidence is compelling enough, minds can change. Sometimes you *do* have to believe it. For example, many people continued to stand by President Clinton and believed his assertion, made before a grand jury during the Starr investigation, that he "did not have sex with that woman," meaning Monica Lewinsky, the White House intern whose relationship to Clinton would become a central issue in the impeachment trial. Then the blue dress appeared, with its telltale stain. Minds changed overnight.

Gilovich's insight as to how we process new evidence has enormous implications for lawyers and the practice of law. It explains, for example, the disturbingly high number of wrongful convictions. Police investigators and prosecuting attorneys generally are not evil people trying to lock up innocent citizens; they typically are convinced they are serving the public by putting away the guilty. The problem is that once they reach a tentative conclusion that someone is guilty, they tend to interpret new evidence in a way that supports that conclusion. In effect, their mental blinders prevent them from giving adequate weight to potentially exculpatory evidence. Even Supreme Court justices suffer from confirmation bias. Especially in the sort of case that gets media play, most justices probably have made tentative decisions, driven by their own intuitions, as to how the case should be decided. Arguments by lawyers that support their intuitions get close attention and full weight, while justices have little difficulty generating objections and reasons to discard arguments that run counter to their intuition-driven tentative conclusions. The difficulty of giving adequate weight to evidence countering our beliefs arises in almost every case a lawyer handles. For example, if a lawyer is attempting to show that a competitor's trademark causes substantial confusion among consumers as to the source of the goods, the lawyer is likely to find data that support a finding of consumer confusion to be highly relevant and well supported, and be equally convinced that data showing little or no confusion is deeply flawed and unreliable. Really, the examples are endless.

Not surprisingly, the different ways we evaluate evidence that supports or contradicts our beliefs explains why we are so often overconfident. If you've been in practice any length of time, you probably have been shocked by a jury that found against your clearly wrongfully injured client, been disappointed by a judge who ruled against your well-supported motion, or discovered that the supposedly airtight contract you drafted had major holes in it after all. Our processing of evidence creates an optimism bias— more on that later.

Today it is easier than ever to find evidence that supports our preexisting beliefs. It used to be hard work for lawyers to track down language in opinions that supported the (objectively quite dubious) claim of their clients. Now Google or Westlaw or Lexis can pull up helpful information in seconds. There's a smorgasbord of information out there, and the pickings are easy.

The confirmation bias that affects our processing of new information is powerful. Law schools have struggled for ways to counteract it, but it is far from clear that they've been successful. Jonathan Haidt goes so far as to say no school "has yet found a way to do it." The reason, he says, is because the bias is "a built-in feature" of our mind, "not a bug that can be removed."[24] Our memory, too, is affected by confirmation bias. Whether new information we encounter ends up in long-term storage depends largely on whether it is consistent with our attitudes and values.

Usually, when we are wrong, we feel perfectly certain that we are right. And usually, when we are forced to confront evidence that proves us wrong, we quickly forget our error and soon come to believe we were always right. Ludwig Wittgenstein, in On Certainty, observed that "'I know' seems to describe a state of affairs which guarantees what is known, guarantees it as a fact. One always forgets the expression, 'I thought I knew.'"[25] We are, as

Kathryn Schulz points out in *Being Wrong: Adventures in the Margin of Error*, "bad at knowing what we don't know."[26] Instead of conceding that we don't have the foggiest idea what the answer to a question is, our minds begin generating hypothesis after hypothesis, and we expend little effort testing their accuracy. Rare is the person who readily says, "I don't know."

USING EXPLORATORY THINKING TO COUNTER CONFIRMATION BIAS

To be a good thinker—or to engage in exploratory thinking, as some writers call it—is to actively test, and potentially reject, "all the incorrect or ill-grounded hypotheses our inner writer is madly generating."[27] Accurate weighing of relevant information is easiest when one feels ambivalent about an issue.[28] On the other hand, when a person is committed to a point of view, even-handed processing of evidence is most difficult. Unsurprisingly, people who are absolutist, who have a strong tendency to see the world in black and white terms, generally have the most difficulty giving fair weight to new information. People who welcome nuance and are comfortable with ambiguity find the task much easier.

Circumstances, of course, can affect how well you consider new evidence. Surrounded by a group of like-minded people, it is ridiculously easy to ignore evidence that runs counter to your own beliefs. On the other hand, you will do your best exploratory thinking when three conditions apply. First, you must know you will be accountable to an audience before you have formed an opinion on a subject. Second, the views of the audience must be unknown to you. And third, you must believe that the audience you are accountable to is well informed and cares about accuracy. When all three conditions apply, you will try to strike a balanced and nuanced position. You will, in other words, do your "darnedest to figure out the truth, because that's what the audience wants to hear."[29]

Good thinking depends on certain mental dispositions and much less on intelligence. Intelligence, it turns out, correlates only very weakly with open-mindedness, diligence, and curiosity, the dispositions that really do affect one's ability to be a good thinker.[30] It helps to have a willingness to collect information and think first about a problem before committing to a position. It requires a mind capable of calibrating beliefs to match the strength of available evidence and weighing the costs and benefits of situations. Above all, perhaps, good thinking requires a willingness to seek out, and listen to, people who might have contrasting points of view.

Although we are perfectly awful at seeking out evidence that runs counter to our judgments, we can employ others to help us do the job. When we enlist colleagues, for example, to challenge the arguments we intend to make in a case, they might "trigger new intuitions, thereby making it possible for us to change our minds."[31] Yes, it is also possible to change your mind through private reflection—but seeking the help of others, especially people you respect, makes the task infinitely easier.

MENTAL BLIND SPOTS

Another lesson of relevance to lawyers comes from research that explores how our fast, automatic information processing system is affected by effortful reasoning. These findings cast serious doubt on the eyewitness accounts of events that are so frequently determinative of litigation outcomes. There is good reason to be skeptical of anyone's account of the world, including our own. In the words of Alan Watts, "Normally we do not so much look at things as overlook them."[32]

The degree to which our unconscious minds can blind us to the seemingly obvious was demonstrated by an experiment conducted by two cognitive psychologists at Harvard. The researchers asked subjects to watch a thirty-second video of two basketball teams passing balls back and forth and to count the number of times the players in the black uniforms passed balls to each other. After the thirty seconds were up, subjects reported the number of passes. Then the researchers asked the subjects whether they noticed anything strange. Only about half did.[33] The researchers then re-ran the tape, this time with no one asked to count anything. Clearly visible, toward the end of the video, is a man in a gorilla costume who walks on to the court, in the very center of the picture, and thumps his chest for nine seconds before walking off. According to Christopher Chabris, one of the Harvard researchers, the "invisible gorilla" experiment left subjects feeling shocked that they could miss the gorilla: "Most people seem to have the intuitive idea that they're going to see this kind of thing and they're really surprised when they find out that they don't."[34]

Intense concentration creates physical changes. Researchers have observed, for example, that pupil dilation is a sensitive indicator of mental effort. Brain imaging shows that when we focus our mental attention on a problem, we use fewer—not more—regions of the brain. Researchers are even able to describe what might be called "Eureka moments": about one second before insight, the visual processing center goes dark, then about 700 milliseconds later, a spike in gamma rhythms appears in the right temporal lobe.[35]

Of course, the gorilla experiment, and what it reveals about selective attention, has significant real-world implications. It suggests, for example, the dangers of multitasking, such as driving and talking on a cell phone at the same time. It also should cause us to wonder whether security screeners at airports really make us as safe as we think they do, or whether radiologists viewing medical scans are picking up all the anomalies. For lawyers, one lesson might be to be skeptical of testimony by eyewitnesses to accidents or crimes, especially if they were giving less than full attention to the scene. It is quite probable that the eyewitnesses missed something critical to the case, even though it would have been blindingly obvious to another observer.

There's another lesson here for lawyers, who are trained to be effortful thinking pros. With all that mental concentration, you're likely to miss a lot of what's happening around you, and some of that might be more important than whatever you've got your effortful thinking system working on. For example, if you are thinking too hard about the next question you intend to ask a witness, you might miss important nonverbal clues. It could be something as otherwise obvious as a jury box full of sleeping people—or even an angry gorilla that just entered the courtroom.

ALL WE SEE IS ALL THERE IS

Our brains are designed to look at ambiguities and make generalizations. Even when a question might not have an answer, we feel as though it must.[36] We have great difficulty accepting that we do not have all the information we need to make a decision, and so we decide based on information we have, however paltry it might be—in short, we act as though "what we see is all there is."[37] Put another way, our brains are lazy. They generally are not looking for extra heavy mental lifting to do, and so when the unconscious, fast-thinking brain generates a conclusion based on sketchy information, our conscious brain is usually ready to endorse it.

We seek coherence using whatever limited information we have. Studies have shown that giving potential jurors even the sketchiest set of facts about a case will set them searching for causal links, constructing stories, and expressing conclusions. When the information provided is one-sided, they will express their conclusion with even more confidence. Generating arguments for the other side doesn't come easy for people, and good stories are measured more by consistency than completeness.[38]

Typically, the more emotionally powerful or salient information is, the more likely we are to overweight that information and ignore other information that might be equally relevant to the problem. This phenomenon repeats many times in law school faculty hiring discussions, where a single memorable comment of a candidate might spell doom or land the job, even when a more objective evaluation of the candidate's overall record—what people today have come to call "the body of work"—suggests a different outcome.

Drawing as we do on the information readily accessible in our memory banks, we often confidently draw very inaccurate conclusions. For example, when I ask first-year constitutional law students to guess what percentage of Supreme Court decisions in recent years have been unanimous, their guesses are invariably too low, typically in the range of 10% to 20%. In fact, the rate of unanimous decisions has consistently averaged over 40% for the past couple of decades,[39] though those are seldom the decisions that get much media attention. The most controversial, and usually most closely decided, cases are the ones we hear or read about in the media, and they are the cases that come most readily to mind for students as they make their guesses about the frequency of unanimous decisions.

Law students, as well as people generally, also tend to underweight prior probabilities and overweight new information. For example, consider these three assumptions, all of which are amply supported by social science research: (1) women are more likely to acquit than men; (2) African Americans are more likely to acquit than whites; and (3) people who have never been crime victims are more likely to acquit than people who have been victims. Now consider Mary, an African American woman who has never been the victim of a crime. What are the odds that Mary will vote to convict in a typical armed robbery case? Presented with this information, most people guess that Mary will vote to acquit; after all, she falls into all three "acquittal-prone" categories. In fact, however, statistics show the likelihood of Mary voting to acquit in such a case is only about 30%. What people ignore is that the vast majority of jurors, about 90% or so, vote to convict in armed robbery cases. The assumptions make clear Mary is less likely than most jurors to convict, and that is primarily what people focus on.[40]

Most people, when they do not have enough information to answer a question, ask another question they *can* answer, and when they don't have all the facts to make a complete story, they supply supposed facts to finish the job. Also, faced with making a decision when some relevant information is readily accessible and other relevant information is more difficult to gather, most people will base their decisions only on the information that is at hand. All they see is all there is.

Of course, this is not what we expect from good lawyers, who confront counterevidence and have a sense for what they don't know. They understand the tendency of most people to underestimate their own level of ignorance, and guard against it in themselves. In short, they know well how to treat knowledge. When presented with a question of the sort faced by the pillow evidence in the Sheppard trial, good lawyers do not rush to conclusions. They think hard before they put a defendant's life or liberty at risk. They gather and assess information, generally from a variety of sources. Only when they've sifted through and weighed all the relevant information do they adopt an opinion, and then one commensurate with the evidence.

ANCHORING

One piece of advice we always give students as they approach their first law school exams is this: "Whatever you do, write the very best first paragraph you can." The reason for that advice is the tendency we all have to anchor our opinions, and then insufficiently adjust from that anchor as new information develops.[41] In other words, first impressions really do matter most. As a professor reads a well-written first paragraph in an exam, an impression inevitably begins to form in his or her mind. "This is really good," the prof thinks, "probably an 'A' paper." From then on it may be all downhill, and the professor's estimate of the exam's worth will decline, but not as much as it probably should: we insufficiently adjust from our anchors. Perhaps the professor chooses to give the exam a "B+." On the other hand, if a student starts out with a poor first paragraph, the professor naturally begins with a low anchor, perhaps a "C." The exam answer might markedly improve from that point on, and the prof ends up giving the exam a better grade than first expected, perhaps a "B-." But again the adjustment from the anchor is likely to be insufficient. In terms of overall quality, the two exams might have been equal, and perhaps both deserving of "Bs," but those anchors meant something. What is true for professors is also true for judges. Hitting just the right notes at the beginning of a brief or an argument can make a disproportionate difference in outcomes.

The anchoring effect is the product of both our automatic and effortful modes of thinking. The automatic system anchors because of what is called "priming," the fact that the unconscious is prone to accept any suggestion that comes its way. If a witness to an accident is asked by an investigator, "How fast do you think the car was going? Eighty miles an hour?" a suggestion has been planted. The witness has been primed to say the car was speeding, perhaps in the vicinity of eighty miles an hour. Of course, the witness might well think that speed to be too high and will make the mental effort to adjust the speed downward. In the absence of any suggestion, the witness might have guessed the speed to be sixty miles per hour. With the suggestion, however, the witness might say "I think the car was going about seventy miles an hour." The witness consciously adjusts the speed downward, but insufficiently. On the other hand, the investigator could have chosen to anchor a lower speed by asking, "How fast was the car going? Forty miles an hour?" In this case, the witness may think the suggestion too low, and offer a higher estimate, say, "About fifty miles per hour."

Every good lawyer at least implicitly understands the anchoring effect. Cases are often won or lost in opening statements, sometimes even during voir dire. In the battle to win the hearts and minds (sometimes more hearts than minds), the trial attorney who first succeeds in establishing a plausible story to explain the case has a big edge. While jurors will adjust their initial views as the evidence is presented, where they begin disproportionately influences where they eventually will come out. Experienced attorneys also know how important it is to anchor a dollar amount for damages in the minds of jurors. Typically, jurors have a specific dollar amount in mind for a damages award when they enter into deliberations. They might move from that number—it could be $2 million, or $70,000, or it could be $0—but where they begin affects where they end. They insufficiently adjust, in the parlance of heuristics talk. The same is true in settlement negotiations, although the anchoring effect is probably lessened because of greater awareness of its role by the more sophisticated participants.

A TROUBLING QUESTION

There is a troubling question here. The anchoring effect is real, but is there something a bit unseemly about exploiting it? When lawyers consciously tailor arguments to trigger irrational thinking, they risk being seen less as key members of a system designed to produce justice than as something akin to Madison Avenue hucksters. When public law schools offer courses that teach students how to anchor their positions in the minds of jurors or, say, take advantage of the poor understanding jurors have of probabilities, some might argue they no longer deserve the support of taxpayers. Critics might note that by emphasizing techniques that exploit the irrational tendencies of jurors, judges, and fellow attorneys, law schools move the legal system away from truth-seeking and toward one that rewards manipulation. Trial advocacy teachers might pretend that attorneys, if they succeed in training them all to become master manipulators, will offset each other's manipulations and leave us with something resembling truthful outcomes (if there is such a thing) in the long run—but that is more a hope than a likelihood. Still, only one conclusion is obvious. The attorney who decides to unilaterally disarm, and swears off any conscious manipulation of human irrationalities, does a disservice to his or her client, the person to whom an attorney's highest duty lies.

All effective persuasion is based on an understanding of how human beings process information. Some techniques of persuasion focus on making the speaker's or writer's message more powerful and memorable. For example, we know that simple messages are more likely to be remembered than complex messages. We know that rhyme makes a message more memorable. (Think of Johnny Cochran's message about the bloody gloves that O. J. Simpson seemingly had difficulty getting his hands into: "If the gloves don't fit, you must acquit.") Can a distinction be drawn between techniques designed to better encode memory in the heads of jurors and techniques built on the knowledge of how jurors are likely to draw unsupported conclusions from certain types of information? You're a lawyer; of course a distinction can be drawn, but almost no one will act on that distinction, and you had better not either.

TOO NARROW FRAMING

The metaphor of the frame is used to describe how we organize the chaos of the world in an understandable way. From the countless bits of information we could choose among, we define those that are somehow worthy of our attention and exclude the rest. Frames, then, tell us what is important and what should be compared to what. The unconscious, with all its biases and tendencies, plays a big role in framing, and there is no "neutral" way to frame. How a problem is framed will generally determine how it is answered because people are, for the most part, passive decision makers. Few people bother to engage in the effortful thinking necessary to see whether a different way of framing the problem might produce a different answer—probably because most people sense that reframing *could* produce a different answer, and they'd rather not face the contradiction.

In general, the broader and more comprehensive the frame is that we use, the better our answers will be. For example, too narrow framing often leads to poor financial choices. By focusing narrowly on losses associated with a single poor performing stock, our natural tendency toward loss aversion inclines us to hold on to the stock, even as it continues its long slide downward, perhaps even to bankruptcy. Experienced traders, on the other hand, are more likely to frame broadly and, as a result, more readily accept losses and move their money to other stocks with better prospects.

The problems associated with narrow framing explain the significant advantage that deep-pocketed insurance companies have over injured plaintiffs in cases, especially in cases where the liability claim is strong. The plaintiff, who quite naturally worries about the small, but non-zero, probability that a jury might ignore the strength of her claim and decide against her, is likely to accept a settlement offer somewhat below the expected value of the award she would get if she took her case to trial. Insurance companies, however, have the luxury of broader framing and can make more "rational" calculations about when to settle based closely on the expected value of the award a jury will give. As a result of the differences in frames, cases in which a plaintiff's case is especially strong almost always result in settlements prior to trial on terms that might be described as somewhat favorable to the defense.

Lawyers employ frames in a variety of ways. In a counseling session, a lawyer might encourage a client to use a broader frame as a way of thinking more clearly about a course of action. Perhaps the lawyer's solid advice might be to accept a small loss, look at the big picture, and move on. In a criminal case involving

DNA evidence, a prosecutor might tell a jury, "The probability of a false match with the defendant is only one tenth of one percent." The defense attorney on the other hand prefers to frame the question in a way that triggers jurors' thinking about reasonable doubt: "One out of every thousand defendants would share this DNA profile, and yet not be the source of this blood." The defense frame conjures the image of a wrongful conviction, while the prosecution's frame is intentionally more abstract.[42]

NEGATIVE IMPLICIT ATTITUDES

We end this discussion of the traps the mind is heir to with consideration of the troubling reality of negative implicit attitudes. A team of psychologists developed the Implicit Association Test (IAT) as a means of measuring the degree to which subjects have negative associations with certain social groups—the elderly, obese people, African Americans, immigrants, and others.[43] The disturbing conclusion of these researchers is that most people, regardless of their political beliefs, do hold negative implicit attitudes toward many social groups. While the explicit values of subjects might be that race or obesity or old age has nothing to do with a person's worth, those explicit values contradict their implicit values. Subjects find, often to their own shock, that it takes them significantly longer to associate a good thing with the face of someone from certain social groups. Brain images can show the conflict. One region of the subject's brain after another lights up as he or she attempts to resolve it.[44] If you think yourself immune from this phenomenon, feel free to take an IAT test yourself at ProjectImplicit.org.

Needless to say, these findings have huge implications for a justice system that promises equality for all. Who you are and what you look like gives you either an edge or a disadvantage in your relationships with other people, including judges, jurors, and other attorneys. The same, of course, can be said for your clients and witnesses.

Simply knowing about negative implicit attitudes could, on occasion, be helpful to an attorney. In the famous McMartin Preschool Abuse trial, as depicted in the 1995 movie *Indictment*, Ray Buckey's defense attorney Daniel Davis asks witness Kee McFarland of Children's Institute International about a series of interviews she conducted with children at the day care center. At one point in his cross-examination, Davis picks up one of the defense exhibits, an anatomically correct black doll. He asks McFarland why, when doing her interviews for the District Attorney's Office with the alleged victims, she chose a black doll to represent Buckey, a white man. One might expect that the three African American members of the jury, if not all twelve of them, listened with great interest to this exchange.[45]

For Jonathan Haidt, the bottom line is that "human minds, like animal minds, are constantly reacting to everything they perceive, and basing their responses on those reactions." If our reasoning system is the rider, and our intuitive system is our elephant, as Haidt calls the two thinking systems of the brain, "within the first second of seeing, hearing, or meeting another person, the elephant has already begun to lean toward or away."[46] It all begins with our intuitions.

IT'S HARD TO KEEP AN OPEN MIND

Intuitions precede reasoning and, for the most part, play the larger role in our decision making, both in our lives and in our professional careers. We use effortful reasoning mostly to rationalize the decisions of our automatic thinking and only rarely to override it. We tend to greatly overestimate our ability to control our unconscious inclinations; for the most part, they control us. Robert Burton observes, "Our mental limitations prevent us from accepting our mental limitations."[47] Fortunately, our intuitions generally serve us well. What good lawyers do, however, is understand when intuitions are not always to be trusted, and they develop strategies for kicking their effortful reasoning into gear when intuitions are likely to lead them astray. Finding the right mix of unconscious and conscious analysis is tricky. What works in one situation often won't work in another.

We need a set of "thinking slow" strategies to avoid falling into cognitive traps. That set should include using checklists and following procedures, a strategy airline pilots now use before take-offs and landings and which has dramatically reduced accident rates. The elements of a lawyer's checklist will vary, of course. The checklist of a lawyer preparing for trial will not be the same as one preparing documents for a merger or acquisition. A second approach might be to enlist others—others who are not "yes people"—to evaluate your strategies and work product. What served President Lincoln so well, his administration's "team of rivals," can work in law firm settings too. Third, lawyers should pay close attention to the way they frame problems. Too narrow framing is a common problem that can cause relevant information to fall off radar screens, leading to less powerful arguments and overlooked legal strategies. Finally, law firms need to encourage a culture in which lawyers are evaluated not just on how their decisions turn out but also on how they are made. Good decisions sometimes yield bad outcomes, and bad decisions sometimes produce good outcomes—law firms need to understand that.

Our intuitions allow us to look at a cumulus cloud and see a rabbit, or to see the image of the Virgin Mary in grill grease. A coroner can see the imprint of a surgical instrument in a blood-stained pillow. Our minds have developed to accept suggestions and find confirmatory evidence more readily than evidence that contradicts our assumptions. Keeping an open mind is one of the hardest things a lawyer, or any other human being, can do.

It also takes a lot of hard work to become an expert—whether a chess grandmaster or a master plumber or a securities lawyer. (Sorry, couch lawyers.) The old notion of genius "being 10% inspiration and 90% perspiration" turns out to be largely right. What many people perceive as genius is really just expert pattern recognition developed and refined through thousands of hours of practice. Just as you should not expect to build stronger muscles without getting off your duff and going to the gym, there is likewise no real short-cut to becoming a better thinker. Stanford psychologist Carol Dweck suggests that we think of the brain as a muscle. Just like your biceps, the brain "changes and gets stronger when you use it."[48] As we learn and face challenges, our brains form new connections.

The good news is that once you know a bunch of stuff it becomes easier to learn even more. As you begin to develop deep knowledge in the field of law, acquiring more legal knowledge becomes easier as the new knowledge finds its place in the framework of knowledge you have already built. An experienced lawyer, in a sense, owns a mental Christmas tree on which new ornaments can easily be hung, while the novice lawyer puts new ornaments in a box, where they easily can become lost or forgotten. Where new lawyers might see only a swirling blizzard of random facts, the expert lawyer sees emerging patterns. The brains of experienced lawyers, like those of experts in other fields, perform a truly remarkable feat: they transform conscious knowledge into unconscious knowledge, and then they let their unconscious knowledge guide their decision making without the expenditure of time and effort that would be required to make use of conscious knowledge.

The cognitive traps highlighted in this chapter are only a few of the many that find ample support in the social science literature, where whole careers have been built on demonstrating the prevalence of various heuristics. In the next chapter, we consider heuristics that can foil even our most confident predictions.

CHAPTER 6

The Good Lawyer Thinks Realistically about the Future

Never make predictions, especially about the future.
—Casey Stengel

AWYERS HAVE SOMETHING IN COMMON WITH METEO-rologists, stockbrokers, and palm readers. People in all four occupations are, to a significant degree, preoccupied with predicting the future. One of the key questions on the mind of every client who seeks out a lawyer is what is likely to happen if various strategies are chosen. A client who feels he or she has been wrongfully injured will ask, "If I sue, am I likely to win?" and "How much money am I likely to collect if I win?" A defendant in a lawsuit wants to know what the suit is likely to cost. Criminal defendants want to know the odds that they'll be sent to prison (and for how long) or, worse yet, sent to their Maker. Other clients want to know how much money they will be able to pass on to their spouse, whether the IRS is likely to audit their tax return, or what will happen if they decide to breach a provision in a contract.

While no lawyer has the ability to consistently predict the future with accuracy, good lawyers distinguish themselves by being better able than most to do so, whether the predictions relate to outcomes of cases they litigate or how another party to a contract they drafted will behave, given a particular turn of events. A lawyer who time and again overestimates his or her prospects of success in litigation, or who is often surprised by events that leave clients unhappy with the contracts he or she drafted, will soon be a lawyer with fewer clients. Predicting the future, of course, is not done with crystal balls or Ouija boards. It is an exercise that requires the lawyer to draw upon knowledge of case law, about the strengths and weaknesses of evidence, about the behavior of particular judges or juries in specific jurisdictions, and about her own abilities and those of opposing counsel. To do the job well also requires a sophisticated understanding of probability and of prediction biases—an understanding, unfortunately, that few lawyers have.

In this chapter, we consider both the difficulty of predicting the future and ways that lawyers might improve their predictive abilities. Making better predictions, especially in the legal context, is not something that comes easy. Compared to the difficulties faced by lawyers, forecasting the weather a few days out is a piece of cake. While meteorologists use computers and ever-growing databases about the physical world to make increasingly accurate predictions, lawyers are left to puzzle about such things as how the life experiences of a judge or a panel of jurors might affect the way they evaluate certain testimony from a particularly emotional witness.

WHAT RESEARCH REVEALS ABOUT THE PREDICTIVE ABILITIES OF LAWYERS

When a team of researchers set out to evaluate the predictive abilities of lawyers, they had reasons to suspect that lawyers would, like most people, be overconfident in their abilities to produce satisfactory outcomes for their clients. Previous research, encompassing a wide range of professions, had suggested that a bias toward optimism led people to expect better results than they were actually able to achieve. While a bias toward optimism keeps people pushing ahead and reduces the risk of depression, it also leads people to undertake tasks for which they are ill-suited and to ignore legitimate risks. Summarizing that research, the team reported, "Psychological studies of human decision-making processes in a wide variety of contexts have revealed overconfidence is a ubiquitous phenomenon."[1] The researchers hoped to measure more precisely than ever the degree to which lawyers were overconfident in their predictions and to see if a particular intervention might cause lawyers to make better predictions than they otherwise would.

The four researchers (Jane Goodman-Delahunty, Par Granhag, Maria Hartwig, and Elizabeth Loftus) persuaded 481 American lawyers in forty-four states to indicate what would be a satisfactory result in a case that each expected to take to trial in the next six to twelve months. Specifically, each lawyer was asked, "What would be a win situation in terms of your minimum goal for the outcome of this case?"[2] For the 70% of civil lawyers in the sample, the "win situation" was most often (but not always) described as a dollar amount they would be happy receiving or paying, either in a settlement or a jury award. For the 30% of the lawyers in the sample who were prosecutors or criminal defense lawyers, the "win situation" was generally described in terms of a conviction, an acquittal, a conviction for a lesser offense, or a mistrial. After defining what would be a "win situation" in their trial, each attorney was then asked to estimate their confidence in achieving that result. Researchers asked, "From 0 to 100%, what is the probability that you will achieve this outcome or something better?"[3]

The good news from the study is that lawyers who were highly confident of achieving a "win situation" were in fact *somewhat* more likely to do so than less confident lawyers—but the difference was less than you'd expect. The more significant finding, however, reinforced the earlier research suggesting that lawyers, whether confident or not, substantially overestimated their odds of achieving a satisfactory outcome. By almost a 2 to 1 margin (44% to 24%), lawyers were more likely to fail to achieve their goal than to exceed it. About one-third (32%) of the lawyers participating in the survey reported the final case outcome matched the goal they had set at the outset. Summarizing their results, the researchers reported, "Far more lawyers were susceptible to the overconfidence bias than to the underconfidence bias. In general, the higher the expressed level of confidence, the greater the overconfidence."[4]

Further analyzing the results, the researchers also concluded, perhaps surprisingly, that predictions did not get better with experience. Nor did, counter to their own hypothesis, asking lawyers to generate reasons for why they might fail to achieve their "win situation" make lawyers' predictions any more accurate. There was no difference in the success rates between criminal and civil lawyers when it came to predicting outcomes. The one thing that did seem to significantly improve predictions was the state of being female; female lawyers seem somewhat less bitten by the overconfidence bug than do male lawyers. The researchers resisted the temptation to speculate as to why female lawyers might make more reasonable predictions than their male counterparts.[5]

Future research might examine the degree to which extroversion and introversion affect the accuracy of predictions concerning legal outcomes. In general, research suggests that introverts, being a somewhat anxious but conscientious lot, are less subject to an optimism bias than extroverts and therefore are more likely to make accurate predictions. Because introverts are overrepresented in the population of lawyers, lawyers as a group probably suffer a bit less from the overconfidence bias than those in most other occupations, from stockbrokers to restaurant owners.[6] If you happen to be an extrovert, consider running your next prediction by your introverted colleague down the hall; you might find your colleague provides a valuable reality check.

Interestingly, despite producing generally unimpressive results in predicting outcomes, most lawyers later reported to researchers that they were nonetheless pleased with the final results of their cases. Almost two-thirds (64%) of lawyers claimed to be "pleased" or "very pleased" with the outcomes of their case even though a considerably smaller percentage of lawyers actually met or exceeded their initial goals for their cases. Only 18% of the surveyed lawyers admitted to being "very disappointed" or "somewhat disappointed" in outcomes, despite the fact that more than twice as many (43%) failed to meet their initial goals.[7] What's going on here? Most likely, achieving a disappointing result caused some lawyers' "psychological immune systems" to spring into action, allowing them to readjust in their mind their initial goals or to give more positive weight to an aspect of the final outcome than they initially might have assigned.[8] Our minds work hard to prop up our egos in the face of failures.

The researchers pointed out some of the implications of their findings. They observed the centrality of predictions about cases to a lawyer's work. What course of action a lawyer takes, whether she takes on a new client or not, and whether she advises a client to accept a settlement offer or proceed to trial, all will turn on a lawyer's perception about probable outcomes. The ability to make accurate predictions about case outcomes affects both a lawyer's financial success and reputation and the satisfaction that a client is likely to have with a lawyer's work on his behalf. In fact, as the researchers noted, the "justice environment as a whole" is substantially affected by these predictions because, "At the end of the day, it is the accurate predictions of the lawyer that enable the justice system to function smoothly without the load of cases that were not appropriately vetted by lawyers."[9]

An earlier study by Brigham Young University law professor Gerald Williams revealed a wild divergence in assessments of a case, even among experienced trial attorneys. Williams asked forty practicing lawyers in Des Moines to read a set of case facts and then participate in negotiations. Twenty lawyers were assigned to the plaintiff's side and twenty to the defense. Despite working from the exact same facts, plaintiffs' attorneys began negotiations with demands ranging from a low of $32,000 to a figure more than *twenty times* higher ($675,000), while defense attorneys' opening offers ranged from $3,000 to $50,000. Settlements ultimately ranged from $15,000 to $95,000.[10] Obviously, case assessment is far from an exact science, but it is startling to find settlements involving the same set of facts vary by a factor of more than six. Probably, even the plaintiff's attorney who pocketed the paltry $15,000 and the defense attorney who coughed up $95,000 walked away from the exercise feeling rather good about their efforts.

Three factors most likely contribute to overconfidence among lawyers, according to the researchers involved in the forty-four state study of actual case outcomes. The first factor they labeled "overestimation," which they described as "the inflated perception of one's ability, performance, or chance of success."[11] Lawyers, and most other human beings, share a strong tendency toward overestimation. The second factor identified by the researchers was "overplacement," or the imagining of one's self as especially competent relative to peers.[12] Most people think that they are better drivers, employees, judges of human nature, and lovers than other people. (This is also called "the Lake Wobegon Effect," named after Garrison Keillor's mythical town "where all the children are above average.") The danger, of course, is that we think so highly of our own abilities to draft documents, negotiate, or present oral arguments that we fail to seek the input of others or subject our own work to critical self-review. Finally, the researchers identified "overprecision" as a factor in overconfidence. Overprecision, they said, is "excessive certainty regarding the accuracy of one's beliefs."[13] Once we adopt a belief, we tend to reinforce it to the point that it becomes harder and harder to dislodge, and the belief moves increasingly in the direction of certainty.

The researchers seemed somewhat disappointed that the tested intervention, asking lawyers to list reasons why their expected outcome might not be realized, failed to produce more accurate predictions. The researchers speculated as to why an intervention that seems to work well for, say, meteorologists, doesn't work so well for lawyers. They noted, first off, that unlike weather fore-casters, lawyers do have some capacity to control the outcomes they are predicting. This fact, they suggested, might lead lawyers to "overestimate their own capacity and neglect the importance of factors beyond their control."[14] Second, they said, "lawyers have a much keener interest in the goals of their predictions than meteorologists."[15] Previous studies have shown that the mere fact of imagining in detail some possible future event increases the likelihood that a person will predict the event will happen. When a plaintiff's lawyer stretches back in his office chair and imagines a jury foreperson announcing that his client will be awarded $10 million, the probability he assigns in his own mind that such an announcement will actually be made goes up. Be careful, the authors of the study warn, what mental scenarios you choose to entertain, because wishful thinking can lead to "painful disappointment."[16]

WE WANT TO BELIEVE THE WORLD IS MORE PREDICTABLE THAN IT IS

Nobel Prize winner Daniel Kahneman has spent a lifetime study-ing how we think. In his best-selling book, *Thinking Fast and Slow*, the world's preeminent cognitive psychologist observes that our minds cause us to "see the world as more tidy, simple, predictable, and coherent than it really is."[17] In Kahneman's view, our tendency to simplify the world and become overconfident in our predic-tions is the result of our desire to reduce anxiety: uncertainty makes us anxious, so we become more certain than the evidence justifies. Optimism puts our minds more at ease, reduces stress, improves performance, and seems even to improve physical health, so there is a good reason that optimism bias is as widespread as it is, but there still is a lot to be said for accuracy. Kahneman contends, "Your intuitions will deliver predictions that are too extreme and you will be inclined to put far too much faith in them."[18]

The illusion that one can predict and control the future is fed, Kahneman says, by another illusion, "the illusion that one has understood the past."[19] When outcomes surprise us, we search for explanations, often fastening on the first one to come to mind. When your football team loses a game you expected them to win, you might conclude that you failed to account for the fact that they would experience "a let-down" from their big win the week before. (A let-down may have been a contributing factor, but so might your quarterback's injured wrist or the stiff wind that blew your kicker's field goal attempt to the left.) When the jury comes back with an unfavorable verdict in the case, you might decide the reason was an inappropriate instruction given by the judge, or a weak performance by your expert witness, while more important factors included your failure to connect with the jury and the strength of your opponent's evidence. The real world is messy and complicated, and usually the contributing factors to an outcome are numerous and difficult to weigh.

Lawyers tend to think that the best possible assessment of a case is one that draws heavily on their own intuitions. As a group, lawyers are not inclined to believe that statistics or outsiders can add much to the accuracy of their predictions. Kahneman tells of once asking his cousin, whom he calls "a distinguished lawyer," what the odds were of "the defendant winning in cases like this one." His cousin replied, with a hint that the question was superficial, "Every case is unique."[20] In fact, Kahneman believes, uniqueness is very much overrated and lawyers can learn much by considering statistics that apply to the sort of case they have. For example, a lawyer who is considering representing a plaintiff in a defamation case against a media defendant might do well to look beyond the specific facts of her case—what outrageous words the defendant used to harm her client—and consider the statistics for defamation suits brought against the media. If she does so, her enthusiasm caused by the specific facts of the case might be tempered by the realization that well over 80% of all defamation cases are dismissed by summary judgments, and even in the small set of cases that do go to trial, 37% of them end up being decided in the defendant's favor. Then only one-third of plaintiffs' verdicts survive intact on appeal.[21] A paltry 4% overall success rate for plaintiffs' lawyers in this type of case should give any lawyer pause—though, of course, some facts are *so* compelling that the long odds can be overcome.

In general, lawyers (and almost all humans) tend to predict outcomes that "are unrealistically close to best-case scenarios."[22] Kahneman observes, for example, that a survey of American homeowners who remodeled their kitchens expected the job to cost less than half of what it eventually turned out to cost.[23] Just as lawyers overestimated their chances of success in litigation, lawyers are also inclined to *underestimate* the time and money that they put into seeing a project through to completion, whether it be representing injured plaintiffs or securing rezoning approval for clients in a real estate practice.

Kahneman believes that predictions can be improved by seeking outside views of experts and consulting statistics or applying algorithms. Kahneman distinguishes between predictions that come out of "high-validity environments" and "low-validity environments."[24] Low-validity environments are ones in which the level of uncertainty is high (for example, the future economic outlook or a political election that is a year away). Lawyers, for the most part, work in low-validity environments, though there are exceptions. A lawyer who practices traffic law in the same municipal court for years can probably make quite accurate predictions as to what will happen to his client who exceeded the speed limit by, say, fifteen miles per hour. For most lawyers, however, uncertainties accumulate to make predictions difficult. "Who will the judge be?" "Will my client be convincing on the stand?" "Can I get the type of jury that I want?" "Will the defendant be willing to settle or insist on taking this to trial?" When questions pile up, you're in a low-validity environment and your predictions are prone to go awry. "In the absence of stable regularities in the environment," Kahneman cautions, "intuition cannot be trusted."[25]

If we can't trust our intuitions to predict case outcomes, where should we turn? Marjorie C. Aaron, in her book *Client Science*, suggests that lawyers carefully consider the facts and arguments that opposing counsel is likely to make. She cautions that this exercise "cannot be passive or casual." It is not enough, she says, "to think (or say), 'Well the other side is emphasizing the credentials of its expert witness and, if he is as smart as they say, that might hurt us.'" Instead, it is necessary "to articulate, in your own words, exactly what the other side's evidence and counter-arguments are."[26]

Kahneman suggests that "a disciplined collection of objective information" can improve the accuracy of predictions.[27] The information that can aid lawyers' predictions is as varied as the types of predictions lawyers make. Before a lawyer predicts the likelihood of the Supreme Court granting cert in a particular case, it might be helpful to know that the Supreme Court's overall cert grant rate is less than 2%, or that the rate rises to 70% when the solicitor general recommends a cert grant. In predicting the outcome of a case pending before the Supreme Court, it might be worth weighing the fact that in over 68% of the cases it takes, it reverses the court below.[28] If you are a personal injury lawyer, you might want to consider that the jury verdict service for your jurisdiction suggests, say, that less than 20% of medical malpractice suits result in plaintiffs' verdicts, or that slip-and-fall plaintiffs win 40% of their suits, if you are representing plaintiffs in either of those types of cases. In other areas of practice, you might find that law review articles or journal stories reporting trends in the decisions of your appellate court could, if properly weighed, facilitate better predictions about case outcomes.

A study by Randall Kiser and other researchers suggests that lawyers for plaintiffs fail to adequately consider overall success rates for the type of case they have and, as a result, frequently misjudge the value of cases when plaintiffs' success for their category of case is rare. For example, Kiser found that plaintiffs' lawyers were about twice as likely to make decision errors in settlements—which they defined as receiving "an award less than or equal to the last offer made by the defendant"—in medical malpractice cases than they are in contract cases. In medical malpractice cases, lawyers made the mistake of rejecting a settlement offer higher than their eventual award in a whopping 81% of cases, compared to a decision error rate of 44% in contract cases. Kiser and his fellow researchers concluded, "In general, an inverse relationship exists between plaintiff decision error rates and win rates."[29]

Another way of improving predictions is to consult outsiders. The predictions of outsiders, as we noted in the previous chapter, are unaffected by "optimism bias." Unlike you, they are under no illusion that they have greater control over the outcome of the case than they do. Consulting a lawyer without a personal interest in your case affords a more objective view of your case than even another attorney in your firm is likely to be able to provide. Of course, where consultation comes at a cost, that cost has to be weighed against the benefits it might provide in sharpening predictions.

There is an abundance of evidence suggesting that group forecasts tend to be more accurate than individual ones, so seeking out a variety of opinions concerning a case's probable outcome is most likely worth the effort. According to statistician and political prognosticator extraordinaire Nate Silver, group forecasts are "between 15 and 20 percent" more accurate than individual forecasts, depending upon the discipline. He warns, however, that there is no assurance that a group forecast will be *good*, only that it is likely to be better than that of a single individual.[30]

HERE COME THE COMPUTERS

Recently a new tool for improving predictions about case outcomes is making waves: computers. "Lex Machina" is Latin for "Law Machine." It's also the name of a tech startup that emerged in 2009 from a Stanford Law School project to help "companies anticipate, manage, and win patent and other intellectual property [IP] law suits."[31] The idea to create a sophisticated database with reliable information about IP suits came to Stanford law professor Mark Lemley after he grew tired of hearing unsubstantiated assertions about patent litigation. "People would make all kinds of claims in policy debates that were presumably testable but were radically different from each other, you know with one saying patent suits are 50 percent of all lawsuits and another saying, no, it's 1 percent."[32] A team of lawyers and engineers put in over 100,000 hours categorizing, tagging, and coding information to produce a database of 150,000 IP cases, 134,000 attorney records, and information about 1,400 judges, 63,0000 law firms, and 64,000 parties from the last decade. Every day the database grows. Lex Machina's crawler, using natural language processing and machine learning tools, continues to extract new data from all ninety-four federal district court sites, the Patent and Trademark Office site, and other sites with IP litigation data.[33]

According to an executive of a venture capital fund that poured more than $2 million in funding into the project, Lex Machina offers clients "previously impossible insights" that "inform winning IP business and legal strategies."[34] Sasha Rao, a partner in the Palo Alto firm of Ropes & Gray, says Lex Machina's rich and easily searchable data "fundamentally improves an IP litigator's chances of winning" by facilitating everything from "initial investigations through trials and appeals."[35] Vicki Veenker, an attorney with Sherman & Sterling, praised the data that "reveal a judge's entire case decision history" in IP cases, information she finds "invaluable for choosing venue, drafting motions, preparing oral arguments and advising on settlement."[36]

For every company executive contemplating initiating IP litigation, the question they want answered is "What are our chances of winning and how much will it cost?" According to the Federal Judicial Center, the average cost of taking a patent case to trial is about $5 million per patent, so companies have strong incentives to carefully assess the odds of success. Joshua Walker, co-founder of Lex Machina, is confident that the technology his company provides will "revolutionize how corporate finance looks at litigation. We've done a number of use cases where we've said, 'Here are the settlement patterns and win rates for these companies'"[37] (Figure 6.1).

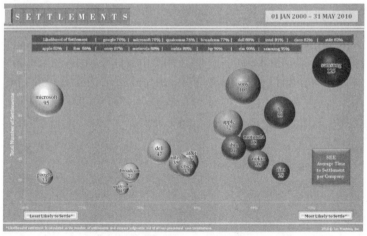

FIGURE 6.1. Lex Machina graph showing the likelihood of settlement in suits involving selected tech firms. Credit: Lex Machina.

Predictive computer databases are likely to make their mark first in legal fields that, like IP, are complex and involve high stakes. (Don't expect public defenders or legal aid lawyers to be using tools like this anytime soon.) The trend, however, is unmistakable. Company executives hoping to hold down litigation costs will have more access than ever before to data that will empower them to participate with their legal counsel in strategizing. Lawyers whose predictions about litigation outcomes reflect overconfidence or other biases can expect to be exposed by the data and abandoned by increasingly sophisticated clients. The lesson for attorneys is clear: make better predictions or lose clients.

BEING SMART ABOUT PROBABILITY

Until computers completely run the show, lawyers can improve predictions of case outcomes by using relatively simple tools such as decision trees. A decision tree depicts a complicated problem, such as the likelihood of various litigation outcomes, by depicting the key events that will shape those outcomes—each key event being, in a sense, a branch of the tree. For example, whether a plaintiff injured in a car accident will prevail in a suit against an allegedly negligent motorist will turn on a number of factors that each can be assigned probabilities. Success could be affected by the composition of the jury, the identity of the judge, new appointments to the appellate court that might review a trial verdict, the likelihood of opposing counsel discovering evidence that blows your case out of the water, or the risk-averseness of your client. When a decision tree is constructed that depicts the key factors influencing litigation outcomes, and reasonable probabilities are assigned to key events, the tree can be very helpful in giving both attorneys and clients a clearer understanding of case outcomes.

Decision trees can be used to produce "the expected value" of cases. Called "the single best measure of the value of a case," the expected value represents a probability-weighted average of all possible case outcomes.[38] An example might be helpful. Assume that you believe the probability that your suit will survive a summary judgment motion, thus allowing you to present your evidence to a jury, is 80%. (Of course, this estimate in turn is based on conclusions about the state of the law and the preferences of your trial judge.) Assume further that you think that if the jury does decide your case, there is a 20% chance your client will be rewarded $1 million, a 60% chance your client will be awarded $400,000, and a 20% chance the jury will decide for the defendant. (In an actual case, of course, there are nearly limitless possibilities in terms of the dollar award, but we're simplifying.) Finally, if the jury does find for your client, assume that the appellate courts are 80% likely to uphold your award. (In some cases, of course, you might also have to assign probabilities to the likelihood that the defendant will have a pocket deep enough to cover your award, even if appellate courts uphold it.)

Once probabilities are assigned to events, determining a case's expected value is simply a matter of math. So long as probabilities of events are independent (that is, the odds of one measured event do not affect other measured events), multiplication of probabilities will produce the odds of an overall outcome. In our example, the odds of a $1 million award for the plaintiff being upheld is 12.8% (.8 × .2 × .8), the odds of a $400,000 award is 38.4% (.8 × .6 × .8), and the odds of getting nothing is 48.8% (100 − (12.8 + 38.4)). The expected value of our case is $281,600 (.128 × 1 million +.384 × 400,000), which becomes a ballpark figure for a possible settlement, after adjustment for the risk-aversion of the client and litigation cost considerations.

Research has shown that people typically overestimate the probability of conjunctive events (events that depend on each of several things working out right).[39] Recovering money in a lawsuit can be thought of as a conjunctive event because several things can happen along litigation road that could prevent you from getting to your final destination. In a study of more than

11,000 cases that proceeded to trial between 1964 and 2005, Kiser and other researchers found that attorneys representing plaintiffs rejected settlement offers that proved to be higher than eventual awards in 61% of cases. At least some portion of those mistakes was undoubtedly the result of sloppy thinking about probabilities. When Kiser and the other researchers looked at just cases in which plaintiffs were represented by attorney-mediators, they found a 21% reduction in plaintiff error rates, presumably attributable to the attorney's experience in dispute resolution and greater cognizance of framing biases.[40]

We tend to assume overall outcomes that depend upon more than one likely event to be more probable than they actually are. Asked to predict whether four heavy favorites will all win their football games on a given Sunday, the average fan is very likely to assign a higher probability to that outcome than the facts justify. Even if, for example, the favorite stands a 4 out of 5 chance of winning each of the games, the probability of all four favorites winning is still a surprisingly low 40% ($.8 \times .8 \times .8 \times .8$). Conversely, people *underestimate* probabilities of disjunctive events (e.g., events that happen if any one of several, perhaps each rather unlikely, events occurs).[41] In general, we are too quick to call certain conjunctive events "in the bag" and too quick to dismiss our chances when we have multiple, but each unlikely, paths to success. Decision trees can help us be more realistic about the probabilities of both conjunctive and disjunctive events.

DECISION TREES, GAME THEORY, AND THE HOPE OF A BETTER SETTLEMENT PROCESS

Some litigation consultants suggest decision trees be shared with opposing counsel to facilitate settlement. Attorneys Ron Friedmann and David Post described a settlement negotiation in which their firm showed their decision tree to the other side: "They accepted our decision tree structure—although not our estimates of probabilities and verdicts—as an accurate estimate of the case." We "encouraged them to choose their own values for certain probabilities," and when they did so, opposing counsel realized "even under their most optimistic scenario, the expected value was much higher than their initial settlement offer." The result of using the decision tree, according to Friedmann and Post, was "structure for what would have otherwise been an unproductive discussion" and "a favorable and cost-effective outcome for our client."[42]

Fair Outcomes, Inc. is a firm offering lawyers lessons from game theory (the study of interactive decision making) to aid lawyers in reaching quicker and less costly resolutions of legal disputes. Jerry Ring, a Boston lawyer, teamed up with academics to tackle the problem that "the vast majority of cases don't settle until you reach the eve of trial." There is too much dancing and posturing. Ring says the reason is simple: "You're not going to get top dollar unless you wait until the last possible minute." Fair Outcomes developed models aimed at moving up settlements to save clients and lawyers both money and time. For example, a model for buyout situations when business partners decide to break up requires each partner to confidentially submit a figure that he or she believes is the company's true worth. The figures are set in stone and no negotiation is possible. The system calls for the partner setting the higher of the two values to be the buyer, with the price paid being the average of the two submitted values. Steven Brams of Fair Outcomes explained the theory behind the model: "They split the difference so each does better than his offer. That's the important thing."[43]

IMAGINING THE FUTURE (AN AMAZING HUMAN TRICK)

Thus far in this chapter, we've considered how lawyers might make better predictions about case outcomes, an important skill if doing right for clients matters, as it surely does. But being a good lawyer also requires imagining your client's future in ways that go beyond simply the "W's and L's" of litigation. To serve clients well means, in part, understanding how various litigation strategies might change your clients' futures, either for the better or the worse. Sometimes what might be classified in litigation terms as a "win" actually causes a client more harm than good. Conversely, clients might sometimes benefit from litigation that by most traditional measures would be labeled "a loss." We all know clients who feel better having had "their day in court" even though their arguments were largely rejected by a judge or jury, and we all know instances in which the stress-inducing demands of litigation caused more harm to clients than they gained from the vindication of their arguments in court. Can lawyers learn to better imagine the futures of their clients and thus make better guesses as to whether litigation really is in their clients' best interest? It is to that question we now turn.

One of the most remarkable abilities of the human mind— probably *the* most remarkable and the one that sets us apart from other species—is our ability to mentally time travel. Harvard psychologist Daniel Gilbert states, "The human being is the only animal that thinks about the future."[44] He notes that other animals may *act* as though they have the future in mind, but that acting is not the same as actually doing it. Gilbert says he will stand by his claim about the uniqueness of our ability to mentally time travel "until a chimp weeps at the thought of growing old alone, or smiles as it contemplates a summer vacation, or turns down a Fudgesicle because it already looks too fat in shorts."[45]

We humans can, at will, go back into our past and dig up (however imperfect they might be) memories of a distant time— our high school graduation or a family trip to Yellowstone or a day spent in the backyard building a fort. Then, in an instant, we can transport ourselves into the future, imagining hiking the Inca

Trail in Peru, arguing a case to the justices of the Supreme Court, or watching a daughter, now just a child, receive her high school diploma.

Backward time travel is the act of remembering; time travel in the direction of the future is an act of imagination. Both are marvelous feats, neither yet accomplished by even our most sophisticated computer, but of the two, traveling into the future—constructing an imagined future—is the more magical. Imagining the future, Daniel Gilbert reminds us, is not the same as predicting the future based on recognizing the similarity between the present and some past event. ("Last time I made this request, the judge granted it, so he's likely to do so this time.")[46] A pet owner might recognize that his dog predicts what you'll do next when you grab a Frisbee and stretch your arm back. We make predictions about the future all the time, and if those predictions prove wrong, we express surprise ("The jury found for *him*? You've got to be kidding!").

What makes humans special is not an ability to predict the future; it is our ability to *imagine* a future—and it's something we do all the time; about one-eighth of our daily thoughts concern the future.[47] For the most part, as you might guess, we imagine ourselves succeeding rather than failing—hearing the jury foreperson announce our $5 million award, winning the acclaim of the press for a brilliant argument before the Supreme Court, getting that well-deserved praise from an important client.

Perhaps more significantly, conscious foresight allows us to become aware of our own mortality. However heavy that awareness might sometimes seem to bear, it is—as many a philosopher and theologian has noted—also what gives our lives meaning and makes the days of our lives seem precious. It is the clay from which wisdom is molded.

Thinking about tomorrow is a function of the prefrontal cortex, evolution's most recent addition to our brains. When a person's prefrontal cortex is damaged by accident or, perhaps, by a prefrontal lobotomy, the result is a seriously impaired ability to plan or imagine any sort of future at all. In some cases, persons with head injuries have retained an abstract understanding of what the future is but have become incapable of imagining themselves in it. They live in "a permanent present." They live life more as an animal might than a fully functioning human being.[48]

Why we, alone among the members of the animal kingdom, developed the ability to imagine our future is a bit of a puzzle, but it does offer two clear benefits. First, it gives us the pleasure of anticipating the upcoming weekend getaway with our lover or next Friday's round of golf at the club. (Of course, it also burdens us with the worry over our bar exam results or next week's scheduled root canal. But even here, there's an upside, as research shows anticipating negative future events usually lessens their pain, if and when the events actually occur.)[49] More importantly, though, our ability to imagine the future offers the possibility of taking actions that might make our future lives better. We suffer the pain of pumping iron, pour money into our 401(k)s, and eat our broccoli all because it offers us the hope of a healthier, happier future than would be the case if we paid tomorrow no mind. We at least believe we have some control over our futures—and a sense of control makes us happy.

THE FUTURE IS HARD TO SEE

Of course, it is one thing to imagine a future and quite another to imagine a future that turns out to be anything at all like the real thing. Humans, it turns out, are not especially good at imagining a future that corresponds with reality. In fact, let us put that more strongly: humans do very poorly when it comes to manufacturing accurate visions of the future. There are several reasons for this, many of which are entertainingly presented by Gilbert in his book *Stumbling on Happiness*.[50]

One tendency we have when thinking about the future is the one we have already considered in the context of predicting case outcomes: we tend to imagine it being rosier than it is actually likely to be. Optimism bias causes us to overestimate our chances of being hired by the city's premier law firm, winning the big case, or getting that sought-after judicial appointment. Of course, there are also people who suffer from the opposite bias: they overestimate the likelihood of negative events. For some of these unfortunate souls, excessive worrying about the future leads straight to a psychiatrist's couch. For others, as we suggested, anxiety about the future has positive consequences, such as motivating them to do something to prevent the feared future—like prepare a case better or sign up for that colonoscopy.

UNDERSTANDING ADAPTATION

Another flaw that affects our thinking about our futures or the futures of others is our tendency to underestimate the human capacity to adapt to new circumstances. Humans have a remarkable ability to adapt to both negative and positive events. Events that you might anticipate would leave you permanently depressed, such as becoming paralyzed below the legs or losing a spouse, are somehow worked through and most people live again to see the sun shine. Similarly, events that you expect will enable you to live happily ever after, such as hitting it big in the lottery, may provide a period of dizzying excitement, but within a surprisingly short period of time your overall happiness is likely to drift back to close to its previous condition. Interestingly, we are better able to adapt to significant adverse events than we are to lesser annoyances, as it seems to take a certain level of adversity to trigger what some psychologists have called "our psychological immune system."[51] Unfortunately, the irritation you experience with that slow elevator to your seventeenth-floor office or that arrogant district court judge is not likely to simply melt away.

On the other hand, it is important to recognize that even a multimillion dollar verdict is not going to turn your injured client's life into a fairy tale, or that your client who is sent to the slammer for five years will not endure five years of pure hell. Big verdicts may bring joy for a while, and prison will take time to get used to, but over time you should understand that your clients' happiness is likely to move back in the direction of—though perhaps not all the way back to—what happiness researchers call their "happiness set points," levels of happiness that are largely genetically determined.[52] By understanding the capacity for adaptation, a lawyer can better judge, for example, whether a trial, which for a particular client might either be satisfying or stressful, is a reasonable litigation strategy, or whether it is better to seek settlement or some other quick resolution of the case.

Understanding Risk Aversion

Understanding how much happiness a client might derive from a big win in court, or the pain that a loss might bring, is a critical part of making a good decision about whether to go to trial. Most people (but certainly not all, as the Las Vegas Strip makes obvious) are risk averse. For most people, the hurt of experiencing a monetary loss of, say, $10,000 exceeds the pleasure of winning the same amount.[53] It is well and good for a cost-spreading lawyer to calculate that the modest chance of a huge jury verdict justifies (from the standpoint of the firm's financial success) taking a gamble on a trial rather than accepting the defendant's disappointing settlement offer. A client, however, might see the matter differently—and it is the client's interests a lawyer is committed to serve. Any lawyer who fails to make an effort to determine his or her client's attitude toward risk is not serving the client's true interests well. Of course, if you are representing a Fortune 500 company, the risk calculation is likely to be very different. Large companies, like people, are generally risk averse, but the fact that they engage in frequent litigation allows them the luxury of making decisions that reflect their ability to balance big wins and big losses, and thus make decisions that turn more precisely on "expected case values."

UNDERSTANDING PRESENTISM

"Presentism" is the word researchers use to describe the natural tendency of humans to allow their current experiences and emotions to shape their views about the future. Daniel Gilbert says the present "thoroughly infuses our imagined futures."[54] In fact, the future usually turns out to be a whole lot less like the present than we imagine. Our present feelings color our imagined futures. When you are feeling depressed, you have a hard time imagining that you will enjoy almost anything in the future, although (with time or proper treatment) you will. When you've just carbo-loaded on a shake, Big Mac, and fries, you might have a hard time imagining enjoying another such meal, but you will.

What's the relevance of understanding presentism for you as a lawyer? First, as you consider the arc of your legal career, understand that what you appreciate and what you find unpleasant about your job might shift over time. Aging has a way of reducing emotional amplitude. The highs you now experience from winning a case and the lows you experience from losing a case are likely to be a bit less high and a bit less low in the future. You will probably value your closest relationships more and money less. You might still empathize with your clients, if you are a good empathizer, but you might feel yourself less colored by your clients' emotions in the future than now. Understanding presentism allows you to better counsel your clients as you help them work through their current problems and concerns to their hoped-for futures.

Using Surrogates to Better Predict the Future

Stephen Hall tells of a study conducted by psychological researchers who at one point in the experiment, used the metaphor of "the fork in the road" to ask subjects what they would do next: take the left branch of the road or the right. An elderly woman surprised the researchers with her reply: "I'd just stand there at the juncture between the two forks and ask people returning what each path was like."[55] She was on to something. Daniel Gilbert suggests improving our predictions about the future by seeking out a person "who is actually *experiencing* the future event we are merely thinking about."[56] Although we all like to think we are unique and experience the world in our own way—we all have a touch of the Special Snowflake Syndrome—people are in fact more alike than different. According to Gilbert, relying on the report of a single, random "surrogate" is likely to produce a more accurate picture of how you will experience a future event than your own imagination.[57] He cites a convincing series of studies in which subjects forced to rely on surrogates to predict future feelings made much more accurate predictions than those who used other means. If you want to know how you will feel after you take a position you are considering accepting, ask someone in a similar position how he or she feels about the job. If you want to know how your client will feel a year after he wins a million dollar verdict, talk to people who won million dollar verdicts a year ago. Gilbert says it is hard for people to accept that a random surrogate is a better guide to the future than their own imagination, but the evidence is clear that it is. "Our mythical belief in the variability and uniqueness of individuals is the main reason we refuse to use others as surrogates," he says.[58] Get over it. You're not as special as you think.

Imagining Our Clients' Futures

When called upon to recommend a course of action for friends or clients, we must imagine their pasts, the key experiences that have led them to the present fork in the road, and the various futures that might lie down the paths ahead. We scan our brains for memories that share commonalities with their present dilemma, and then fast-forward through the memory file to learn what the consequences were of the choice we made: "My client wants to know whether to fight for full custody of her kids, just as I did in my own divorce proceeding. What happened when I did so?" "Sarah wants to know whether she will be happy at Able & Baker. Do I see her making partner, finding friends, enjoying my firm's particular culture? Will she have kids and will they be happy at the public school in our city?"

Wise lawyers draw on a broad collection of memories that can be called upon to provide guidance in making the choices that matter. They acknowledge that those memories might have been distorted over time. They also know, however, that what they imagine about the future is the result of a process that has bent that imagined future in quirky but somewhat predictable ways. They understand just how cloudy crystal balls can be, but they know enough to polish them up as much as possible. Lawyers become better counselors for their clients when they use empathetic capacity, understand adaptation and presentism, recognize the keys to human happiness (meaningful relationships and a sense of control being at the top of the list),[59] make efforts to determine risk tolerance, and seek out surrogates.

For the lawyer whose job it is to help plan clients' futures (including estate planners and business planners), the future becomes his or her main preoccupation, even if it might not be for clients. Most humans apply a sort of temporal discounting that causes them to focus too much on immediate gratification and too little on their more distant years.[60] Retirement day will come for your clients; someday your clients' businesses may collapse or be sold. Time will march on and bring new concerns to the fore. The job of the lawyer planner is to remind clients of the costs and dangers of underweighting their futures. You should be the "providential ant" who serves your client, "the impetuous grasshopper."[61]

Presentism, optimism bias, misunderstanding of probabilities, and the failure to understand adaptation are but a few of the many ways we misjudge the future. But perhaps the most important thing to understand about the future is how darn difficult it is to predict, at least where the "big picture" is concerned. In the movie *Charlie Wilson's War*, which focuses on the efforts by the United States to end the Soviet invasion of Afghanistan in the 1980s, there is a scene near the end of the film in which CIA operative Gust Avrakotos, played by actor Philip Seymour Hoffman, tells Congressman Charlie Wilson (whose determination led America to take up the Afghans' cause and who is played in the movie by Tom Hanks) the story of a Zen master and a little boy. Gust tells Wilson that on the boy's sixteenth birthday he "gets a horse as a present. All the villagers say, 'How wonderful!' The Zen master says, 'We'll see.' One day, the boy is thrown from the horse and is hurt and can no longer walk. All the villagers say, 'How terrible!' The Zen master says, 'We'll see.' A short time later, war begins, and all the young men of the village are taken away to be soldiers, but this boy can't fight, so he is spared, and all the villagers say, 'How wonderful!'" Charlie Wilson finishes Gust's story: "And the Zen master says, 'We'll see.'"[62]

A good lawyer has something of the wisdom of the Zen master. The good lawyer knows how difficult it is to predict the future and how events that seem now like terrible setbacks might actually make for a better future, and that the reverse might also be true for events that seem unambiguously positive. Recognizing how hard the future is to see gives wise lawyers the perspective they need to help clients deal with problems that might to them seem overwhelming. Let clients know that "this too shall pass." Understand what causes expectations about the future to mismatch with reality and think about how you can develop a more accurate picture of what awaits you, and the people you care about and advise, in the years ahead.

PROMISE KEEPING

There is one prediction that every lawyer should be able to make with confidence: a promise made will be a promise kept. That means, of course, that promises should only concern things within your control. A good lawyer doesn't promise a client that a judge or jurors will see things their way, or that a contract will prove to be airtight, or that a patent will be issued. A good lawyer might, however, promise to return a client's phone calls, complete a certain document by a specific date, or charge so much and no more for a particular service. A good lawyer might promise a client, simply, "I will do my best." When a promise is made—barring an extreme event such as Hell freezing over—it must be kept. Keeping promises, both explicit and implied, is what builds trust, and trust is the most important building block in a good relationship or a satisfying job.

Promise-making and keeping, a key principle of a life well lived, is possible only because of our ability to time travel in our minds. A promise takes our minds to the future, to the time when we will do as we say we will do. And with every *kept* promise, the mind of another is taken into the past, to the time of your promise, and that person's trust in us is deepened.

A BALANCE BETWEEN KNOWING AND DOUBTING

Lawyers use knowledge to make predictions about outcomes and as a basis for making decisions between various courses of action. To answer the question, "Will the appellate courts ultimately decide in my client's favor if we litigate this issue?" a lawyer may weigh information about prior court decisions on the same or a similar issue, consider the composition of the court that will decide the issue, measure his or her own ability (and the ability of opposing counsel) to write compelling appellate briefs, and ponder the social-political context in which the case will be decided. If the case could involve a jury trial, knowledge about the likely composition of the jury and probable attitudes of possible trial judges (such as how the trial judge might rule on a key evidentiary question) will have to be considered. Perhaps the possibility of an administrative or legislative action before final decision complicates the analysis.

The answer of whether an appellate court will favorably decide a case will rarely be "yes" or "no." Almost always the answer, like a weather forecaster's prediction for rain next Thursday, will be expressed in probabilities. The lawyer, after weighing what he or she knows—and thinking about what might not be known— might conclude that there is, say, a 40% chance of prevailing on the issue in the highest court the case is likely to reach. But even that oversimplifies the analysis. Appellate courts don't just hand out wins and losses. The decision of an appellate court can be an all-out victory or defeat, but it can just as likely be something in between—the half a loaf decision.

As complex as the lawyer's analysis might be when considering the odds of prevailing in an appellate court, that is only a part—and maybe a small part at that—of the reasoning process that must precede selection of a course of action. For example, the lawyer might feel the need to ask, "Would litigating this issue in the courts be more likely to help or hurt the true interests of my client?" To answer this question, the lawyer might draw on knowledge from prior encounters with the client to make predictions about how the litigation process might affect his or her emotional state. Will the client find the process stressful, either because of anxiety over its outcome or concern over high litigation costs? Will litigation adversely affect relationships that are important to the client? Think about how much there is to know before a question like this can be confidently answered: it requires knowledge of another person's mental and emotional state, knowledge of another person's relationships with others (and a sense of how important certain of those relationships are), knowledge of how relationships might be strained by litigation, and knowledge of the client's financial situation—perhaps both now and how it might evolve over the course of the litigation. And really, there's much more that might be helpful to know.

Before deciding whether to file suit, a lawyer might ask some inward-looking questions, especially if the case is difficult and will consume much of his time: "Is this a case that I am fully prepared to handle, or might my client be better off with a different lawyer?" "Do I have the skills, the knowledge, the time, and the enthusiasm to do right by my client?" To answer these questions, the lawyer must draw on yet another body of knowledge, one that will carry his or her mind back to similar cases handled in the past, and also into the future, as the lawyer imagines previous commitments and makes predictions about his or her future emotions and attitudes.

Finally, the lawyer might compare the benefits of taking the client's case to other work or activities that might have to be passed up as a result. "Will work on this case be consistent with my own values?" "How likely is it that work on this case will tempt me to take morally dubious actions?" "Do I have more socially productive ways to spend my finite amount of time?"

The essence of wisdom lies in treating knowledge the right way. The wise lawyer uses knowledge to make predictions about the future with confidence, but not with too much confidence. In the words of John Meacham, the wise person believes "knowledge is fallible" and strives "for a balance between knowing and doubting."[63] When it is the future we are considering, the balance ought to tip—more than it commonly does—toward doubting.

CHAPTER 7

The Good Lawyer
Serves the True Interests
of Clients

At the heart of any code of professional ethics is the injunction to put the client's interests first.
　　　　　　　　　　　　　　　　—Barry Schwartz and Kenneth Sharpe

HAT ARE YOU TRYING TO ACCOMPLISH AS A LAWYER? Is it your goal to achieve a seven-figure income or win the acclaim of your peers? If so, you've bought the wrong book. Perhaps you have no clear idea of what you are trying to do from day to day other than keep malpractice suits at bay. If so, you're probably in the wrong profession. Just as you won't break par without knowing where to aim your tee shot, you can't be a good lawyer without knowing where to put your effort.

Many lawyers practice law without giving much thought to whether their aims are the right ones. A good lawyer, at the very least, moves in the right direction. In the end, it is not the size of the judgments we win, the number of people we send to jail, or even the bar association rankings by our peers that are the best measure of our effectiveness as a lawyer. Rather, your worth as a lawyer is determined by how well you serve the true interests of your clients.

Courtroom victories attract attention and might be the result of effective legal work, but being a good lawyer is so much more than winning the big ones. As a profession, we have placed too much emphasis on being "zealous advocates" and too little on being "good counselors." It is from our counseling that we find our direction. The good lawyer, as counselor, wrestles with clients' problems in a deep and expressive way. The goal is to develop strategies that not only meet the clients' stated objectives but also might benefit them in ways they might not have considered, preferably while doing no harm to the larger public interest. Virtually every serious discussion between lawyer and client has moral content. From the many strategies that can be deployed to resolve a client's problems, some are likely to do less collateral damage than others. Some strategies might actually be "win-win" opportunities for all concerned. The good lawyer recognizes this and views visits with clients as opportunities to offer moral insights.

Anthony T. Kronman, dean of the Yale Law School, lamented a spiritual crisis which he believed had taken hold of the legal profession in the last generation. Kronman worried about a collapse of values that had sustained the profession for decades. The collapse, he feared, left lawyers thinking they were just a "specialized tool" for realizing the desires of clients.[1] Lawyers, he argued, "have a responsibility to help clients make a deliberatively wise choice among goals."[2] It is not enough, if you want to be a good lawyer, simply to supply information and implement the client's stated goals, however selfish or poorly considered those goals might be.

A STORY OF A WISE LAWYER

Estate planning is a practice area in which the potential difference between the asserted interest of the client and the true interest of the client can sometimes be obvious. Consider the story told by Orville, who practices estate and tax planning in rural

Iowa. Orville describes a meeting he once had in his office with a long-time client, Hilda.

Hilda announced, in a voice that held no hint of doubt, "I want Harold taken out of my will. I'd like you to rewrite my will so the farm goes only to Judy and Glen, not Harold." Orville had done legal work for Hilda for over thirty years, and this was small-town Iowa where secrets didn't last long, so he didn't need to ask the reason for the change, but he did anyway. "It's Donna," Hilda said. "I just can't stand that woman he married. She shows me no respect whatsoever. The thought of even a penny of my money going to that woman makes me sick." "Hilda," Orville asked, "what will Harold feel like when he finds out you've left him out of your will?" "Well," Hilda replied, "he won't like it, of course, but he made the decision to marry that arrogant woman." "How about your other kids, Judy and Glen? Will they think it is fair when their brother gets nothing and they each get half? Do they want their brother punished because of Donna?" "Well, maybe not, but they're not the ones that have had the run-ins that I have." "Let's talk about our overall goal. Do you think our goal should be fairness? Is that what we should be shooting for? Or is it more important to tell Harold how upset you are?" "Well, I guess fairness is more important—but I do want to send a message." "You know, Hilda, when someone thinks they haven't been treated fair, they often think about suing. Now, I'm not sure Harold would do that, but you are in your late eighties and sometimes questions get raised. When there's a suit, the will becomes a public document that anyone can see, and lots of money ends up going to lawyers. All of your kids could pay a price, in time, stress, and money." "I see that; it could make a mess of things. But I just have to—maybe I'm not as good a person as I should be—but I just have to get back at Donna for what she's done to me." Orville paused before proposing a solution to Hilda's problem. "How about this, just as an idea: let's leave the rest of the will the way it is for now and we add a provision telling Harold how disappointed you've been with the way Donna's treated you. You could write whatever you want, anything you're comfortable with, and we can put it right in the will." Hilda thought for a minute before she answered, "That seems good to me. I'll write something up."[3]

Let's consider what happened during this exchange in Orville's office. Rather than immediately agreeing to Hilda's request to remove Harold from the will, Orville first sought to determine the reasons for his client's request. He then asked her to consider the effects that her decision would have on others—to imagine the future she was creating. Then, once he thought he understood her true interests, Orville suggested an inventive course of action that left Hilda satisfied and prevented harm to others. In proceeding as he did, Orville sent Hilda out of his office happy and most likely averted a lot of family divisiveness and disappointment in the future, but the skills he used to do so are not those generally taught in law schools. The typical Trusts and Estates course explicates rules relating to intestate succession or revocation of wills, but rarely does a professor take the time to discuss when it might be a good idea to encourage a client to write a provision into a will that has *no legal effect whatsoever*. If Orville drew only on his law school education, Harold would likely be out of the will and there's a decent chance all hell would break out when the contents of Hilda's will became public. Alerting Hilda to the possible consequences of her stated goal and looking for options that might produce happier results was the right thing for a good lawyer to do (Figure 7.1).

We might describe the advice Orville gave to Hilda as "wise." Of course, it required some basic knowledge of the law. Orville had to know, for example, that the sort of declaration he suggested that she write would not void the will or have some other adverse legal effect. But the heart of wise lawyering is not knowledge or intelligence; rather, it is an attitude. While what constitutes wise

FIGURE 7.1. Orville Bloethe, at age ninety-four, by his Victor, Iowa, law office. Credit: Douglas Linder.

lawyering is subject to debate around the edges, at its core is a concern for the well-being of the client and the community of which she is a member. You might ask, "Doesn't every lawyer center concern on client and community?" The answer, unfortunately, is "no." Changes in the nature of practice over the past few decades have left lawyers confused about aims. Asking clients to consider the effects that their decisions might have on others can make both the lawyer and the client uncomfortable. Some clients might, in fact, be made so uncomfortable as to decide to look for lawyers who support, and do not challenge, their stated goals. You have to be okay with that.

BEING CLEAR ABOUT AIMS

When it comes to the proper aims of a lawyer, let's begin with the basics. It's not all about you. It's not even mostly about you. You don't write briefs or argue to juries to win fame and glory and riches (though they might come); you write briefs and argue to juries for your client. You're not there to please the cheering crowds, garner press attention, or satisfy your own ego; you're there to hear (you hope) that one quiet voice say, "Thanks for helping me out."

The time for your interests and those of your firm to be in play is the time *before* you say "I'll represent you." Up to then, you can run the calculations. "Will this case likely pay off?" "Is this the type of case that interests me and will help develop my talents?" "Can I square representing this client with my own values?" "Will this case derail my summer travel plans?" In fact, you might even ask, "Will this case win me fame and glory?" We don't suggest that such concerns should prevail over others; we just note that the time for them to be a factor is before you agree to take on your client's problem.

When you agree to represent your client, you agree to focus on the interests of your client, not yourself or your firm. The question then becomes: "What exactly are the interests of my client?"

ADVOCATES AND COUNSELORS

There is, of course, a major distinction between the two main roles of a lawyer: the lawyer as advocate and the lawyer as counselor. A counselor's job is to identify the client's interests and create a plan for their pursuit. An advocate's aim, on the other hand, is to represent the identified interests of a client to others, preferably in a way that convinces them to support the client's position. The role of the advocate is straightforward in a way the role of the counselor is not. While the advocate seeks to find the strongest arguments that can be made on the client's behalf, whether based on law or facts, the counselor has a more imposing task. The counselor tries to uncover—through moral conversation—the client's *true* interests, interests that might not even be apparent at first to the client. It's a task that requires empathy, patience, and wisdom.

Not everyone agrees with the distinction we are making here between the client's asserted interests and true interests. Many lawyers assume that they have no duty to question clients about their stated goals, at least so long as those goals are lawful. (Depending upon how one defines "duty," they might be right about that.) Then there are some lawyers who go even further and argue that lawyers have no business pushing clients into a moral conversation they never asked for and which might make them uncomfortable. Just as lawyers have the freedom to choose what clients they will represent, clients in the end are free to choose their lawyers. If a client merely wants a mouthpiece, he or she likely can find one.

THE FOUR POSSIBLE AIMS OF LAWYERS

Thomas Shaffer and Robert Cochran Jr., in *Lawyers, Clients, and Moral Responsibility*, suggest that a lawyer can choose to seek one of four goals for her client: client victory, client autonomy, client rectitude, and client goodness. Shaffer and Cochran contend that "client goodness" is the superior goal among the four, but their reasons for rejecting the other three illuminate the wisdom of their choice.[4]

If client victory is the aim, then the choices all belong to the lawyer—the acknowledged expert in how to win (and preferably, win big) in whatever context the client's problem arises. The win might be measured in a jury's award (or nonaward) of damages. It might be in the form of a contract that effectively discourages disgruntled employees or customers from bringing lawsuits. Or it might be in the form of an administrative decision that allows the client's project to move forward. Regardless of what form victory might take, the lawyer considers the narrow stated interest of the client and does what he can to bring home the "win." In this story, the client simply defers to the lawyer's decisions. Moral growth is not the issue.

When the aim of the lawyer is client autonomy, roles shift. The choices become the client's and the lawyer is simply the "hired gun," jumping through legal hoops and hurdles in the order and manner that the client dictates. Because the choices all belong to the client, the lawyer frees herself (or so she may think) from any burden of responsibility for the harm her actions cause others: "The client made me do it."

In the third story, where client rectitude becomes the aim, the choices belong to the lawyer, but the lawyer seeks to resolve the client's legal problem by "doing the right thing." The lawyer considers all the human consequences of various possible courses of action and then chooses the one that she thinks is best for everyone affected. The lawyer here is really the lawyer–guru, the maker of moral choices on behalf of her client.[5]

Finally, when the lawyer's aim is client goodness, "the lawyer and client together wrestle with and resolve the moral issue."[6] In this story, the lawyer has, in addition to securing a satisfactory solution to the client's problem, two other considerations. The lawyer weighs the impact her decision will have on others and, at the same time, acts as the client's friend, helping him to become a better person, while still recognizing the difficulty of knowing what the right thing to do is.

Let's consider the appropriateness of each of these four possible aims lawyers can have. Don't be surprised when the favored choice turns out to be the last one.

WHAT IS WRONG WITH "WINNING IS EVERYTHING"?

A football coach once said, "Winning isn't everything; it's the only thing." The oft-used quote did not originate, as is widely believed, with famous Green Bay Packer coach Vince Lombardi, but with

UCLA Bruins coach Henry "Red" Sanders, who first used the phrase in 1950.[7] (Lombardi, for the record, insisted that what he told his players was: "Winning isn't everything, but the will to win is everything.")[8] In the years since, countless coaches in dozens of sports, not to mention a lot of lawyers, have found inspiration in Coach Sanders's words. But is winning really everything? If that's true, then the well-being of your client, your own well-being, and the well-being of everyone else affected by your case is nothing.

Lawyers with a winning-is-everything philosophy make assumptions about what their clients want. In particular, they assume that what their clients most want from them is a win. They assume their client is selfish. They live in a simplified amoral universe where, after the game is played, their clients want only to look up at the scoreboard and see the bigger number under their name. They assume their clients want a jury foreperson to say, "These millions are for you" or hear a judge declare, "You get the kids," or sign a contract that gives them everything and the other party nothing. This worldview, of course, necessitates a loser.

Since the winning-is-everything lawyer is content to operate on assumptions, he maximizes his own opportunity to control the game. He feels free to use whatever trick plays and devious tactics are in his well-used playbook without pausing to ask whether his client might have ethical reservations about his game plan. Unilateral resolution of questions is efficient. There is rarely reason to contact clients, since their input seldom matters. You are the person with the technical skills and knowledge to get the job done—and you know, or think you know, what that job is: to win. You believe that a client's potential moral qualms only get in the way of what he or she really wants from you, so it's ultimately in your client's own interests not to be bothered.

The lawyer focused solely on winning regardless of the harm those choices might bring to others could be compared to the Godfather of Francis Ford Coppola's films. ("It's not personal, Sonny. It's just business.")[9] If you question the winning-is-everything lawyer about morality, he is likely to suggest that when aggressive lawyers like him, representing both sides in a controversy, fight it out on the legal battlefield, justice in the end is well served. Reminiscent of Social Darwinists, he sees society improved when the strong survive and the weak die—or at least their claims do. Those represented by less skillful lawyers (including persons with limited financial resources) and those affected who have no lawyer at all have only themselves to blame. The harm to others inflicted by win-at-almost-all-costs advocacy gets but a shrug.

Our law schools are filled with students focused exclusively on "winning" for their client, regardless of the costs to others. Shaffer and Cochran described what happened at an American Bar Association client counseling competition some years ago. The competition involved a client whose live-in girlfriend wanted "to keep her baby." In the interview, the client hinted "that he wanted to be fair to his girlfriend and accept his responsibilities toward his child." Nonetheless, all the competing students seemed to dismiss these moral reservations and charge toward the battlefield. Shaffer and Cochran describe the final round of the national competition:

> None of the student teams—not one—seemed to hear the murmur of conscience in their client....The judges of the final round, all distinguished lawyers, hardly mentioned the point. Instead, the young man's lawyers, the best American law schools produced that year to be counselors-at-law, and their judges, talked about influencing the girlfriend toward abortion, about litigating the issue of paternity (an issue the client had not raised), and about minimizing his financial responsibilities to his girlfriend and their child. It seemed as if conscience had no place in a law office, not even when the client put it there.[10]

Every client deserves, at the very least, the respect of having an opportunity to identify his or her own interests and goals in all their messiness. It should not be the function of a lawyer to override his client's interests, and if the client is never asked what those interests really are, there is a serious risk that might happen. Moreover, simply being asked about interests and goals is likely to make the client feel better about the process. The lawyer who assumes he knows the client's true interest treats his client more like a child than an adult.

Finally, even if financial benefit were to be the sole measure of success, empirical evidence suggests that the Godfather model is not the best way to achieve it. The embarrassing fact, for gladiator lawyers, is that the lawyers who take account of noneconomic interests of their clients produce better results, even if measured solely in economic terms![11]

LAWYERS AS HIRED GUNS: WHAT'S WRONG WITH MAXIMIZING CLIENT AUTONOMY?

The narrow view of what counselors or advocates should do is that they should simply do their best to help clients realize their objectives—at least so long as these are lawful. (No reasonable lawyer, as we see it, would view his role as properly including aiding perjury or hiding evidence of a crime, for example.) The Lawyer as Mere Tool of Client has only two responsibilities: supplying the client with the information he or she needs about legal consequences of various courses of action and then implementing the plan the client chooses. In this model, the client is the only real decision maker. It makes for a neat division of labor and spares us the second thoughts and blame that might come if we were real participants in the decision-making process.

Hired guns or, less pejoratively, expert tools of our clients: What, if anything, is really wrong with this vision of lawyers? Isn't empowerment—everyone seems to be in favor of it these days—a good thing for clients too? Who are we to question our client's morality?

According to some commentators, there is nothing wrong with maximizing client autonomy. Monroe Freedman, a legal ethics professor, writes, "The attorney acts both professionally and morally in assisting clients to maximize their autonomy." He sees this approach as showing "respect for the dignity" of the client.[12] Lawyers, as he envisions them, ought to get out of the way and let clients make their own moral choices, then help them implement those choices.

The problem with too much client autonomy is that people can get run over. If lawyers are just chauffeurs, driving in whatever direction the client points, whoever is in the car's way is at risk. We toss our consciences out the window and speed along, but people other than our client do matter. We should at least pause to consider what will happen to the tenant we help evict or the supplier we've injured by squeezing through a loophole in a contract.

Being neutral and nonjudgmental might get you through life with a minimum of fret and hassle. It seems to be a much-favored approach in the world of psychotherapy. Lawyers, however, should not encourage clients to make self-serving choices, which they inevitably do by not raising questions about the consequences to others of a client's preferred path. If your client is a pharmaceutical company and an executive asks your help in keeping a competing, but much cheaper, life-saving drug off the market, you need to ask the executive to at least consider the public health implications of the company's proposed course of action. It's possible that the executive can explain why the availability of the cheaper competitor *won't* save hundreds of lives—but wouldn't you want to know that before you act?

The wise lawyer, we believe, sees the conversation between lawyer and client as a moral one. Whatever path is chosen, you both choose. Whatever the human consequences of that choice, you both bear them. Stanford law professor Deborah Rhode made that point when she wrote: "Those who refuse to pass judgment on a client generally seem to assume that it is value-free. But individuals cannot market their loyalty, avert their eyes to the consequences, and pretend that they have not made a normative decision. To decline to take a moral stance is in itself a moral stance."[13]

Attempting to raise moral questions about what a client proposes is not an easy thing to do. The temptation is to go along, for friendship as much as anything. But friendship should not govern all our choices, as Robert Bolt suggests in *A Man for All Seasons*, his play about lawyer Thomas More and his refusal to compromise his integrity, even with his head on the line. At one point in the play, the Duke of Norfolk urges More to take the Oath of Supremacy, which would recognize King Henry VIII as the head of the Church of England, and accept his remarriage. He presses More to do so for fellowship's sake, despite his legal and moral qualms. More replies, "When we stand before God, and you are sent to Paradise for doing according to your conscience, and I am damned for not doing according to mine, will you come with me, for fellowship?"[14]

We want to be good. We want our friends to be good. And we should want our clients to be good, too. Moreover, most clients— most clients that you or I would want to have, anyway—aren't looking for legal advisors who value, above all else, neutrality on moral issues. Rather, they want their lawyer to be wise.

Involving our clients in a moral conversation might not only help our clients become better persons, but it will make us better and happier people as well. One of the key contributors to career satisfaction is a sense that you are doing your bit to make the world a better place—and moral conversations have the potential to do just that. On the other hand, the guilt that comes from doing what you believe to be morally dubious or wrong can be painful. One female lawyer described it as "sort of professional prostitution."[15] Another, using a similar metaphor, said, "It's like being forced into a sex relationship you didn't anticipate. It's a screw job. It feels horrible to do something you wouldn't do normally."[16]

GURU LAWYERS: WHAT IS WRONG WITH SIMPLY DOING RIGHT AS THE LAWYER SEES IT?

Some lawyers are willing to make moral choices for their clients. They feel comfortable telling clients what they ought to do, not just what the law requires them to do. In a sense, they assume the role of "guru."

Noah Parden, the courageous Chattanooga lawyer we met earlier, played moral advisor to his clients, insisting that they tell the truth and strongly urging them to accept their punishment when he thought they were guilty. Some clients, undoubtedly, paid a stiff price for following his advice. Parden's commitment to the truth was so great that it might have blinded him to the effects his advice had on the lives of his clients.

We can all agree that Noah Parden was an admirable man who stepped up to meet his responsibilities. But was he a wise lawyer? Lawyers often are smart, leaders in their communities, and people with a developed sense of right and wrong. It's only natural that they might be tempted, in their role as lawyer-counselors, to push their clients to look past their own selfish interests and "do the right thing." And when they do so, given their status within the community, clients are likely to give in, even when their own life, liberty, or property is on the line.

A proper sense of humility would have lawyers understand that they have no monopoly on moral truth. Often, the right and true path is not clearly marked. Lawyers should admit the possibility that their clients have moral insights as good as their own. Two is better than one when it comes to grappling with problems that have moral dimensions. Moreover, as the next section suggests, the very act of wrestling with a problem might benefit a client—and even the lawyer—in not insignificant ways.

Worse, of course, is the arrogant lawyer who makes little if any effort to even determine what the real interests of clients might be. Richard Susskind, in his book *The End of Lawyers*, criticizes corporate lawyers who "are generally not alive to the culture of client organizations, the ways in which lawyers are regarded, the appetite for risk, the extent of internal bureaucracies...and, more importantly the *realpolitik* and broader context of business disputes and deals that are being advised upon."[17] Susskind writes that "partners from law firms are reported to pontificate at meetings without pausing for a breath, rather than focusing their energy on what is actually on the minds of their clients." Often, he believes, clients simply want their lawyers to walk in their shoes and get the big picture, while lawyers are determined to supply answers to questions that don't even exist. In Susskind's appraisal, "law firms are from Mars while clients are from Venus."[18]

LAWYERS AS FRIENDS: AIMING FOR CLIENT GOODNESS

Shaffer and Cochran contend that good lawyers view counseling sessions as, at least in part, moral conversations.[19] In *The Lost Lawyer*, Dean Anthony Kronman endorses this approach: "The most demanding and also the most rewarding function that lawyers perform is to help their clients decide what it is they really want, to help them make up their minds as to what their ends should be."[20] Kronman places this "enterprise of co-deliberation" at the very "center of the lawyer's professional life."[21]

The good lawyer enters into what theologian Martin Buber would describe as an "I-Thou" rather than an "I-It" relationship with his client.[22] Rather than act merely as a hired gun, he respects his client's autonomy in the higher sense. He does not charge off to pursue the client's stated selfish interest, but instead he makes the inquiries necessary to ensure that he serves the client's true, more fully informed, interests. "Have you considered the effect your decision will have on others?" he might ask—and then wait as his client ponders that question. This is the way friends treat friends. This is the way the lawyers should treat clients.

Each decision made by lawyer and client can be like the Amazonian butterfly in James Gleick's book *Chaos*.[23] As the butterfly flutters its wings, it adds a small amount of pressure to the breeze, and breeze builds on breeze, just as decision can build on decision, until the hurricane blows or the clouds part. Choices that might at first seem insignificant can have major consequences, few decisions between lawyer and client affect only those two people, and if the client isn't fully aware of that fact, he should be made so. The truth may be painful, but it is your job to tell it as you see it, accepting—and explaining—that your own vision can be cloudy and that value judgments can change over time. It may not be easy or even possible to puzzle out all the implications of choices, but we need a stubborn faith that the effort is well worth it.

A good lawyer is willing to offer suggestions based on her own morality, but she is also willing to listen. She's not manipulative. She accepts that her client has moral beliefs of his own—and that they might be different in certain respects from hers. Ultimately, she understands that it is her client, not her, who must balance self-interest with morality and choose the direction for the legal work. When a client does not reveal the ethical basis for a decision under consideration, lawyers can and should ask for it. "Why are you considering that option?" is one simple phrasing of the question—or, perhaps, "Why do you have such strong feelings about going in this direction?"[24]

The good lawyer cares about the client in the most complete sense. (Of course, caring about your client's life doesn't mean you need to play matchmaker, lend money, or cheer on your client's kids at soccer matches. You are a *lawyer*, after all.) Yes, it matters whether or not the client "wins" as a matter of law. Yes, respect for the client's autonomy is important. Yes, it matters whether the client does the right thing. But it also matters—it matters a great deal—that the client becomes the best person he can be.

Unfortunately, many forces today conspire to limit opportunities for lawyers and clients to enter into deep moral conversations, as friends might do. Law schools, too often, do little to prepare lawyers for these conversations—and sometimes even suggest that they are not the lawyer's job. Law firms, with the increased specialization of practice today, are less likely to allow lawyer and client to build a history that encourages and enlightens a true moral conversation. Many clients now call on lawyers only in times of crisis, to help them with their truly exceptional problems, and not with a wide range of more routine problems. It is, sadly, harder than it used to be to be a friend of your client.

ESTABLISHING TRUST

Nothing—and we mean nothing—is more important in the lawyer-client relationship than mutual trust. Most clients do, in fact, trust their lawyers—but perhaps not as much as they should. A 2010 survey of Canadians (who probably are at least as trusting in general as Americans) found that 38% rated lawyers as highly trustworthy, while 11% gave lawyers low marks for trustworthiness, and another 47% put them somewhere in the middle on the trustworthiness scale. These numbers compare with 50% who thought highly of the "expertise" of lawyers and 44% who thought them as being highly "respectful of clients."[25] Clearly, there is room for improvement. Saying, "Trust me, I'm a lawyer," won't always cut it.

Trust takes time to develop. It evolves through the repeated making and keeping of promises, whether explicit or implicit. You build trust in a client by getting back to her when you say you will, treating her with respect, preserving her privacy, sending her copies of all pleadings and correspondence, charging a fair price for your services, and producing results that fall within your range of predicted outcomes. Conversely, each unreturned phone call, each questionable item on a bill for legal services, each disappointing and unexpected result can undermine trust. Be careful what you promise, but then keep your promises, whatever they may have been.

Trust also is built upon honesty. Good lawyers tell their clients the truth, even when it is not what they want to hear, and they offer their honest opinions on matters of settlement, litigation strategy, and the potential costs of litigation. Of course, delivering bad news to a client is never fun and requires great sensitivity. Clients have a natural tendency to either reject or be disoriented by bad news, so it is essential to take the time to know that they fully comprehend reality. When a judge has ruled against your client or you've concluded that your opponent's arguments are compelling, you need to be both direct but attendant to your client's emotions. There is a second circumstance in which lawyers need the courage to be honest. When you believe your client is making a mistake, perhaps by insisting on an aggressive litigation strategy or continuing an ethically questionable business practice, you need to make that clear to the client.

Take, for example, a scenario that may occur all too often behind closed doors. Transactional practice, no less than litigation, brings lawyers into contact with clients who may want to push the envelope. One tax lawyer in the Midwest says that "there are people who wouldn't even think about violating other laws, but they view tax laws as something different, more of a game." The tip-off, he says, are some of the questions clients ask: "Doesn't everybody do it?" "What are the chances of getting caught?" "We just won't put that in writing." "I probably shouldn't tell you this, but…" He gives an example of a two-person partnership that wanted to borrow some money to finance its operations. One partner is in a high tax bracket and the other pays little or no tax. (Under the Internal Revenue Code partnership liabilities are allocated among the partners as if they personally owed the debt, and a key factor in properly allocating the partnership liability among the partners is their relative personal economic risk of loss if the partnership itself were to be unable to repay the loan.) The two partners inform the lawyer representing the partnership that they want to allocate 99% of the liability in question to the partner in the high tax bracket so that he can deduct the lion's share of associated tax losses but have an oral side agreement that if the liability ultimately has to be paid by the partners personally, the partner in the lower tax bracket would kick in half, not just 1%. It is up to the lawyer to tell the client: "You can't do that, and I'm not going to participate in that. The fact that we don't put that in writing doesn't make it nonfraudulent."

Of course, it is also up to our clients to earn *our* trust. We should be generous about extending it, but not careless. Client reputations, if they are known to a lawyer, are a starting point, not an end point. Reputations can be spot-on, but they can also be exaggerated or simply wrong. Give your client the opportunity to earn your trust. Ask for promises, and then see if they are kept. If you ask your client to provide information about others potentially affected by your course of action, see if that information seems consistent with what you know about these other people and their interests. If your client assured you that she would reveal all she knew about some matter, does it seem as though she did that—or was something held back? Trust is no game, and there is no battery of simple tests that can be devised to determine whether it is merited. Like so many things in life, knowing who to trust and when to trust comes easier with experience—like your mother always told you, "There's no substitute for experience."

One of the sad consequences of the specialized nature of modern practice is that lawyers today generally have fewer opportunities to interact with individual clients over a wide range of client problems. You might handle a client's merger but probably not his copyright problem or his lease negotiation. You might be called upon to help a client work through a difficult divorce, but you don't work on his estate plan or his licensing problem. When your only encounter with a client is the one you are having now, the trust that is essential for a good lawyer-client relationship won't be there. Trust doesn't walk in the door—it has to be built.

INVOLVING THE CLIENT IN THE PROCESS

A client might come to a lawyer expecting to simply dump her problem in his lap and hope that he can somehow solve it. "After all," the client might think, "he's the legal expert; I'm not." Even if the client expects to play a role in the decision making, she might expect it to be limited to a few big calls—"Should I take the settlement offer or not?" The wise lawyer lets clients know, early in the visit, that he expects them to be fully involved in the process. Whatever key decisions lie ahead will be joint decisions. The lawyer and client need to wrestle together with the problem.

One impediment to client involvement might be the client's feeling of awe for the lawyer. The client sees those framed certificates hanging on your office wall and thinks about all the education it represents. "What can I really offer?" the client wonders—and adopts a posture of deference. You need to let clients like this know that you might have a J.D., but that doesn't qualify you as an expert on all the matters that should be considered before choosing a course of legal action. You can do this by stressing that the decisions to be made will have not just legal implications, but economic, moral, psychological, or social implications as well. You, as a lawyer, have important knowledge and skills that can be brought to bear on the problem, but it will take the two of you to really get the answer right.

"We" is a word that should pop up many times in a conversation between a lawyer and a client. "We have some decisions to make." "We need to identify our options." "We have to think about the impact each alternative has on other people." You can add emphasis to your invitation to have your client join in the decision-making process by reminding her, "Whatever we decide will affect you far more than it will me." There is an inherent power imbalance between lawyer and client, and dropping the prideful "I" in favor of the more humble "We" ameliorates that imbalance to at least a small degree.

The client is often uniquely positioned to assess the effects that any course of action will have on her and/or on others. Lucie White tells a story about when she was a legal aid lawyer representing a client on welfare, Mrs. G.[26] A caseworker had erroneously told Mrs. G. that a $600 insurance settlement from a car accident did not have to be reported as a set off against her monthly benefits. At the administrative hearing, Mrs. G. refused to use the "estoppel" argument, suggested by her lawyer, that her caseworker had misled her. She also departed from the script that she was forced to spend the money on "necessities" such as shoes and said instead that she wanted her grandchildren to have nicer shoes for church. Lucie White learned from Mrs. G.'s self-assertion that the client had her own truths to tell: she did not want to blame her caseworker; she did not view shoes as a material necessity, but she wanted to tell the hearing examiner how important religion was to her. The hearing examiner's office allowed Mrs. G. to keep the benefits.[27]

In many areas of practice, clients are likely to have relevant information that won't come out unless you ask for it. If the matter at hand involves estate planning, the client knows far better than you the interests and concerns of various family members. If the issue involves the client's business, the client will know, certainly more than you, how a particular decision might impact employees, clients, and competitors. An effective way to involve the client is by asking her to identify other potentially affected people, and to consider how each of those people might respond to alternative legal actions and outcomes. You might ask, for example, "How do you think Betty might react if we propose raising her rent (or changing her rental terms or not renewing her lease)?"

A good lawyer knows how to fully engage clients in the decision-making process, both because it can produce better legal outcomes and because it can make the client feel better, regardless of the outcome.

CATEGORIZING AND FRAMING THE ISSUES

What is left outside of a frame can be as important as what is put inside it. The proper frame, the way we choose to describe a problem, is what allows room for all the important issues to be addressed—be they legal, economic, social, or moral. A frame that encompasses only the discrete legal questions raised by a problem most likely will produce both bad answers for the client and bad answers for society. Because most people are relatively passive decision makers, there is a strong probability that the frame you choose will influence your client's chosen course of action.

The probability of a wise resolution of a client's problem is increased when you frame it as a search for a win–win (or win–draw, or at least win-not-lose-to-the-point-of-wanting-to-kill-the-winner) course of action. Using "us" versus "them" framing will make it less likely that your client will feel any obligation to weigh the costs that come with various approaches to his problem. If a client comes to your office complaining he was denied a promotion because of age discrimination, for example, you have a choice of whether to frame the problem as "us" (you and the client) versus "them" (the bastard that decided not to promote you, his bosses, and the company as a whole) or you can frame the problem in terms of a disappointed employee trying to find a path to the best possible future with a company he still cares about. You can lay out the legal options—sue, don't sue (but intercede and negotiate)—or you can ask your client whether anything other than his age might have played a role in the decision not to promote him. The second way of framing the problem might suggest the value of an attitude adjustment, a heart-to-heart meeting with the supervisor, a renewed effort to meet and exceed a supervisor's expectations—any of a number of possible courses of action that might produce less scar tissue than a bruising court battle. Of course, in the end, filing suit might be the only real option, but making sure that is the case is worth the effort.

For some clients, litigation is less an economic issue than it is a matter of principle. They may wish to punish someone they think has been a bad actor, or they may wish to send a message to future litigants that they shouldn't expect settlement offers. Clients are within their rights, of course, to draw lines in the sand and make decisions that may seem objectively unreasonable from a dollars and cents standpoint. In the end, of course, litigation is the client's call, but lawyers should frame problems in such a way as to make clients aware of all the possible costs of standing on principle.

Framing is critical when you present clients with possible settlement options. Even subtle changes in how an offer is characterized might affect a client's decision of whether to accept or reject it. Most people are risk averse with respect to gains: there is a general preference for "the bird in hand" over "the bird in the bush." People value the peace of mind that can come from taking a certain gain and calling it a victory rather than rolling the dice for a potentially much larger gain. Also, most people are risk seeking with respect to loss: there is a tendency to risk additional losses rather than accept a known loss.[28] Accepting a loss, even when it is the economically rational thing to do, can cause a client psychological pain. Given these tendencies, how a lawyer frames an offer—and many offers can be framed as *either* a gain or a loss—may well determine the client's decision. The lawyer who makes the effort to fully understand both a client's economic situation and his risk preferences can frame offers in ways that maximize the chances that a client's true interests will be well served by his decision on a settlement offer.

IDENTIFYING AND SERVING THE CLIENT'S TRUE INTERESTS

With the issue properly framed, lawyer and client can hope to chart a course that best serves the client's true interests. The conversation that ensues might convince the client that the approach he first favored was flawed. Perhaps the client insufficiently accounted for the harm that his approach might cause others within the community. Perhaps it was the harm to him—in the form of stress, anxiety, and guilt—that was not part of his initial calculus. You, as a lawyer, need to help the client know what he does not know, doubt what he thinks is certain, and think about what he has not thought about. If you're doing your job right, you're guiding your client through a jungle of moral and factual ambiguity. You do so with the faith that even when the client ultimately remains unmoved in his beliefs, he will be better for having taken the journey.

At the end of your conversation, which sometimes might resemble moral wrestling, you should have a clear perception both of what your client wants you to do and what you want to do. Most often, you will be able to arrive at a point when you both want to do the same things. In rare cases, however, your client might want you to do what you, in good conscience, cannot do. No one made you take an oath that said, "My client, right or wrong." When a little bird lands on your shoulder and whispers, "Don't do it," it's best to listen—even if the rulebook suggests it might be okay. Codes of professional ethics merely tell us what lines we should not cross over; we have to decide for ourselves how close we can get to lines and still feel comfortable.

THINKING LIKE A JUDGE, NOT A LAWYER

It's no doubt occurred to you that the approach to knowledge that we've tied to wisdom is very much like the attitude your first-year law professors (or at least the good ones) worked so hard to instill. You felt humbled when they questioned your off-hand conclusions and forced you to concede there was another equally valid way of deciding the cases. You got frustrated when they seemed to be constantly "hiding the ball" rather than revealing the "right answer" or "right principle" that should apply in a given situation. They knew, as you should now, that you can't take a clear picture of a fuzzy object—and that law, or large parts of it, are fuzzier than Tabby's hairballs. If your professors did their job, you left law school understanding that neither you, nor anyone else, has a monopoly on the truth—and that truth itself doesn't come with a capital "T."

You've heard—probably too often—the observation, "Law school teaches you to think like a lawyer." In an important sense, however, it really teaches you to think more like a judge.[29] A lawyer wants to know how to make the best possible arguments for his or her client, but many of the questions you were asked in law school really asked how a particular legal question should be decided. The question of how a case should be decided—the question that judges ask themselves—puts the focus on doing best for the community, not one party or another. There is a reason for forcing law students to consider the societal implications of alternative decisions. Put simply, those implications matter and should be weighed in a properly constructed conversation between a lawyer and client. In the end, the client might very well decide, "To hell with everyone else; this is what I want to happen," but a wise lawyer should suggest that those consequences for others be considered. This discussion of proper aims that should occur in law offices can be tricky and may require improvising, something like an intricate piece of jazz.

In the next chapter, we shift our focus from aims to movement and consider what it means to pursue justice with integrity. We will discover that justice should be pursued differently depending on one's place in the legal system. What constitutes "justice" and what actions are consistent with "integrity" are not always the same for prosecutors (whose "client" is the state) and defense attorneys, or for divorce lawyers and corporate lawyers. We also will consider what it means to be "honest," a virtue that is closely related to (some might call it part of) moral courage, a topic we addressed in Chapter 2.

CHAPTER 8

The Good Lawyer Pursues Justice with Integrity

Justice, justice you shall pursue.

—Deuteronomy 16:20

REMINDERS OF THE IMPORTANCE WE PLACE ON JUSTICE are everywhere. Statues of Lady Justice, blindfolded, and holding the scales of fairness in her right hand and a sword in her left hand, grace our courthouses. In many classrooms across the country, children begin each school day by standing and pledging allegiance to a flag and a republic that promises "liberty and justice for all." Despite the fact that we're all hot for justice, we argue over what that means. "Justice" is a word of a thousand meanings.

Speakers at law school commencement ceremonies urge graduates to go forth and serve the cause of justice—but in very different ways. For example, Lawrence Lessig, best known as a champion of the free flow of electronic information and now director of Harvard's Edmond Safra Center for Ethics, told graduates to prove wrong those who say the profession "cares too little about the justice it was meant to serve, and too much about the wealth it increasingly defends." Lessig encouraged the grads to do "People Law," not "Inc. Law." Leave the profession better than you find it, he advised: "Not just rich, but just." After all, he concluded by asking, "What the hell is being a lawyer for?"[1] Justice Clarence Thomas, on the other hand, told graduates that society was awash with whining and it was the job of lawyers to buck up and fight the trend. "Today as the fabric of society is saturated with complaint and protest, each of you has the opportunity to be a hero," he said. Justice Thomas concluded, "Do what you know must be done."[2] What must be done, apparently, is to join "Inc. Law" and fight the "People Law" lawyers who represent whiny people in baseless lawsuits.

While competing notions of justice are debated in college classrooms and featured prominently in popular culture, nowhere are they on clearer display than in the legal system, where the hard work of dispensing justice is done. Lawyers on opposing sides of cases implicitly or explicitly each claim the mantle of justice. You might well ask, "Is justice really only in the eye of the beholder?" In this chapter we consider how lawyers pursue justice in a world that assigns justice many conflicting meanings.

A FRAMED CORDUROY JACKET

Representing Justice is one of the most unusual books about the law ever published. In it, Yale law professors Judith Resnik and Dennis Curtis consider the idea of justice and how that idea has been represented in courthouses and plazas and art galleries from Australia to Zambia. Readers will discover images of courthouses of all sizes and styles, as well as dozens of images of Lady Justice, in a variety of poses and dress. One photograph from St. Paul, the home of Peanuts cartoonist Charles Schulz, even shows a statue of Lady Justice in the form of Lucy, blindfolded, with scale and swords, and a big smile. Another statue, placed near a federal courthouse in Portland, Oregon, depicts Lady Justice as a bird perched in a tree, with sword uplifted and scales held behind its back. Most often in the collected images, however, Lady Justice cuts a majestic pose, wearing the flowing robes and serious expression you expect of the icon. The book contains other representations of justice as well, including a gruesome painting from the fifteenth century depicting the flaying of a corrupt judge and an abstract work by the contemporary artist Ellsworth Kelly consisting of nine rectangles of bright hues in an array—the artist says—governed "by measure and balance."[3]

Of all the representations of justice that Resnik and Curtis discovered in their far-ranging travels, one stood out in their minds as the most powerful. Before speaking on the subject of courthouse architecture at an Eighth Circuit conference in Minneapolis, the two professors traveled through the small northern Minnesota town of Grand Marais, hard by Lake Superior and just thirty-five miles from the Canadian border. Visiting the town's courthouse on a hill, with its multistory ionic columns, they asked the first staffer they found, who turned out to be a probation officer, if any icons of justice were displayed. The probation officer immediately led them to the second-floor courtroom and pointed to a wall with a plaque and framed, well-worn, corduroy jacket. The jacket belonged to the county's long-time public defender, James A. Sommerness (Figure 8.1). In his more than two decades of defending the poor, Sommerness—according to the judge who spoke at an informal ceremony honoring the public defender— "probably appeared in this courtroom thousands of times." The judge described the lawyer as "a top-notch advocate" noted for his "professional kindness," and said his work "was a good thing, a thing we should do as a community."[4] The plaque next to the jacket commended Sommerness for his commitment to the "human dignity of others" and his hard work in "improving and delivering volunteer legal assistance to the poor."[5] Resnik told a

FIGURE 8.1. Display honoring James A. Sommerness, Cook County Courthouse, Grand Marais, Minnesota. Credit: Douglas Linder.

reporter for the *New York Times*, "We've seen a lot of representations of justice over the years, but that one will always be pretty hard to top."[6]

Resnik and Curtis argue in their book that the ways in which governments choose to represent justice "provide windows into their aspirations."[7] Statues of Lady Justice gracing courthouses from sea to shining sea tell us that governments place importance on the idea of judges *dispensing* equal justice. The rarity of displays such as the corduroy jacket in a northern Minnesota courthouse honoring a defender of the poor should make us ask whether governments, and society as a whole, value enough the idea of *seeking* justice for all, regardless of their station.

In the more than half century since the Supreme Court declared, in *Gideon v. Wainwright*, that lawyers in criminal courts "are necessities, not luxuries,"[8] the promise of equal justice for all accused has not been realized. In 2012 in Cook County, Illinois, public defenders handled "an average of 685 cases per lawyer."[9] In such circumstances, lawyers cannot properly interview clients, file the motions that should be filed, investigate cases thoroughly, or adequately prepare for negotiations with prosecutors.

U.S. Attorney General Eric Holder says that public defenders around the country face "overwhelming caseloads" in "underfunded and understaffed" public defender offices.[10] Given the current lack of political will to provide additional funding to these offices, the situation is only likely to get worse. To do good work for an indigent client today, journalist Karen Houppert writes in *Chasing* Gideon: *The Elusive Quest for Poor People's Justice*, requires "a herculean effort few could sustain."[11]

SEEKING JUSTICE FOR PEOPLE

Many law students come to elite law schools with plans to work for public interest organizations and then leave school to do high-paying work for corporations. Corporations undoubtedly deserve legal representation, and defending them can be an honorable and important thing. Lawrence Lessig observes that most corporate lawyers go home at the end of the day feeling that the system works: "Their clients got the process they were due. Their arguments were heard. Their interests were fairly considered. If through litigation, the litigation took place in a federal court with great judges, beautiful carpets, and clean bathrooms. If through a transaction, the deal was cut in a conference room at the Four Seasons."[12]

Lessig says, however, there is another part of the law that does not work so well, the part he calls "People Law." In addition to our seriously underfunded public defender systems, which leave indigent criminal defendants without adequate legal representation and risk—nightmare of nightmares—wrongful convictions, other areas of "People Law" practices reveal a justice system in crisis. For example, as Lessig notes, "There is no one in housing law who believes it is what law was meant to be."[13] According to bar studies, the legal needs of 80% of low-income Americans and a majority of the legal needs of middle-class Americans go unmet.[14] Many residents in rural areas must travel great distances to find any lawyer at all to assist with their probate, property, or family law problems. In South Dakota, where citizens in some portions of the state live more than 120 miles from the nearest working attorney, the state recently enacted legislation providing annual subsidies to lawyers choosing to live and work in rural areas.[15] Where the law affects ordinary people, Lessig believes, "we've seen an accelerating retreat." Courts, as he sees it, have become less open to small claims and "less relevant to most Americans."[16] We need to do better. Justice is promised to *all* Americans, not just the wealthy or privileged.

Good lawyers, whatever the nature of their own practice, support efforts to provide adequate funding and staffing for public defender and legal aid offices, and they welcome their own duty to help ensure equal justice for all. Helping to provide access to justice for society's underdogs is a duty that flows from the professional autonomy and self-regulation lawyers have been granted. Professional service requirements for unpaid work should be accepted with the understanding that such work not only provides personal satisfaction but also helps preserve the independence of the bar. Too many lawyers, however, don't see public service that way. For them, it's a bother, not a badge of honor.

One place to start changing attitudes is in the law schools. Deborah Rhode, director of Stanford's Center on the Legal Profession, notes that the problem of unequal access gets little or no attention in the traditional core curriculum. One survey of law graduates showed that only one in a hundred could recall any discussion of pro bono obligations in either orientation programs or professional responsibility classes. Rhode urges schools to con-sider offering at least one course focusing on access to justice issues. She argues that "all law students should have some exposure to the expertise that it requires" to assist the poor, including "not only substantive knowledge, but also cultural competence and related skills."[17] A push from bar examiners might help. Rhode notes that bar questions about pro bono obligations or limited rights to civil assistance would "undoubtedly prompt greater cur-ricular coverage."[18] She sees sponsored lectures, workshops, and mentoring programs as additional ways of addressing a problem that is too important for society to ignore. Rhode says that "the nation with the world's highest concentration of lawyers" should be able to provide "assistance to those who need it most."[19]

Dealing with the problems of real people should—at the very least—be seen as important as greasing legal wheels and creating wealth for Google, Coca-Cola, or Citibank. A family facing an unjust eviction order, a woman seeking protection from an abusive husband, or a couple needing help getting credit for their small retail operation all need lawyers. The monetary rewards to lawyers for doing such work might be relatively small, but research makes it abundantly clear that lawyers who find work that aligns with their values will be rewarded with increased career satisfaction.[20]

Unfortunately, too many lawyers are doing work that does not align well with their values. When the ABA conducted a poll to find out how the reality of practice met the expectations of lawyers, the biggest disappointment by far turned out to be that the lawyers' jobs failed to provide the opportunities they hoped they would to do good. Only 16% of lawyers surveyed indicated that their "ability to contribute to the social good" matched their expectations when they began practicing law. A full quarter of lawyers reported, on this measure, that their expectations were "not at all" met in their jobs.[21] Rhode suggests that attorneys experience "the greatest disappointment when they feel they are not contributing to the public good."[22]

Of course, nothing is simple about finding a job that matches your values. You might be representing a client with a plan to save the world one day and defending Uncle Scrooge the next. You may want nothing more than to end the sorrow of animal cruelty but find that the jobs allowing you to help do that just aren't out there and you have to settle for something else. If you have a cause you care deeply about, by all means search for jobs that allow you to champion it, and if you find that job, beg for it; but the reality for most lawyers is that compromises will have to be made. Some jobs will align with your values much better than others (though not perfectly), and those are the ones that will provide the better emotional connection to your work. Remember, as Eduardo Punset reminds us, "Without emotion, no project is worth its salt."[23]

Nothing we've said here should suggest that a lawyer cannot find emotion and meaning in doing good work on behalf of corporate clients. Corporations are (for some constitutional purposes) and are not (biologically) people, but it's obvious that corporations are *run* by real people. Lawyers perform a valuable service when they steer corporate executives toward actions that benefit the larger community. Stephen Bainbridge, a corporate law specialist at UCLA Law School, is surely right in recognizing the value of a good corporate lawyer when he says, "If his corporate client was doing the right thing, he helped him do it, thus creating better lives for employees and customers. And if his corporate client was doing the wrong thing, he told him to stop it and do the right thing, thus also serving the public interest."[24]

CHATTANOOGA REVISITED: ONE LAWYER'S SENSE OF JUSTICE

In Chapter 2 we told the tale of Noah Parden, the courageous Chattanooga lawyer who sought justice first for Ed Johnson, and then for those who lynched him. Protection for the innocent and punishment for the guilty: the two halves of our classic notion of justice, and Parden believed passionately in both; for him, it was a matter of faith.

Moses, in Deuteronomy 16:20, says, "Justice, justice you shall pursue." The occasion was the impending arrival of the Israelites into the Promised Land. Moses called his people together for some final words of advice. He counseled them to appoint judges and officials who "shall govern the people with due justice." Justice, Moses explained, had two aspects: rewards, or at least protection, for those who kept the laws, but also punishment for those who broke them. The two verses that follow his command to pursue justice emphasize punishment. Moses warns his people that justice includes laying down the law against anyone who sets "up a wooden Asherah pole beside the altar you build for offering sacrifices to the Lord your God" or who erects "a sacred stone," which "the Lord your God hates."[25]

Noah Parden was no less motivated by his belief that crimes deserve punishment than his conviction that the innocent deserve protection. As a result, the fearless defender of the innocent arguably became a less than ideal lawyer for those clients he knew or he believed were guilty. Some fellow defense attorneys believed Parden failed in his duties for the typical criminal defendant—that is, the defendant who in fact had done just what he stood accused of doing. Defense lawyers criticized Parden for not aggressively defending his guilty clients. His usual approach in criminal cases where his clients were guilty—which was almost all the time, mind you—was to urge them to plead guilty and accept their punishment. How's that for great defense work? Parden's religious beliefs led him to the conclusion that the guilty should pay for their crimes and, in fact, it was in their own best interest to do so.

If law school does anything, it preaches the need for lawyers to pursue their clients' interests as well as they can within the bounds of the law and their ethical obligations. Parden's approach comes uncomfortably close to the view of many nonlawyers, who believe that there really is no need at all to defend the guilty. Lawyers are expected to believe that the criminal justice system works best when the government is made to prove its cases beyond a reasonable doubt and that the presumption of innocence stands as a bulwark of protection for the guilty and innocent alike. Lawyers are taught to look for mitigating circumstances and to poke holes in prosecution cases—not to roll over and pack their clients off to jail. Harvard's Alan Dershowitz expressed the view of most defense lawyers in his *Letters to a Young Lawyer*: "Zealous advocacy requires subordinating all other interests—ideological, career, personal—to the legitimate interest of the client. You are the surgeon in the operating room whose only goal is to save the patient, whether the patient is a good person or a bad person, a saint or a criminal."[26]

Parden's sense of justice, shaped by his religious beliefs, led him to conclude that guilty defendants deserved punishment and, in fact, *became better people* by accepting their punishment. He did not *force* clients to plead guilty; he merely used his power of persuasion to convince them this was their best option. Pleading guilty was for Parden part of a package leading to redemption: you pay your debt to society, you find God, and from this point on, you hew to the straight and narrow. By following this prescription, Parden believed, his clients in the long run could look back on their lives with some pride. For Parden, the *presumed* interest of his client might be to avoid punishment, but the *true* interest of the client was something else.

Can we say with certainty that Parden was wrong to push his clients toward guilty pleas, at least in cases where there was a real hope of charges being dropped or an acquittal? Should we now say Parden was a *bad* lawyer? Most readers might agree that Parden still qualifies as a good lawyer, but he is Exhibit #1 for the argument that the question "What makes a good lawyer?" is both confounding and important. The same values that made Parden a fierce defender of the innocent and those wronged by unscrupulous insurance companies made him a terrible choice for people who had committed crimes and hoped to skate free. No one could deny that Parden pursued justice, but some would blame him for not recognizing that pursuing justice isn't always his job.

IS THE PURSUIT OF JUSTICE NOTHING MORE THAN HELPING YOUR CLIENTS?

What sets Parden apart from most lawyers was the intensity of his belief that he should, regardless of cost, be a warrior for the cause of justice. Most lawyers believe something else: that they should represent the interests of their clients. Many defense lawyers belong to religious communities that believe, like Parden, that justice requires evildoers to pay a price for their actions. Thomas and Mary Shaffer note that the law and the legal profession is "in tension" with what they call "the community of the faithful."[27] Lawyers who draw sustenance from religious communities must maintain good relationships within those communities. Without their support, it becomes almost impossible for religious lawyers to maintain the strength and emotional balance that good work requires. For the religious lawyer, there may come times when fellow believers find his or her decision to serve the interests of a client to be misguided, or even immoral. In the book *American Lawyers and Their Communities*, Thomas Shaffer describes how members of his church reacted when he was legal counsel for a Nazi and, later, accepted a court appointment to represent a man who had been convicted of raping a child:

> My sister and brother Christians who talked to me about what I was doing in those cases were conscious of our memory of the Resurrection. They knew that the memory of the Resurrection defined the destiny of the defendant in the rape case, and of the Nazi, as well as my destiny, as it also defined the significance of

the American constitutional law I would use to represent my clients. What the community of the faithful did, with me, was look out, *from* the church, at these people and at the account of human existence that is to be found in American constitutional law....God finds us where He puts us. We talked about this in the church and then I went on downtown and tried to do something as a lawyer for my clients.[28]

For lawyers, whatever religiously based sense of justice they might have must be modified by their fundamental obligation to serve the interests of their clients. Your friends, neighbors, or fellow congregants come to their conclusions about justice from a different place—and you just have to accept that.

Of course, agnostics and atheists have no such worries. America's most celebrated legal defender of the poor and other of society's underdogs, Clarence Darrow, was an outspoken agnostic who pooh-poohed the whole notion that justice really mattered. Darrow saw justice not as "a lofty ideal" but rather as the simple adjusting of "human claims and human conduct to the established customs and institutions of the world." Justice, he wrote, "has no wings." What drove Darrow, instead, was his belief in charity, sympathy, generosity, and understanding. "Without these," Darrow said, "man is dead." What Darrow seemed to be saying was that true justice is beyond the poor ability of humans to define, so we define justice simply by what we do—by what actually happens in our courts and elsewhere. By Darrow's definition, justice is neither good nor bad; justice is merely "the law."[29] Rather than focusing on what is truly just, something we can't figure out anyway, Darrow argued that we should work for legal outcomes that reflect kindness and understanding. Darrow might deny that he worked for justice, and his vision of good legal outcomes differed considerably from those of most of his fellow citizens (he never met a client whom he thought deserved jail time), but something gave him the motivation to raise his voice so eloquently on behalf of the damned and the downtrodden, and it wasn't his sharp intellect. Darrow's passion for justice (let's call it that, even if he wouldn't) sprang from his determinist leanings and his "feeling" that "men and women [should] use their best efforts to help their fellow travelers on the road, to make the path brighter and easier as we journey on."[30]

"BIG PICTURE" JUSTICE

If, as we've suggested, your job is to represent to the best of your ability the true interests of your client, not to secure justice as you see it, then doing good for them, and not for the world at large, should be your focus. In fact, in some cases, doing your job well will produce more social harm than good. The story is told of a defense attorney who e-mailed a client with news of his case. "Justice has prevailed!" the lawyer reported. "Appeal immediately" was the reply from his client.

You, as a lawyer, quite naturally—if you're a decent person—would like to feel that your hard work is contributing to making the world a better place, and some days it just won't feel like that. You might have just used a technicality for your corporate client to defeat an otherwise perfectly legitimate claim filed by a starving widow. Perhaps you've just cleared the way for your behemoth client to grow its market share at the expense of some struggling mom and pop operations.

As we noted earlier, when work aligns with your own values, when you feel your efforts are making things better, you are likely to be happier. According to a study of 190 occupations, there is a reason why members of the clergy, occupational therapists, and firefighters find the most satisfaction in their work.[31] In each of these jobs, it's easy to believe that you are helping people. You see the positive effects of your work directly. For most lawyers, that's not always true. So how *do* you sleep better at night?

It is helpful to think of law as an imperfect process that produces a more just and stable society than would be possible in its absence. When you take on the role of a private lawyer, you give up certain options. You have implicitly promised to put the interests of your client ahead of those of society as a whole. And so has the attorney who will represent your opposing party. And so have the tens of thousands of other private attorneys out there. The good lawyer seeks ways of bringing the interests of clients and the larger community into closer alignment, but the fact remains that the interests of the client trump.

In theory, of course, effective representation of all clients' interests, an objective judiciary, and clear thinking jurors will combine to produce a better approximation of truth and justice (and maybe even the American way) than any other system man has yet devised. That's the theory, at least. John W. Davis, one of the most prominent lawyers of the twentieth century, described well the contribution lawyers make: "We smooth out difficulties; we relieve stress; we correct mistakes; we take up other men's burdens and by our efforts we make possible the peaceful life of men in a peaceful state."[32]

It's an imperfect system. Not all clients can afford, or can find, highly effective legal representation. Quite often, deep-pocketed clients outspend, wear down, and ultimately prevail over more deserving opponents with fewer resources. As we suggested earlier, if you want to help redress the balance, take Lawrence Lessig's advice and do "People Law" instead of "Inc. Law," but don't delude yourself into thinking that choice puts you on the right side of every case. Truth rarely lies on only one side of a dispute. Sometimes corporations deserve to win.

Remember also that a lawyer can refuse to represent a client. If a client seeks your help in achieving an end that you truly believe to be too socially destructive, you can take a page from Nancy Reagan and simply say "no." Your instinct to refuse to do the client's bidding could, of course, be the start of a conversation rather than its conclusion. But when the tension between your client's interests and your own sense of justice becomes great, you are unlikely to give the case your all—and zealously presenting your client's case within the bounds of the law and ethics is your first obligation. Knowing when to say "no" and when it's okay to say "yes" to a valued client is perhaps the most difficult call a lawyer ever has to make: "The hard thing in life is to know when to hold fast to one's principles and when it's acceptable to bend them a little."[33]

Lawyers rarely flatly turn down clients—and that's a good thing. The noble tradition in the United States of having a bar committed to fighting for the interests of every client, big or small, rich or poor, popular or unpopular, is one of which we are rightly proud. Consider the alternatives.

WHEN IT IS YOUR JOB TO DO JUSTICE

For a relatively small group of lawyers, doing justice really is their job description, though they do not always act as if it were. Prosecutors, unlike defense attorneys or attorneys in civil cases, should strive for the truth and not focus solely on winning their cases. It is tempting for prosecutors to place winning cases above everything else. Lawyers value their reputations, and they assume that the public will assess their performance based on their win-loss record more than a track record of resolving all ethical issues in favor of doing justice.

Wrongful convictions are, tragically, often the result of prosecutors who are too sure of themselves and value winning too highly. Even as evidence accumulates that the wrong person has been charged with a crime, they refuse to dismiss charges; instead, they attempt to do whatever it takes—sometimes even presenting evidence that the prosecutor suspects is unreliable—in order to secure the conviction. Errol Morris, in his documentary *The Thin Blue Line*, tells the compelling story of how Randall

Adams, an innocent man, was convicted by an overzealous Dallas County prosecutor. As the movie made clear, Adams was wrongfully convicted after police focused on him, rather than the real sixteen-year-old killer, who, unlike Adams, could not have been charged with a capital crime. Adams served thirteen years in prison and came within three days of being executed for a crime he did not commit. Interviewed in the film, defense attorney Melvin Bruder said, "Prosecutors in Dallas have said for years, 'Any prosecutor can convict a guilty man; it takes a great prosecutor to convict an innocent man.'" Bruder added that he thought Douglas Mulder, the prosecutor in question, "believes the Randall Adams conviction was one of his great victories, probably because of some reservations he has about Randall Dale Adams's guilt."[34] Appeals Court Judge M. P. Duncan, in an opinion setting aside Adams's conviction, knew who was to blame for the miscarriage of justice: "The State was guilty of suppressing evidence favorable to the accused, deceiving the trial court during Adams's trial, and knowingly using perjured testimony."[35]

When things go wrong in criminal trials, it is generally because police and prosecutors, convinced that they have found their man, either fail to turn over to defense attorneys potentially exculpatory evidence or skate near (or over) ethical lines by plugging holes in their cases with suspect evidence and testimony—evidence or testimony that the prosecutor strains to find credible. Blinders firmly in place, the prosecutors fail to give full weight to evidence that calls into question the defendant's guilt, while at the same time overweighing evidence that supports their prosecutions.

Worse yet, prosecutors sometimes put on the stand witnesses they know are lying, or they attempt in closing arguments to fill in or obscure gaps in the state's case. In one case resulting in a wrongful conviction overturned years later, the victim of a brutal rape met with the prosecutor before taking the witness stand. When she told the district attorney she was "90% certain" that the defendant was the rapist, the prosecutor responded, "When you're on the stand, you better say 100%."[36] Alan Dershowitz argues that most prosecutors believe their misconduct is consistent with the "search for truth." According to Dershowitz, "they see their actions as calculated to produce a true verdict: the conviction of a guilty defendant."[37] Hundreds of innocent people sit in jails because of these sorts of actions by prosecutors.

Because of what he has seen in criminal courtrooms, Dershowitz tells his Harvard Law students there are "few higher callings than an honest prosecutor with a real sense of justice." If they really want to improve the justice system, he advises students, "They should become prosecutors who care about justice."[38]

THE EVOLUTIONARY ROOTS OF OUR NOTIONS OF JUSTICE

Stepping back from the specific context of what justice means in the courtroom, let's consider how general notions of morality and justice are shaped. The shaping process, it turns out, has been going on for the last several hundred thousand years of human history. In *The Descent of Man*, Charles Darwin offered his views on the origin of morality, and nothing in the past century and a half suggests the great man got it wrong. In his view, primeval tribes with "a great number of courageous, sympathetic, and faithful members," who stood ready to warn, aid, and defend each other, outcompeted tribes dominated by "selfish and contentious people."[39] As Darwin saw it, group selection on the African savannah explains both human cohesiveness and our moral instincts. He wrote that "our moral sense" originates "in the social instincts, largely guided by the approbation of our fellow-men, ruled by reason, self-interest, and in later times by deep religious feelings, and confirmed by instruction and habit."[40] Our sense of justice is, for the most part, preloaded or innate owing to our savannah ancestors who practiced cooperation and survived droughts, disease, and occasional attacks by warring bands to successfully pass their genes on to subsequent generations.

Although Darwin's theory of group selection still has its skeptics, Jonathan Haidt is not among them. In *The Righteous Mind: Why Good People Are Divided by Politics and Religion*, Haidt says the result of this process is that humans have become "the giraffes of altruism."[41] Our evolutionary path has left us as "one-of-a-kind freaks of nature" when it comes to our willingness to engage in selfless behavior for the benefit of our groups.[42] Recently, brain scans have allowed us to see how behavior consistent with our own sense of justice activates our reward (dopamine-driven) systems. In short, seeing justice done makes us feel good.[43]

But, as the psychological research makes clear, our sense of justice also is significantly affected by our culture and experiences, beginning at a very early age. As children, we learn through experience how to recognize unfairness (in an uneven distribution of cookies, perhaps), cruelty (in the unprovoked beating of a friend by a bully), and how to distinguish appropriate lies ("white lies") from those that are contemptible. In the hundreds of social situations that present themselves to us as we age, we learn, through our successes and our failures, which behavioral responses are most likely to produce the most satisfying results.

EMOTIONS, REASON, AND OUR SENSE OF JUSTICE

The more researchers learn about the human brain, the more persuaded they are that emotion not only influences our perceptions and thoughts but is also integrated into the processes of thought at the level of our neurological circuitry. As we suggested in Chapter 4, our moral judgments, including our sense of justice, emerge from a bath of emotions. That is not to say, however, that reasoning has no role to play. If reason and our sense of justice were completely disconnected, it would be hard to account for the existence of the countless courses in ethics and moral reasoning that appear in college catalogs.

Neuroscientists at Princeton used brain scans to see whether emotions or reason mattered more in determining how people deal with moral dilemmas. The Princeton researchers administered MRI scans to subjects while presenting them with "the Trolley Problem," a moral dilemma first posed by philosophers in the 1980s. The researchers asked what should be done when a runaway trolley is about to hit and kill a group of five people, but where a nearby switching device could, if pulled, divert the trolley car unto a sidetrack, saving the group of five but—and here's where the dilemma arises—dooming another person who is standing on the sidetrack. Presented with this situation, the vast majority of respondents pull the switch, sacrificing the single individual but saving the five. When the facts are changed, however, and the group of five can only be saved by pushing an obese "stranger" onto the tracks, thereby causing the train to derail before the imminent collision, most people come to the opposite conclusion: they choose not to act, dooming the five, but sparing the life of the stranger.[44]

What's going on here? Brain scans showed that the thought of pushing a person onto tracks in front of an onrushing trolley caused emotional parts of subjects' brains to light up like crazy. Even for those subjects who ultimately decided to make the push, the decision took considerably longer to make than when the question was whether to pull the lever. The lesson is that it takes time and effort for our cognitive brain to overrule our emotional brain, and the more active our emotional brain is, the longer the delay will be.[45] As the Trolley Problem research shows, our emotional brains and cognitive brains sometimes point in opposite directions. For every Mr. Spock who sees saving five for one as the right choice, there is someone else who is thankful we have brain circuitry that gets so tangled up at the thought of killing people that we choose not to.

We make moral judgments only after processing by both the emotional and cognitive parts of our brains. Some people, because of their brain circuitry, will incline toward utilitarian (less emotion-driven) judgments, while others make judgments guided more by guilt, compassion, and other emotions. Despite what law professors and others might have told you, there is no reason to assume that the more "reasoned" a judgment is, the better it is. Although we sometimes say the person who makes the more "impersonal" decisions has "risen above" her emotions to reach the right result, it is just as likely that she is making a serious mistake. Evolution had reasons for bathing our decision-making process in emotions. In law school you were supposedly taught "to think like a lawyer"—but we should give ourselves permission to think, first and foremost, like humans. This is especially true when a lot is on the line. Sigmund Freud might have had it about right when he said, "In the most important decisions of our personal life, we should be governed, I think, by the deep inner needs of our nature."[46]

Morality is concerned with "should" questions: Should I agree to represent an unpopular defendant when to do so might damage my practice? Should I tell the police about my concerns that my client is planning a fraud? Should I demand that opposing counsel provide me with a huge stack of documents, even though I know the costs of assembling that information far outweigh whatever small benefits they might have for my case? We use both reason and emotion to decide these moral questions, but mostly we use emotion.

Your sense of justice as a lawyer, although refined by years of law school and legal experience, is still—like everyone else's—strongly influenced by your emotional brain. When opposing counsel comes back with an insultingly low offer, your brain will flash "punish the bastard!" before—if there is a before—your cognitive processing kicks in and you begin to weigh the possible costs of a punitive response. Being a good lawyer, in no insignificant part, comes from learning—through trial and error—when to punish and when to forgive, when to fight and when to retreat, when to raise your voice and when to lower it, when to empathize and when to detach.

PURSUING JUSTICE, BUT WITH INTEGRITY

Lawyers, more so than most any other professionals, need strong moral cores because of the temptations they regularly face to lie, deceive, or fudge. Being straight about the facts of a case or being honest and direct in dealing with a valued client who proposes an ethically questionable course of action is often the harder course to take.

"WE DON'T BLUR!"

Earlier we met John Doar, who worked courageously for the cause of equal rights in the Deep South of the 1960s. Doar was also a great respecter of truth. One of his former assistants at the Justice Department, Howard Glickstein, remembered discussing strategy in a voting rights case with Doar. There were two ways of presenting the case to the court, Glickstein recalled. One way was to straightforwardly present the facts. The other way was to blur the facts in a way that somewhat strengthened the government's position. When Glickstein suggested to Doar that they adopt the second approach, Doar sat up straight in his chair. "Absolutely not!" he said. "You just present the facts as they are. We represent the United States of America. We don't blur!" Doar was so sincere and so well prepared that judges "took anything that came out of his mouth as the Gospel truth."[47] His careful, thorough approach and soft-spoken arguments bordered on being dull, but "with all the emotionally charged rhetoric of the time, being dull could be very effective."[48]

THE IMPORTANCE OF HONESTY

Blurring tempts all lawyers at various times in their careers, but Doar did the right thing for a Justice Department lawyer (especially) to do. To blur or not to blur: that is a moral question? Yes, choosing to be completely forthright in a brief—not "blurring" the facts, as Doar insisted—might reduce the chances for a favorable court decision (or might not, with astute enough judges), but for Doar, principle trumps the desire to win.

Honesty has long been considered an important value, of course. We all have heard the (apocryphal) story involving a young George Washington and the cherry tree he supposedly chopped down. Telling his father he cut down the tree required overcoming fears about a probable punishment. But young George, guided by a moral principle that would help lead him to future greatness, tells the truth anyway. Another president, Abraham Lincoln, also placed a high value on honesty. In 1850, Lincoln offered this advice to new law students: "There is a popular belief that lawyers are…dishonest. [But]…[l]et no [one] choosing the law for a calling…yield to the popular belief—resolve to be honest at all events; and if in your own judgment you cannot be an honest lawyer, resolve to be honest without being a lawyer."[49]

The belief among the public that lawyers as a group are dishonest has changed little since Lincoln's time. A 2011 Gallup Poll that asked over 1,000 Americans to rank professions by their "honesty and ethical standards" found that only 19% of respondents thought the honesty and ethics of lawyers ranked either "very high" or "high." In comparison, 84% of the public thought nurses had very high or high levels of honesty. Judges did considerably better than lawyers (47% thought them honest in a similar 2010 poll), and even real estate agents, bankers, and reporters scored better than lawyers.[50] Only a handful of jobholders, including advertisers, members of Congress, car salespeople, and lobbyists, were thought to be more dishonest and unethical than lawyers. Clearly, we have some work to do in the area of public perception.

Cheating sometimes helps you win, as most lawyers know. Not every trial judge will impose sanctions, even when he or she strongly suspects a lawyer deserves them. And, of course, many times cheating won't be discovered at all, or it will be discovered too late. When a lawyer is not punished for being dishonest and the client benefits from his dishonest actions, the inclination is strong for the lawyer to keep doing it. No one wants to lose a case or an important client. Doing the right thing takes courage. We need to remember the words of one experienced trial lawyer, who said the goal of great lawyers is not just to win—it is to win "with honor."[51] "Honor" may have an old-fashioned ring to it—the American sense of morality has evolved—but character still matters, especially in the legal profession, where both the opportunities and incentives for justifying ethically questionable conduct are great.

CAN LAWYERS BE HONEST ALL THE TIME?

Of course, it is possible to be honest in one aspect of one's life, but not another. For all we know (though we doubt it), John Doar might have cheated like a bandit at poker. Or, if scrupulously honest in his card games, perhaps he took more than his share of "mulligans" on golf courses. Cognitive psychologist and best-selling author Dan Ariely contends that we're all prone to a little dishonesty from time to time. In his book, *The (Honest) Truth About Dishonesty*, Ariely argues that most people are dishonest—but only to the point at which they can still reconcile their dishonesty with their image of themselves as basically honest people.[52] Precisely where that point is will vary from person to person.

Being a consistent truth-teller is not only difficult for good lawyers but quite likely impossible. No lawyer tells the whole truth. It can't be done, and no lawyer wants to try, anyway. Lawyers select from a universe of facts those facts that advance their causes and omit those that don't. The adversary system is built on the assumption, not always correct, that each side will find and present the facts that best make their respective cases, and from the resulting clash of facts, and from the conflicting interpretations of the law that each side supplies, some semblance of the truth will emerge and some form of justice will be done. It's a nice theory, one that calls to mind Winston Churchill's quip about democracy being the worst system of government except for all the others.[53]

While Justice Department lawyers can generally present the truth as they see it, other lawyers don't have that same luxury. If traversing morally ambiguous terrain is not your thing, don't become a criminal defense attorney. For the criminal defense attorney, shading the truth is part of the job description. When cross-examining a prosecution witness, a defense attorney will often know that the witness in direct examination has told the truth, or something very close to it. The witness really did see the defendant enter the convenience store, or the witness really did discover the defendant's blood at the crime scene. Does anyone of a certain age believe that O. J. Simpson's "Dream Team" doubted for a minute whether the bloody glove offered into evidence by the prosecution—the glove "that did not fit"—was worn by their client on the night of the double murder? On cross-examination, defense attorneys will do whatever they can—within the limits of professional ethics and sometimes outside them—to convey the mistaken impression that a witness didn't see what she saw, or didn't really find the damning evidence he thought he did. Yale law professor Stephen L. Carter, in his book *Integrity*, notes that a defense lawyer "can do nothing else" than attempt to "fool the jury into disbelieving a truthful witness," which is "nothing but an expedient lie."[54] The threat of misleading jurors is sometimes the only leverage a lawyer has.

With an obvious bad taste in his mouth, Carter justifies the deceptions of lawyers as a necessary consequence of the special lawyer-client relationship, which he compares to a marriage. In the best of marriages, one partner can tell the other his or her deepest and darkest secrets without fear that they will be repeated to others. And when one partner gets in trouble, the other will do his or her darndest to get the partner out of it, even if it means doing and saying things that person would never consider in other circumstances.

The public often knows full well what attorneys are up to when they lead clients through loopholes, dissemble, and obfuscate. And for the most part, they don't like what they see. Stephen Carter observes, "The lies we are forced to tell, and the convoluted arguments we must offer to justify them, virtually ensure that lawyers will be not only disliked but distrusted." What we lawyers do, he says, may be consistent with our "vision of integrity, but the shared vision is sufficiently unattractive that we must excuse our fellow citizens for dismissing it as bunk."[55]

HONESTY IN THE PRACTICE

Morality, like art, means drawing a line somewhere.
—Oscar Wilde

If complete honesty is neither possible nor even desirable in the advocacy setting, can we at least agree that it should be our goal in other aspects of our legal practice? Yes, but remember even worthy goals are sometimes unrealistic.

Dan Ariely argues that we're all (or almost all) dishonest to a point. Specifically, we're dishonest to the degree we can still maintain our self-image as basically honest people. In other words, most of us cheat, but we don't cheat too much. Take, for example, billable hours. (Yes, please take them!) You probably are unlikely to report putting in twice as many hours on a brief or a client meeting than you actually did. You might, however, consistently round your billable time up to the next fifteen-minute increment. Or you might feel justified in billing time spent pondering a case during your morning shower or during your drive to work, even though during those times your mind wandered to the golf game scheduled for Saturday. It's all the easier to justify bill-padding because you suspect (probably rightly) that most of the other lawyers in your firm are doing the same thing. "If I were 100% honest in my billing," you think, "I'll be the poor schmuck who gets penalized when the final accounting comes."

For some lawyers, cheating comes naturally. Although intelligence is not correlated with cheating, Ariely cites evidence that creativity is. Creative people tend to be a bit more dishonest because they use their creativity to conjure rationalizations for a degree of dishonesty that would be too much for less creative types to swallow. Ariely writes, "Creativity can help us justify following our selfish motives while still thinking of ourselves as honest people."[56]

Several environmental factors also can influence how much we cheat. For example, being mentally depleted makes dishonesty more likely. Research suggests that resisting the temptation to cheat takes energy, and as our energy levels are drawn down by long hours of mental work or intense physical activity, we cheat more. "Think of your willpower as a muscle," Ariely suggests, and consider that "if you wear down your willpower, you...wear down your honesty as well."[57]

Dishonesty also increases when others around you are being dishonest, so if you want to be an honest lawyer, join a firm where honesty is valued. You choose your environment, and then your environment shapes you. Cheating is contagious. If you don't want to catch the flu, stay away from sick people, and if you don't want to become dishonest, don't choose to work with people who cheat. That lesson extends to your choice of a practice area. If you work in a field of law where you suspect widespread cheating by your adversaries, you are much more likely to engage in similar conduct yourself. For example, if you suspect opposing attorneys are consistently putting witnesses on the stand who they know or suspect are stretching the truth, you become more inclined to do the same yourself. Unilateral disarmament rarely seems an appealing option.

In addition to our contact with unethical peers, dishonesty is also more likely when the cheating is done to help another person ("altruistic cheating," in Ariely's terminology).[58] This suggests, of course, that if you want to be an honest lawyer, you should choose to work for clients or causes you could care less about. (No, don't—but it does have this one benefit.) When you empathize with your client (say, an accident victim) or care deeply about a cause you are working for (say, environmentalism), you become very tempted to do whatever you can to help the client or the cause—even if it means cheating. Ariely notes, "Sadly, it seems altruism can have a dark side."[59] When you help someone you really care about, it becomes easy to cheat and at the same time still think of yourself as a basically good and honest person; it's harder to do that when you cheat for selfish reasons. "Great," you are probably thinking, "I have to choose between being an honest lawyer and doing work I really believe in." Not exactly: you can be an honest lawyer and care about the results you achieve for your clients; it's just more challenging. Do you like challenges?

Finally, studies show that cheating increases in morally ambiguous situations (where there's "more room for justification"),[60] and after cheating has begun and further cheating is an option (Ariely calls this the "what-the-hell effect").[61] For lawyers, who more than most professionals toil on morally ambiguous ground, the best advice for those who wish to stay honest is to establish firm ethical lines and to never cross them. Once you cross a line you never expected to cross, however compelling the justification seemed at the time, crossing that line a second time becomes a whole lot more likely—and line-crossing comes even more naturally the third and fourth time you do it. To prevent that first dangerous crossing, Ariely offers a few suggestions. Moral reminders, he says, can be surprisingly effective. If all lawyers in the Justice Department had signs on their desks that said "I shall not blur," there would be a lot less blurring. Simply by requiring lawyers to sign a statement stating "All the billing time indicated above is a true and honest reflection of actual hours billed" in fact makes it more likely that hours will be accurately accounted for. (In a study involving mileage reports on the expense reports of salespersons, simply adding a similar statement and a signature line to the reporting form reduced cheating by 15%.)[62] When witnesses swear on a Bible that they "will tell the truth, the whole truth, and nothing but the truth," the odds significantly increase that they will do just that. When we sign our names, hold up our hands and take oaths, or pledge our sacred honor, we are not simply going through meaningless gestures. We are making it more difficult to lie, because we are reminding ourselves of the standards we set for ourselves.

One other approach has been proven effective at increasing honesty: close supervision. If you have a mentor who demands honesty and checks your work to see that it reflects that, you're likely to be more honest. Careful judges and scrutinizing opposing counsel can also help keep you in line. Of course, it's easier to feel better about yourself if it's your own internal police that have you in their sights, but—as we've said—they tend to fall asleep on the job from time to time.

Ariely believes that "acts of honesty are incredibly important for our sense of social morality."[63] To build a society in which honesty is the rule and dishonesty the rare exception, we'd do well, he argues, to set our tolerance for cheating at a very low level. When we let the little things go, he says, the big things are sure to follow.

"LET JUSTICE BE DONE THOUGH THE HEAVENS MAY FALL"

We end this chapter with another story, one that depicts a judge who believed justice and integrity mattered more than his own judicial career.

In 1933, Judge James Horton presided over the retrial of Haywood Patterson, one of the so-called Scottsboro Boys. Alabama officials accused Patterson, a nineteen-year-old African American, of leading a gang rape of two white women on a freight train as it passed near Scottsboro, in northern Alabama. Patterson and eight other black teenagers had been hastily tried two years earlier, all nine found guilty, and eight of them sentenced to die. When the verdicts were announced to a huge crowd outside the courthouse in Scottsboro, a band had struck up the tune, "There'll Be a Hot Time in the Old Town Tonight." Hot times had to wait, however, because the U.S. Supreme Court reversed the convictions, concluding that a mere fifteen minutes before trial with a drunk local lawyer who hadn't tried a case in decades failed to meet the Constitution's requirement that states provide defendants competent counsel in capital cases.[64]

In the second trial, Samuel Leibowitz, the attorney for Haywood Patterson, tried the case the only way he knew how to try them: full-throttle. When Leibowitz, a Jewish defense attorney from New York, subjected the complaining witness to a tough cross-examination, the town boiled with anger, a few angry southerners even threatening the defense attorney with death. As the trial continued, it began to seem as though it didn't matter to the twelve white jurors that one of the two women who initially claimed rape now said that it never happened. Nor did it matter that some of the alleged attackers were too young or too weak to have possibly done what they were accused of doing, or that the medical evidence strongly suggested that no rape took place. When it came time for closing arguments in the Haywood trial,

Wade Wright, the county prosecutor, gave the jury the only reason he thought they needed to convict. "Show them," Wright thundered while he pointed at Leibowitz, "that Alabama justice cannot be bought and sold with Jew money from New York."[65]

In his instructions to the jury, Judge James Horton reminded them of their duty: "You are not trying whether or not the defendant is white or black....You are not trying lawyers, you are not trying State lines."[66] Despite Horton's admonition, the jury convicted Patterson and sentenced him to die in the electric chair. The verdict stunned Leibowitz. When he recovered from the shock, he approached the bench, grasped Horton's hand, and said, "I am taking back to New York with me a picture of one of the finest jurists I have ever met. But I am sorry that I cannot say as much for a jury which has decided this case against the weight of the evidence."[67]

A few weeks after the trial, and before rulings on post-trial motions, an emissary from Montgomery visited Judge Horton. The man from Montgomery reminded the judge that if he were to annul the jury's verdict, he would have little or no chance of being reelected. Horton smiled. "What does that have to do with the case?" he asked.[68]

Northern Alabama was in the grip of a record heat wave when Judge Horton convened court on the morning of June 22 in the Limestone County Courthouse of his native Athens, every seat taken for what were anticipated to be arguments on a routine motion of the defense for a new trial. Everyone present seemed to think that the motion had almost no prospect of success. Judge Horton took his seat and, without any opening remarks, the judge began reading in a low, steady voice: "Social order is based on law, and its perpetuity on its fair and impartial administration. Deliberate injustice is more fatal to the one who imposes it than to the one on whom it is imposed....The vital ground of this motion, as the Court sees it, is whether or not the verdict of the jury is contrary to the evidence. Is there sufficient credible evidence upon which to base a verdict?"[69] Sixty-five minutes later,

Horton's reading came to an end: "The testimony of the prosecu-trix in this case is not only uncorroborated, but it also bears on its face indications of improbability and is contradicted by other evidence....It is therefore ordered and adjudged by the Court that the motion of the defense be granted; that the verdict of the jury in this case and the judgment of the Court sentencing this defen-dant to death be set aside and that a new trial is hereby ordered."[70]

Despite knowing that setting aside the Patterson verdict would likely mean an end to his judicial career, the decision for Horton was not a difficult one. A judge must do his duty. "My mother early taught me a phrase she said was her father's motto," Horton later recalled. "It has frequently come to mind in difficult situations." The phrase Horton learned on his mother's knee was "*Justitia fiat coelum ruat*"—"Let justice be done though the Heavens may fall."[71]

Although he had last won reelection to a six-year term without opposition, Horton announced that he would not seek reelection as circuit judge. Shortly afterward, a group of Athens, Alabama, lawyers showed up on the colonnaded porch of Horton's residence carrying a petition signed by every member of the Athens bar. The petition read: "We, who comprise the entire bar of Athens, Ala., your home town,...recognize in you a judge of unimpeachable character and integrity; we know you are untrammeled by politi-cal considerations in the exercise of judicial functions; unflinching in the faithful discharge of your duties as judge, and recognizing the fact that you have the fortitude to do right, we are unwilling to see you leave the bench. We, therefore call upon you, as your friends and neighbors, to give us the privilege of putting your name before the people of the Eighth judicial circuit of Alabama for re-election as judge of our court."[72]

Horton agreed to run for reelection. He received a level of support in his home county that surprised most Alabamians. Birmingham columnist John Temple Graves explained how many continued to support Horton despite his unpopular decision. Graves wrote: "Horton is their own good man, no matter how foreign the occasional company his conscience makes him keep. They feel it because he himself feels it. He has little or no thought for the liberal and other groups which acclaim him from a distance. He does the right thing as he sees it, with no particular sense of the scene about him, but with an enormous sense of right-doing ancestors gone and example-bound descendants to come. His 'social conscience' is vertical rather than horizontal."[73]

Local support, however, was not enough. Outside his home county, an outraged population exacted its revenge. Horton lost his race. Horton worked briefly for the Tennessee Valley Authority, then retired to a farm where he raised prize Aberdeen-Angus cattle. He grew old. He spent afternoons playing Rook, Hearts, and dominoes with other farmers at a cotton gin near his home. Every so often, historians or area school children visited his farm to ask about his recollections of the Scottsboro Boys trials. He died in 1973, at age ninety-five. Shortly after Horton's death, county officials installed a plaque on the south wall of the second-floor courtroom in which he read his opinion setting aside the jury's verdict in the Patterson trial. I visited that courtroom. In raised bronze on the plaque are inscribed words from the judge's instructions to the jury in the Scottsboro case: "So far as the law is concerned it knows neither native nor alien, Jew nor Gentile, black nor white. This case is no different from any other. We have only to do our duty without fear or favor."

PURSUING JUSTICE WITH PASSION

Every lawyer worth his or her salt wants to see justice served in the abstract, but what that means in an individual case depends on where the lawyer stands. For federal and state prosecutors, pursuing justice means punishing the guilty but never the innocent. For government lawyers working on civil issues, pursuing justice means helping to evenhandedly execute the law. For judges, it means, as Judge Horton emphasized, ensuring "the fair and impartial administration of the law."[74] Private attorneys, however, understand that the interests of their clients will not always be consistent with their own sense of justice. The client of a criminal defense attorney might seek to avoid incarceration for a crime he committed, and the client of a defense attorney in a civil case might hope to avoid compensating a party she negligently injured. The client of a plaintiff's attorney might wish to recover far more damages than her injuries justify, or seek to punish a defendant to a degree not justified by his actions. In these cases, attorneys will experience tension between their duty to their client and their own sense of justice. Of course, they can rationalize the conflict by persuading themselves that justice in the big picture is best served by the effective representation of each party in court, and that they are just playing their part in the system. Good attorneys may have doubts about that rationalization, but they'll still do their best for their clients—and they'll do it within the rules. They know that few things are more important than protecting their own reputation for honesty and have strong moral cores that guide them across ethically ambiguous terrain.

In the next chapter, we consider the topic of persuasion. Your pursuit of justice, no matter how you define that task, is unlikely to be successful unless you make an effort to master the sometimes subtle (and sometimes not) art of persuasion.

CHAPTER 9

The Good Lawyer Is Persuasive

Character may almost be called the most effective means of persuasion.
—Aristotle

EVERY LAWYER BENEFITS FROM BEING PERSUASIVE. IN fact, the ability to be persuasive is arguably the best predictor of a lawyer's success—at least if success is measured by the results a lawyer achieves for his or her client. And lawyers know this. It explains why plaintiffs' lawyers flock to continuing legal education programs to learn how to persuade jurors to award injured people millions of dollars, and why defense lawyers share strategies designed to convince jurors to give people little or nothing for their injuries. Because their cases depend on persuading judges that their view of the law is the correct one, appellate advocates agonize over every turn of phrase they intend to use in the thirty minutes or so allotted for oral argument, while other lawyers—wanting the best results for their clients—yearn to uncover the secrets of "getting to yes" in negotiations. Even lawyers drafting contracts are acutely aware that they cannot include terms most favorable to their client without persuading other lawyers that their proposed terms are fair or essential to completing the deal.

Because of its central role in good lawyering, a chapter about the art of persuasion could easily become the longest in this book, but it won't. Whole books have been written on how best to persuade jurors, judges, and other lawyers. Readers who want to learn the finer points of how to structure an appellate brief or, say, how to be persuasive in a negotiation should seek out books that address those specific questions.[1] The literature about persuasion is vast and growing. Many authors offer readers a numbered series of tips which, if followed, will result in winning virtually any argument, or so they claim. For example, famed defense lawyer Gerry Spence, in his *How to Argue and Win Every Time*, lists his "Ten Elements of the Great Power Argument."[2] David Ball, in a book called *Theater Tips and Strategies for Jury Trials*, has his "Ten Commandments of Court Conduct."[3] Robert Cialdini, author of *Influence: Science and Practice*, prefers his six "influence cues or weapons of influence."[4] Turn to the Internet and you can find WikiHow offering its thirteen "steps to the art of persuasion."[5]

As you might expect, scientists also have invaded the subject. Papers are now being published in the new field of the neurobiology of persuasion.[6] Read these articles and you can learn, for example, that when research subjects listen to arguments they agree with, the left prefrontal areas of their brains are especially active; conversely, when they hear an argument they oppose, their right prefrontal area lights up more.

Here, in this chapter, rather than attempting a comprehensive survey, we consider how several of the virtues or visions discussed in previous chapters can prepare you to be your most persuasive possible self. Our focus primarily is the art of persuasion in trial and appellate courtrooms, but much of the discussion has general application to other settings in which lawyers seek to achieve favorable outcomes for their clients.

BEING HONEST AND COURAGEOUS

In our chapter about pursuing justice with integrity, we told the story of John Doar, who insisted in no uncertain terms that a Justice Department brief in a voting rights case not "blur" the facts in a way favorable to the government's position. By developing a reputation for honesty and sincerity, in the words of his colleague Howard Glickstein, judges "took anything that came out of his mouth as the Gospel truth."[7] For Doar, a reputation for honesty became a persuasive tool, and it can become one for you as well. Jurors value honesty no less than judges, and like all people, they are very effective at detecting strings of words that might commonly be referred to with a barnyard epithet. Gerry Spence says "if one is not credible, one might just as well preach to the pelicans."[8]

The great lawyer Louis Nizer, in his classic book *My Life in Court*, wrote of what he called the "rule of probability" that all juries and judges use to test the words that come out of the mouths of attorneys and witnesses. Juries, Nizer contended, accept "one version as against another because it accords with its own standard of experience."[9] Stories must be plausible, and when they aren't, everything else the lawyer or witness says will be viewed skeptically. The lawyer has a certain freedom to choose the facts that will be used to tell a story; what the lawyer should never do is make up facts and then expect them to feel right.

In some situations, people are so conditioned to expect dishonesty and spin that when statements ring true, they have a power disproportionate to their probative value. Winston Churchill understood this power, remarking, "What people really want to hear is the truth—it is the exciting thing to speak the simple truth."[10] Spence urges lawyers to have the courage "to stand naked."[11] For him, that might mean sharing his deepest feelings about a case—perhaps his fear of failing his client. Don't worry too much, he advises, about false starts and bad syntax in your opening or closing argument. What matters is that your words seem credible. David Ball makes essentially the same point. "Stay in character," he advises, "and the character you stay in is *you*."[12] He says that "only when you are yourself are you credible and persuasive. Theater and movie audiences don't believe acting. Neither do juries."[13]

Louis Nizer offers a story to illustrate the power of being yourself. Interviewing a key witness before trial, Nizer learned that the defendant had tried to bribe him to change his story. Nizer asked, "What did you say?" The witness, matter-of-factly, answered that he told him he wouldn't do it. Pressing the question, Nizer asked what words he actually used when the dishonest proposal was made. The witness answered, "Well, you don't want me to tell you what I really said, do you?" When assured that it was what Nizer wanted, he "cut loose with a series of expletives that would have made even the most hardened briber blush with shame." Nizer told the witness that when he testified in court he should simply say that he told the defendant in no uncertain terms that he wouldn't change his story. As expected when the witness testified, opposing counsel objected to the characterization as vague and demanded a more precise account of the conversation. When he got it, Nizer said, "The effect in the courtroom was explosive...because the truth of the whole incident became evident from the outraged naturalness of the man's retort."[14]

BEING EMPATHETIC

In our chapter about empathy, we stressed how lawyers can use empathy to tell more persuasive stories about their clients. Stories move people in ways that other strings of words simply can't. As psychologist Jonathan Haidt observes, "The human mind is a story processor, not a logic processor."[15]

Gerry Spence argues that a good story begins with the lawyer "crawling into the hide" of his client "and from that dark and frightening place shout to the world what we see."[16] He offers the example of how he might prepare to represent a quadriplegic in a personal injury lawsuit: "I might spend several days with my client, live in his house, get up with him in the morning, see him struggle to get out of bed, see him fight to get his pants on, see him exhausted before the day begins from the tasks we complete automatically every morning."[17]

Listening and interpreting body language, two skills that allow us to understand—and then better influence—the thinking and emotions of others, receive nothing like the attention each deserves. Only by listening to a client can a lawyer understand what the client wants and develop a theme for a story that might help the client achieve her goal, and listening carefully to a judge's questions or remarks is essential to the process of addressing any concerns the judge might have with your argument. People, of course, send signals with their bodies, not just with their words, and being attentive to the body language of clients, witnesses, jurors, and judges also can be critical to a lawyer's success. Sometimes lawyers are so focused on covering each of twenty points on the outline of an argument that they don't see the judge or juror stifling a yawn, raising eyebrows, or crossing arms; these are all signals that the lawyers are going seriously off track and need to change course. Defense lawyer F. Lee Bailey, describing the work of another lawyer he admired, said that he kept his eyes "ever on his audience." Bailey continued, "The slightest quizzical brow, a mere change of impression of a single juror, these would be a sign from which he could shift and bear down on a point, paraphrase it if he thought the first shot hadn't gotten through, or shift his topic if he thought attention was starting to drift."[18]

APPEALING TO MORAL INTUITIONS

In our chapter about moral intuitions, we discussed research that shows people's decisions are determined far more often by moral intuitions than they are by reason. Louis Nizer liked "to think that the scales which the blindfolded figure of Justice holds in her hands are the symbol of scales within each of us." He believed, as social science research later established, that people weigh right and wrong "not by erudite legal processes, but by simple moral precepts. Their source is varied, partly untraceable, and cloaked within the mystery of conscience."[19]

If you don't think moral intuitions play a large role in judging, try judging a moot court case. More often than not, after reading the facts of a case, you'll find you have a gut feeling as to who should win. Briefs for that party will seem more persuasive because we pay special attention to arguments that confirm our visceral feelings. The other party's brief will seem to be full of holes. In oral argument, you will have trouble generating anything but "softball" questions for the lawyer representing the side you favor, while one skeptical question after another will pop into your mind when the lawyer for the other side argues. It's remarkably easy to find support for positions that agree with a gut feeling; it's remarkably hard to justify a position your gut inclines you against.

The implications and the challenge for the advocate are clear: the goal must be to target, as early as possible in the process, the moral intuitions jurors and judges use for measuring right and wrong. "If they are activated favorably...they are irresistible," Nizer contended. In his view, the actual state of the law matters far less than the moral intuitions of a judge or jury: "Precedents, no matter how hoary, and rules of law, no matter how firmly established, will yield before them."[20]

A Failing of Legal Education

In his 1936 essay "How to Pick a Jury," Clarence Darrow observed that a "skillful lawyer" does not waste time "hunting for learning or intelligence in the box" because "if he knows much about man and his making, he knows that all beings act from emotions and instincts, and that reason is not a motive factor." In Darrow's indelicately phrased view, which finds support in recent scientific research, "Assuming that a juror is not a half-wit, his intellect can always furnish fairly good reasons for following his instincts and emotions."[21] There are exceptions, but the reality—not just for jurors but for all humans—usually is "intuitions rule." As Jonathan Haidt puts it, "Moral reasons are the tail wagged by the intuitive dog."[22]

Darrow's central insight, that moral intuitions determine outcomes more often than reasoning, runs counter to the message generally conveyed in law schools. Even though they sometimes pretend otherwise, law professors know—as does any good lawyer—that reasoning plays the backup role in most decision making. Despite this knowledge, law schools too often worship reason and distrust the passions. They select students based on their reasoning ability. High scorers on the LSAT have the ability to think logically and generate impressive lists of reasons for positions that they already hold, but there is little evidence they are especially adept at the art of persuasion. If the decision makers that we are trying to persuade make decisions based primarily on their gut feelings and then fabricate justifications to support them—and the evidence is that they mostly do—then emphasizing reasoning in our legal training mainly trains students to help decision makers previously inclined to agree with their positions come up with longer lists of justifications for their decisions. For the most part, law schools do not train students to change the minds of decision makers.[23]

Law schools discount the importance of moral intuitions in decision making in the legal system in part because what their professors are good at doing is reasoning—and teaching students how to reason better is easier than teaching them how to be more persuasive. The situation is reminiscent of the story about a boy who is found looking for a lost ball some distance from where the ball was lost, and explains it by saying "the light is better here." Learning to effectively trigger moral foundations in decision makers is difficult, so we seldom bother to try, even though it might be the only means possible to move the decision maker to where we want him to be. Haidt, who favors the metaphor of elephants (our moral intuitions or gut feelings) and riders (our reasoning power), says that to change minds, don't talk to the riders, "talk to the elephants first."[24] Yet, with few exceptions and political symbolism aside, law school faculty doors are still closed to elephant trainers.

The Moral Intuitions of Judges

Donning a black robe doesn't change the basic way in which a person makes a decision. Judges, despite their best efforts to convince us otherwise, are as much influenced by moral intuitions as anyone else. On some politically charged issues, they simply cannot be moved. Alan Dershowitz quotes a lawyer who said about arguments before the Supreme Court on big ideological issues such as abortion, capital punishment, or race, "It's like arguing with a vending machine that took your money and didn't give you a Coca-Cola."[25] What distinguishes judges from the rest of mankind is their ability to justify their intuition-based decisions with reasons that might strike readers as neutral or "objective." In cases that trigger the moral intuitions of judges, intuitions rule.

Despite this, if you ask any Supreme Court justice what role politics plays in judging, the answer you are likely to get is the same answer Justice Scalia gave to Piers Morgan in a 2012 interview on CNN: it plays no role at all. Scalia insisted that "not a single one" of his colleagues acts in a politically motivated manner. "I have ruled against the government when the Republicans were in the administration and I've ruled for the government when the Democrats were in the administration—I couldn't care less who the president is or what the administration is." Even the case most frequently cited as having been decided on a political basis, *Bush v. Gore*, was for Justice Scalia not about politics, but rather something else: "So the only question in *Bush v. Gore* was whether the presidency would be decided by the Florida Supreme Court or by the United States Supreme Court. That was the only question, and that's not a hard one." He advises people who don't like the decision "to get over it."[26]

If you accept Justice Scalia's narrow view of politics, he is almost surely right about its having a negligible role in Supreme Court decision making. (Decision making on state and local courts, where candidates for judgeships sometimes trumpet their politics in television advertisements, is another matter.) Justices rarely, if ever, vote the way they do to bolster a political party; they vote the way they do because of their "judicial philosophy." And as it happens, conservatives are much more likely to have a judicial philosophy like Justice Scalia's, one that assigns great weight to fidelity to constitutional text as it was originally understood. Without exception, the most conservative members of the Court, all appointed by Republican presidents, have judicial philosophies that make them skeptical of federal power, less protective than other justices of rights claims that lack a long history of protection, and more inclined than their liberal brethren to protect corporate and religious speech.

The choice of a judicial philosophy is a political choice, and we can assume that the conservative moral foundation of Justice Scalia, rather than pure reason, led him to his strongly textualist approach to judging. Very smart people have very different views as to how the Constitution and statutes should be interpreted. There is no "right answer" (though there may be *wrong* answers). Justice Scalia rationalized his way to a judicial philosophy that, in turn, makes it easier for him to rationalize decisions that are consistent with his conservative values. Similarly, the liberals on the Court gravitated to judicial philosophies that facilitate their rationalization of decisions that promote liberal values. Conservative presidents and liberal presidents, after all, nominate people to the

Supreme Court because they expect them to produce decisions that will generally support their political views. So Justice Scalia uses his judicial philosophy to support his values relating to the sanctity of life or marriage, while Justice Ginsburg's judicial philosophy, supporting her concerns about compassion and fairness, leads her to protect the privacy rights of pregnant teenage mothers and the beneficiaries of affirmative action. Most cases that come before the Court are "close cases," and any justice worth his or her salt is perfectly capable of rationalizing a decision consistent with his or her moral foundations. (This is not to say that justices won't occasionally feel compelled by their judicial philosophy to reach a result they dislike, but it happens rarely.)

Reasoning and Being Reasonable

However, to be perfectly fair to judges, there are cases in which reasoning really matters. It's not enough just to appeal to moral intuitions. In the less high-profile "intellectual puzzle" cases in which judges have no clear intuitions about who deserves to win, reasoning can make the difference. In fact, most cases probably are decided, in some sense, "on their merits." A case, for example, involving the question of whether a piece of property belongs to this or that owner, or one turning on the meaning of an arcane provision of the Internal Revenue Code, belong to the category of puzzle cases and are likely to generate much agreement and little heat among judges. In cases such as these, judges really do put on their logical thinking caps, and an advocate's arguments must squarely and fairly address the applicable case law, statutes, and regulations.

Being an effective advocate requires being able to tell strong arguments from weak arguments. Some lawyers can't. Jim McElhaney tells the story of a young lawyer who jumped up to object when opposing counsel offered into evidence a photo of the same kind of locomotive that hit a man's car. Not the "best evidence," he insisted. McElhaney wryly observed that no judge is likely to insist that the lawyer introduce the *actual* locomotive into evidence, as the lawyer's objection seemed to demand. Lawyers need to understand that every argument they make must pass what McElhaney calls "the giggle test": "Never make an argument unless you can say it with a straight face."[27]

Appealing to Judges with Different Moral Intuitions

Lawyers on both sides of the liberal-conservative divide underestimate the potential resonance of arguments emphasizing a moral foundation that is not weighted heavily in their own value matrix. We are often blind to the power of arguments by our opponents that appeal to judges with political beliefs that differ from our own. One constitutional law professor, for example, admitted that when word of litigation broke in the Florida recount of 2000, he told his students that one thing the Supreme Court would "never [do] in a million years" was take up the case, much less stop the recount.[28] Similar overconfidence might have affected White House lawyers, who seemed unable to fathom the possibility of a serious constitutional challenge to the Patient Protection and Affordable Care Act of 2010, and thus failed to propose modest changes in the legislation that could have strengthened their legal arguments, though perhaps at a political cost—such as calling the consequence of failing to purchase individual health insurance "a tax" instead of "a penalty." (Thankfully, from the standpoint of the Obama administration, Chief Justice Roberts, unlike his four conservative colleagues, did not see the choice of label as fatal to the taxing power argument, and Roberts provided the fifth vote to uphold most of the Act.)[29]

One consequence of the fact that liberals largely lack moral receptors for purity and authority is that conservatives turn out to be significantly better able to predict liberals' positions on a range of issues than liberals are able to predict the positions of conservatives. Conservatives have all the "receptors" that liberals do, even if some—such as the compassion and fairness receptors—might not be as keen as those of liberals, so they generally understand where liberals are coming from, even though they might disagree with their positions. Liberals, on the other hand, can be at a loss when it comes to predicting conservative responses because they are insensitive to facts and arguments that "light up" loyalty or purity receptors.

If conservatives are better able to anticipate the concerns of liberals, doesn't that mean conservative lawyers are in a better position to argue cases that trigger moral intuitions? After all, conservative lawyers can play all the notes to strike the right melody in briefs or oral argument, while liberal lawyers are more likely to flounder about, mystified as to what arguments might move a conservative judge. While the phrases "the sanctity of marriage" or "respect for the flag" or "common decency" might seem empty to the liberal lawyer, they hold a lot of meaning for conservative judges. The liberal lawyer arguing a case before a conservative judge faces many risks. The lawyer might misjudge the importance that a conservative judge places on deference to the military, or underestimate the readiness with which a judge detects a threat of subversion, or miscalculate a judge's attachment to institutions such as private property or private associations. Conservative lawyers face risks too, of course, when they argue before liberal judges, but they come better equipped, given that their moral receptors include all three found among liberals (plus three that aren't) to handle them.

Being an effective advocate means understanding not just your own value matrix but also the value matrices of the people you are trying to persuade. Liberal attorneys start off with a handicap, but by understanding the roots of political differences, they can activate the moral intuitions that push decision makers in their direction, even when they don't share their value matrix. If you lean liberal and are trying to persuade moderate or conservative decision makers, it is critical to remember that values dear to them—sanctity or order or loyalty, for example—might influence where they come down in your case. Even though these values might seem to you relatively unimportant, if they matter to the people you are trying to persuade, you need to address them. A good liberal lawyer knows what moves a rock-ribbed conservative judge, just as a good conservative lawyer knows what moves a flaming liberal.

THE MORAL INTUITIONS OF JURORS

Almost no one suggests that the moral intuitions of jurors are irrelevant to their decision making. A whole industry, jury consulting, has been built on the assumption that the deeply held values of jurors are predictive, to a large extent, of how they decide cases.

Long before there were jury consultants, Clarence Darrow offered advice on how to pick a jury that will show compassion for criminal defendants and underdogs. Today, many of Darrow's generalizations about ethnic and religious groups seem shockingly sweeping or stereotypical, but they reflect how the famous defense attorney approached the task of jury selection—in his mind, the most crucial stage of almost any trial. Darrow wrote that any attorney representing an injured plaintiff or criminal defendant "would be guilty of malpractice" if he or she "got rid of" potential jurors who were Irish, who Darrow believed to be naturally "emotional, kindly, and sympathetic." The English, Darrow contended, were not as good as the Irish, but still not half bad either for having "come through a long tradition of individual rights" and being willing "to stand alone." He was less keen on Germans and Scandinavians. Darrow advised excusing a Presbyterian "with the fewest possible words before he contaminates the others" because Presbyterians "know right from wrong" and "seldom find anything right." Methodists, on the other hand, Darrow believed were "worth considering" because their "religious emotions can be transmuted into love and charity." He warned defense lawyers to avoid Baptists and Lutherans, and to look instead for Unitarians, Universalists, Congregationalists, Jews, and Agnostics. "Keep them" all, Darrow advised, "especially Jews and Agnostics."[30] While more than a kernel of truth could be found in Darrow's stereotyping at the time he published his piece on jury picking in *Esquire*, today most of his suggestions would be considered laughable. The assimilation of European immigrant groups has erased distinctions that previously existed among Irish, German, and Scandinavian populations, and most differences that once might have separated Methodists and Presbyterians also have long since melted away.

Jury consultants now are much more likely to focus on core value differences than race or religious affiliations. They use labels such as "authoritarians" to describe tendencies of jurors to weigh certain core values more heavily than others.[31] Depending upon the cause and who they represent, attorneys will either seek to put people with certain values on the jury or to keep them off. For example, jurors who place a high value on order and security are generally believed to be better prosecution jurors than ones who give more weight to care and compassion.

Attorneys understand that getting the right people on the jury is half the battle; equally important is the job of activating the moral intuitions that they hope are prevalent among the jurors. Experienced trial lawyers always have made—and always will make—appeals to the moral intuitions of jurors. The reason is simple: they want to win. As longtime fans of famous trials, we cannot resist offering here two examples of impressive attempts to juice the moral intuitions of jurors, one aimed at a liberal moral foundation, and the other aimed at a conservative moral foundation.

In 1907, Clarence Darrow traveled to Idaho to defend "Big Bill" Haywood, who stood accused of ordering the assassination of Idaho's former governor, who had crossed Big Bill's Western

Federation of Miners. Of Haywood's guilt, there can be little doubt, but Darrow ended his closing argument to the jury with an emotional appeal. "Gentlemen," he said, "it is not for him alone that I speak. I speak for the poor, for the weak, for the weary, for that long line of men who in darkness and despair have borne the labors of the human race."

He continued:

> The eyes of the world are upon you, upon you twelve men of Idaho tonight. Wherever the English language is spoken, or wherever any foreign tongue known to the civilized world is spoken, men are talking and wondering and dreaming about the verdict of these twelve men that I see before me now. If you kill him your act will be applauded by many. If you should decree Bill Haywood's death, in the great railroad offices of our great cities men will applaud your names. If you decree his death, amongst the spiders of Wall Street will go up paeans of praise for those twelve good men and true who killed Bill Haywood. In every bank in the world, where men hate Haywood because he fights for the poor and against the accursed system upon which the favored live and grow rich and fat—from all those you will receive blessings and unstinted praise.
>
> But if your verdict should be "Not Guilty," there are still those who will reverently bow their heads and thank these twelve men for the life and the character they have saved. Out on the broad prairies where men toil with their hands, out on the wide ocean where men are tossed and buffeted on the waves, through our mills and factories, and down deep under the earth, thousands of men and of women and children, men who labor, men who suffer, women and children weary with care and toil, these men and these women and these children will kneel tonight and ask their God to guide your judgment. These men and these women and these little children, the poor, the weak, and the suffering of the world will stretch out their hands to this jury, and implore you to save Haywood's life.[32]

FIGURE 9.1. Clarence Darrow, on the left, with William Jennings Bryan at the Scopes trial, 1925. Credit: *The Scopes Trial*. Original painting, 2002, by artist Trevor Goring, www.imagesofjustice.com, in the private collection of Jeff and Julie Anderson, Saint Paul, MN.

Nearly two decades later, Darrow turned up in a courtroom in Dayton, Tennessee, to defend John Scopes, accused of teaching the theory of evolution in a high school classroom in violation of a recently enacted Tennessee law. On the prosecution team was William Jennings Bryan, the nation's most prominent opponent of evolution (Figure 9.1).

In his closing argument written for the Scopes trial, Bryan said "Science is a magnificent force," but warned "it is not a teacher of morals." Bryan continued:

It is for the jury to determine whether this attack upon the Christian religion shall be permitted in the public schools of Tennessee by teachers employed by the state and paid out of the public treasury....The case has assumed the proportions of a battle-royal between unbelief that attempts to speak through so-called science and the defenders of the Christian faith, speaking through the legislators of Tennessee. It is again a choice between God and Baal; it is also a renewal of the issue in Pilate's court....Again force and love meet face to face, and the question, "What shall I do with Jesus?" must be answered. A bloody, brutal doctrine—Evolution—demands, as the rabble did nineteen hundred years ago, that He be crucified. That cannot be the answer of this jury representing a Christian state and sworn to uphold the laws of Tennessee. Your answer will be heard throughout the world; it is eagerly awaited by a praying multitude. If the law is nullified, there will be rejoicing wherever God is repudiated, the savior scoffed at and the Bible ridiculed. Every unbeliever of every kind and degree will be happy. If, on the other hand, the law is upheld and the religion of the school children protected, millions of Christians will call you blessed and, with hearts full of gratitude to God, will sing again that grand old song of triumph: "Faith of our fathers, living still, In spite of dungeon, fire and sword; O how our hearts beat high with joy Whene'er we hear that glorious word—Faith of our fathers—Holy faith; We will be true to thee till death!"[33]

Both Darrow and Bryan end their arguments by targeting squarely the moral intuitions of their jurors. Perhaps *too* squarely: they just don't make closing arguments like those anymore—and we're not recommending you try to imitate them. Jurors a century ago had different expectations of lawyers and less cynical outlooks. What works in one era does not necessarily work in another.

COMMUNICATION THAT STICKS

In our chapter on cognition, we noted that only a tiny percentage of our brains' sensory inputs actually get encoded in our memories.

The old adage that most things go in one of your ears and out the other turns out to be true. The challenge for the advocate, therefore, is to make the really important points of his or her argument sticky enough to make it into the long-term memory of jurors and judges. While it is not the place here to delve too deeply into the science of memory, two points bear emphasis. First, human memory is primarily associative, meaning that new information is more likely to be remembered later if it can be bundled in some way to knowledge that is firmly encoded—that is, deeply anchored in our memory. Second, when the new information is *personally meaningful*, when it is identified as especially relevant to our plans or those we care about, it is more elaborately processed in the brain, resulting in effective encoding and improved recall.

It is because memory is primarily associative that stories—stories that emotionally connect your audience with your client's cause—are more effective tools of persuasion than recitations of facts strung together. Stories are stored in memory as symbols, and research shows that while people retain only 20% of what they read, they recall 80% of the symbols they encounter.[34] Stories become sponges, absorbing new information that would otherwise be lost. Given even the sketchiest plausible story, so long as the story is consistent with known facts, jurors will begin to draw causal connections and generate conclusions that fit the story.

So how is a good story constructed? Perhaps cognizant of research that shows rhymes to be especially memorable (remember the gloves that didn't fit?), Gerry Spence advises lawyers to "stick with the action—avoid the abstraction."[35] Stories should have a strong narrative drive. Use the present tense to describe action whenever possible and keep the story moving toward its (hopefully dramatic) conclusion. Resist the temptation to wander down some intellectual path that you might find beguiling but your audience won't. Perhaps most importantly, a good story is told using the words of everyday language—words that are likely to be associated with previously acquired knowledge in the brains of your listeners. Especially in a jury trial, plain talk also establishes a closer connection with the people you need to move and enhances your credibility. Remember that people are groupish creatures, and if your words suggest you belong to another group (for example, the stuffy Ivy League lawyer group) than your audience does, your message is unlikely to be well received. Obviously, the language that is appropriate in oral argument before the Supreme Court might not be language that works well with a blue collar jury. Louis Nizer called words the "weapons" of the trial lawyer, and like all weapons, it is important to understand their range and their effectiveness, given the composition of your audience.[36]

A good story is built around a theme, of course, and the theme is best advanced using emotional or visual content that a judge or a jury will remember. Justice Sonia Sotomayor, in her recent memoir, recalls a lesson she learned while working in the Manhattan district attorney's office. She came to see the state's case as "the story of the crime" and saw as her job identifying the "particulars that make a story real." Sotomayor writes, "In examining witnesses, I learned to ask general questions to elicit details with powerful sensory associations: the colors, the sounds, the smells that lodge an image in the mind and put the listener in the burning house."[37] A single vivid image can become the focus of a jury's discussion, as defense attorney Barry Slotnick, defending Bernhard Goetz, who seriously injured four men in a subway car, discovered when he compared his client's actions to that of "a trapped rat," not a "Rambo."[38] Clarence Darrow, attempting to avoid the death penalty for two teenage killers, Nathan Leopold and Richard Loeb, needed to have the judge imagine the consequence of his imposing the death penalty. He took Judge Caverly right to his clients' executions: "I can picture them, wakened in the gray light of morning, furnished a suit of clothes by the state, led to the scaffold, their feet tied, black caps drawn over their heads, stood on a trap door, the hangman pressing a spring, so that it gives way under them; I can see them fall through space—and—stopped by the rope around their necks."[39]

Images, because they induce a more elaborate or associative encoding in brains than do words, are remembered far better than words. (Humans can remember pictures with 90% accuracy in recognition tests over several days, even when the images are presented for only a short time during learning.[40] Just try that with words.) Images are so essential to effective communication that David Ball contends that a "trial attorney without images is like an art book without pictures."[41] Competitors in memory championships (yes, there is a circuit of memory competitions around the globe) know that creating unusual and vivid visual images is the best technique for encoding information in their brains. They frequently employ "memory castles" in which every room is the site of an activity that triggers an association with a thing sought to be remembered. Gerry Spence once took the unusual approach of filing a brief with the Court of Claims that consisted entirely of a few pages of cartoons drawn for him by his brother. Even though the brief lacked a single citation to a reported case, he won the case—probably to the amazement of his opponent. Spence argues that lawyers' papers "should be fun to read."[42] We do not endorse, by the way, reducing every argument to a series of cartoons, but boring judges or jurors out of their minds breeds resentment and cannot be helpful to your case. In the right case, photographs, charts, or diagrams can make a brief more understandable and compelling. Adam L. Rosman, general counsel of Willis Group Holdings and a strong advocate for using well-crafted images in briefs, contends "there's every reason to think that courts would welcome innovative displays of information."[43]

Finally, research into the science of persuasion shows that the voice a lawyer uses may be no less important than her choice of words. Gerry Spence goes so far as to suggest that "the sounds always carry the argument better than the words."[44] Sounds convey emotional content and help determine your credibility. If your voice fails to communicate urgency or emotion, if you speak in a flat monotone, you risk conveying a sense that you don't care about your client's case—and if you don't, why should a judge or jury? Even a halting speech with poor syntax can be powerful if your audience senses it comes from the heart. Pauses, trembles in voices, changes in volume, or anything else that conveys real emotion moves audiences and results in information being more firmly anchored in memory. Research shows that emotions are contagious—and this is a time you want to spread a contagion.

ANCHORING AND FRAMING

This chapter is also the place to remind you of the anchoring heuristic: the tendency of people to draw conclusions early, and later, when additional information calls those conclusions into question, to make insufficient adjustments.[45] Good advocates try to anchor their client's story as early as possible. In trials, this does not mean in opening statements, but rather in voir dire. Although technically a forum designed to produce a fair jury, attorneys on both sides see voir dire as their first chance to educate potential jurors about why their client deserves to win the case. Awareness of the tendency of people to anchor beliefs also should lead other advocates to devote disproportionate time to making sure the first paragraphs of briefs, or their first words behind the lectern, or the opening gambits in a negotiation session are carefully crafted to produce desired effects. Don't save your best stuff for later; start out with your strongest points.

Advocates also need to consider the importance of another tool discussed in our chapter on cognition: framing. A single point can be made in multiple ways. Many different elements can be chosen to tell a particular story and a storyteller might emphasize either a goat or a hero. A consequence can be somebody's gain or it can be somebody else's loss. To better appreciate the importance of framing in advocacy, consider a case in which you represent certain family members who wish to disconnect a feeding tube from a loved one in a persistent vegetative state. Should you frame the question as one about caring family members who desire to be free from the pain of witnessing their loved one's condition, or is it better instead to suggest that the issue is the plight of the comatose patient trapped in the jail of her own body? If you represent the state opposing the same request, should you frame the case as one about the rights of other disabled people to be free—potentially—from the selfish desires of relatives to see them through the door, or should you instead stress the sanctity of all life, including one so impoverished as a patient in a vegetative state? Framing matters and good advocates frame in ways that get their audiences leaning in their direction.

Proper framing begins with digging. Louis Nizer said, "The lawyer's task is to reconstruct past events and adduce the persuasive facts for his client. He is the archaeologist who must find and exhume old evidence."[46] Sifting through the collected facts, the lawyer considers them all, asking which facts advance the story he or she plans to tell, and which can do so in ways that trigger the moral intuitions of jurors.

RESPECTING OPPONENTS AND MAKING STRATEGIC CONCESSIONS

Showing respect for opponents elevates you in the eyes of jurors and judges. Name-calling, insults, and sarcasm almost always are counterproductive. This undoubtedly seems like trite advice, but in the heat of battle it often is forgotten, sometimes with disastrous consequences. The Golden Rule is widely recited for good reason. Treating others, even cantankerous opposing attorneys, as we would wish to be treated ourselves, makes you more likable and persuasive. Common decency also, as we discussed earlier in the book, has the very important side benefit of helping to preserve the sense of legal fraternity which all lawyers should value.

If respecting your opponent helps you seem like a reasonable person, so does making strategic concessions. Once again, the old advice about choosing your battles wisely seems self-evident, but it is frequently ignored in practice where some lawyers reflexively say "no" to everything, whether or not the point really matters. If something is true, even if it is harmful to your client, it is generally better for you to make the concession than to have it exposed by your opponent. If your client was legally drunk when he got plowed over in a crosswalk by a pizza delivery van, concede the intoxication but argue like hell that your client's condition was no excuse for the defendant's negligence. The last thing you want decision makers to suspect is that you are participating in a cover-up or—in the case of contesting everything—playing the obstructionist in a process that's supposed to be about justice and truth-finding.

PREPARING THOROUGHLY

Gerry Spence's phenomenal success with juries led to suspicion by some lawyers that he must be using trickery of some sort to win over jurors. Spence tells of one defense lawyer who actually accused him of "hypnotizing" a jury. The real key to his success, according to Spence, was simply hard work. Spence writes that the accusing lawyer "had little idea of the weeks, indeed, sometimes the months that I spend in lonely isolation preparing my case." While he "watched the reflection of the rising sun on my computer screen," Spence claims, his opponents have "slept their lives away peacefully, so peacefully."[47]

You'd be hard-pressed to find a good lawyer who doesn't attribute a large part of his or her success to a solid work ethic. Nizer, for example, said "proper preparation is the be all and end all of trial success."[48] And, of course, lack of preparation generally spells doom. Alan Dershowitz, who as an appellate lawyer, claims to

have reviewed "as many transcripts of losing criminal trials as anyone," says "if there is one common theme" in those trials "it is lack
of preparation."[49] Gathering facts, analyzing both facts and law,
organizing materials, considering how to present arguments in
the most powerful way, anticipating questions, seeing issues from
all possible angles: these things take time, effortful concentration,
and lots of willpower. All those things, in turn, depend upon caring—caring about your client, caring about justice, and caring
about your own career.

We end this discussion with two final thoughts about persuasion. First, understand that inexperienced lawyers will lose
even some winnable arguments because advocacy skills take
years to develop and hone. No one is born a great advocate.
Second, don't expect to win every argument. Some arguments
aren't winnable.

CHAPTER 10

Seeking Quality in a Rapidly Changing Profession

I believe that lawyers, in order to survive and prosper, must respond creatively and forcefully to the shifting demands of what is a rapidly evolving legal marketplace.

—Richard Susskind

QUALITY IS ELUSIVE, WE WARNED IN THE PREFACE. IT is something glimpsed out of the corner of your eye. In the first nine chapters we have wandered from the Jim Crow South, where we considered the nature of courage, to Thunderhead Ranch in Wyoming, where we pondered the spectacle of weeping lawyers participating in psychodrama sessions. We have speculated on the significance of the launch of Lex Machina, a tech start-up promising to improve lawyers' case assessments, considered whether a lawyer's religious beliefs should determine the advice given to a client, and explored ways in which conservative and liberal lawyers might learn to get along better. We have asked whether lawyers can learn to be more open-minded, seen the benefits and pitfalls of intuition, offered advice for avoiding the emotional traps that prevent a lawyer from doing his or her best work, and stressed the importance of developing mature adaptations to setbacks. In short, we've been all over the map, all over the field, and covered a big swath of recent social science research.

In this last chapter, we offer a series of perspectives on what it means, personally and professionally, to strive to be a good lawyer in a profession undergoing an upheaval unlike any it has experienced before. We will consider the challenges posed to high-quality legal work by the evolving nature of modern legal practice and restructuring trends among law firms. Finally, we examine the personal costs and rewards that come from making the effort to be a better lawyer.

THE TRAJECTORY OF CAREERS

Every fifth October, I board a westbound plane to spend a few days at a law school reunion. Just like reunions of all kinds, these gatherings are bittersweet affairs that keenly remind us of the passage of time. We see the physical toll that five more years have taken on our former classmates: the added pounds, the new wrinkle lines, the more deeply hollowed cheeks, and the graying hair. After a certain number of these reunions, you begin to worry whether you might see a particular classmate the next time around: "Why, Fred doesn't look too good; I hope he found a cardiologist." But there's a football game in the autumn sunshine to be enjoyed, toasts to be made at one of our old haunts, and funny stories to be told. It's really great to be back where our legal careers began.

At my first few law school reunions, much of the chatter was about the trajectory of our careers. We talked about making partner, moving from one firm to another, or our hopes of joining the judiciary or the legal academy. We shared our courtroom triumphs and defeats, complained about senior partners, and wondered how to balance family life and our professional careers.

At more recent reunions, our conversations—especially our late evening conversations over fine California wine—took on a very different tone. We no longer talk as much about where our careers are going as where our careers have taken us. We wonder whether our lives in the law have made us better people, whether we have made a difference in our clients' lives, and whether—if given a second chance at life—we'd do it all over again.

As we've entered a more reflective phase of life, we've worried less about money, fame, and real or perceived slights by peers. External measures of success matter less and less. Instead, we now fret about whether we are meeting the internal standards of quality we have set for ourselves. The attitudes, virtues, and skills considered in this book have become our ever greater preoccupations.

In a sense, we—at least many of the classmates I am proud to call my friends—have come full circle. We started our legal careers thinking about quality, about aligning work with our values, and having careers that made a difference. Then, for a couple of decades, those thoughts for many of us were swept away by our quests for partnership, tenure, judgeships, monetary success, and professional acclaim. The buzz and swirl of life left little room for reflection. Now, as we approach the end of our careers, quality again becomes our focus, though perceived differently than from our naïve twenty-something perspectives.

While in law school, many of us associated quality with a particular political vision—typically a liberal vision. Older and wiser now, quality seems to have no political agenda. Like the Zen master, when asked to consider the consequences of political change, we are more inclined to say, "We'll see." We also know that good lawyering is not confined to big firms or to big cities or to big cases. There can be as much quality in the career of a small town tax lawyer as that of a Wall Street firm mergers and acquisitions hotshot. Increasingly, we place our faith with attitudes and virtues we once considered old-fashioned or optional, depending on one's lifestyle. We value honest lawyers more and, with less to lose, probably *are* more honest ourselves. We recognize the importance of our relationships—and sometimes ask ourselves if anything really matters *other* than relationships, and so we become a bit more forgiving and a bit less judgmental. We've had setbacks in our careers and come to appreciate resilience. We've taken professional losses, as well as victories, and realized that some of our losses made us better and some of our victories diminished us. Money drives us less, and so we have less reason to cut ethical corners. We've become *wiser*, even with a few less brain cells to show for ourselves.

We also congratulate each other on having the foresight to have attended law school at a time when virtually every graduate could expect to have choices among job offers and when starting salaries offered by large firms seemed wildly disproportionate to our meager practical skills. Today, we note, over a third of all law graduates cannot find *any* work requiring a law degree, and average starting salaries over the past five years have actually dropped 15%.[1] Moreover, we complain the practice isn't what it used to be for those lucky enough to find work. "It's just a business now—all about the bottom line," one of us opines. "There's no time for reflection or building relationships," another of us adds. "Thank God I'm not a new associate who has to meet our billable hour requirement," says another. Typical old fart stuff, perhaps, but few will deny the practice has changed dramatically in the past decade or two, and mostly for the worse. College students seem to have gotten the memo. Applications to law schools nationwide have dropped by a startling 46% in the last nine years.[2]

One thought keeps recurring as I wind my way through reunion weekend: most of these old classmates, each in their own sometimes circuitous way, have become good lawyers. They are lawyers I could recommend to anyone—but, I wonder, is their kind becoming more endangered every year? Would I want my college-age daughter to attend law school?

THE CHANGING NATURE OF PRACTICE AND WHAT IT MEANS FOR QUALITY

The world needs good lawyers far more than it needs more lawyers with impressively filled memory banks or genius-level IQs. Key positions in the field for too long have gone to people of great intelligence and knowledge, without adequate regard for the soft skills and attitudes that are even more important to the practice of law. Top corporate law firms often look no further than the nation's premier law schools to fill vacancies, usually culling from that crop only the Order of the Coif/Law Review cream. According to an analysis in the *ABA Journal* of the "obsession with pedigree" found in elite firms, there is little statistical evidence that their hiring practices are justified, especially if the measure of a good hire is the quality of legal work that an associate performs. Instead, as the authors conclude, hiring preferences appear to be "largely rooted in vanity and identity."[3] Mark Britton, founder of Avvo, a Seattle company that rates lawyers, says that hiring partners use law school as a "shortcut" to judge "quality and affinity." Hiring partners, he says, "look at resumés for common elements and to better gauge whether that person is someone they can relate to." As a result, Britton concludes, "the brain moves to thinking about school."[4] Elite schools, relying heavily on LSAT scores, select students more for intelligence than they do for other traits that are useful in the practice of law. Social science literature makes clear that differences at the upper part of the IQ scale are far less predictive of professional success than are certain character and personality traits. UC Berkeley professors Marjorie Shultz and Sheldon Zedeck conducted a landmark study of lawyers that resulted in the identification of twenty-six competencies that underlie quality lawyering.[5] Remarkably, only eight of the twenty-six competencies turn out to be tied in any way to either LSAT scores or law school grades. In fact, high first-year law school grades and LSAT scores are actually *negatively correlated* with skills in networking and business development and service to the community.[6] Moreover, high undergraduate grades are negatively associated with empathy, integrity and honesty, and relationship-building skills.[7]

Producing better lawyers will require bucking some trends. Arguably, it has never been harder than it is today for associates in large law firms to develop the skills critical to serving clients well. The legal profession has undergone a tremendous transformation in just a generation. Purchasers of legal services today are calling the shots, and what they want is "better, faster, cheaper." The desires of clients for cost savings have not brought down the hourly rates charged by lawyers. In fact, billing rates are higher than ever and profits are seen as the measure of a successful firm. Former Stanford Law School dean Larry Kramer notes, "Twenty years ago, most lawyers would have scoffed at the idea that profitability—much less profits-per-partner—should be the measure of success for firms, but that's where we are now, with the given standard to be bigger, to bill more hours, to open more offices, to be more profitable."[8]

With both clients and law firms focused to an unprecedented degree on the bottom line, the delivery of legal services has changed in predictable ways. Many smaller and mid-size firms, where lawyers shared common values and goals, have merged or closed their doors. Today, when most people think law firm, they think of the mega-firm with hundreds of lawyers plying specialized practices and with offices in a variety of states and foreign countries. Both jobs and salaries have been cut.

"Thirty years ago if you were looking to get on the escalator to upward mobility, you went to business or law school" said William D. Henderson, a law professor at Indiana University. "Today, the law school escalator is broken."[9] Over time, markets right themselves; and supply and demand in the legal world will once again be in balance. A growing, complex economy will require more lawyers to grease its wheels and smooth out its problems, and advances in technology can only reduce research time, not eliminate it altogether. If the demand for lawyers is ever to grow significantly, however, it will happen only when we recognize that there are vast numbers of poor and middle-class Americans with unmet legal needs and that we, as citizens of one of the wealthiest nations on the planet, can no longer tolerate that fact. Providing adequate legal representation for all will require figuring out how to provide a high-quality—yet affordable—legal education and, most likely, a greater commitment of public resources in a time when politicians generally are not looking for more ways to spend taxpayer money.

The desire of clients to reduce costs has shifted much legal work from corporate firms to in-house counsel. Some Fortune 500 companies have gone so far as to adopt the presumption that all of their legal work will be handled in-house. Even when corporations do turn to large law firms for help, the nature of lawyer-client interaction has changed. Whereas lawyers formerly might have worked with a client on a wide range of legal problems, they now might deal with a client only when a crisis arises that falls within their narrow area of expertise. Moreover, work that traditionally was done in corporate law firms, such as the drafting of a contract, is now frequently done by general counsel. Relegated to reviewing a contract drafted by the in-house counsel, pushed to spot only problems with the contract as drafted, the lawyer's opportunities to exercise wisdom have diminished. The lawyer who might have suggested a dramatically different approach to drafting the contract, and had very good reasons for doing so, instead takes out a word here and adds a sentence or two there—because that's all that's expected (and wanted).

Another dramatic change in recent decades has been the increased specialization of practices within larger firms. We have gained better mastery of narrow areas of law, but we have lost something more important. When a lawyer had the opportunity to solve a variety of legal problems for a client, the two could develop trust. Trust can only build over time, through the process of promise-making and promise-keeping—and trust is all but essential to a relationship in which wise advice is given and acted upon. In the new, more specialized law firm, we have sacrificed the repeated interaction with clients concerning problems big and small that allowed attorneys to understand the nature of a client's business, key relationships, and goals. Previously, each subsequent interaction could build on the knowledge gained in previous meetings, and in this way a deeper understanding of the true interests of clients emerged. Now, when a client comes to a lawyer, it is often for a one-day ticket. The client wants help today, but expects there will be no tomorrow. Good lawyering emerges from client relationships that have both pasts and expected futures but, sadly, those relationships are less common in the modern firm.

Finally, in large law firms, cost consciousness has made purchasers of legal services reluctant to foot the tab for the work of junior associates, who traditionally had their training costs underwritten by clients. Without adequate training, the life-or-death struggle of associates to achieve basic competency denies them the opportunity to develop the moral skills associated with wise counseling and advocacy. Increased price competition among firms is likely to be a permanent fixture of the new legal marketplace, at least according to 92% of law firm leaders surveyed in 2012.[10] The situation is aggravated by escalating billable hour requirements that further reduce the time available for younger lawyers to hone their wisdom-dispensing skills. Technology is gobbling up what used to make up much of an associate's billable work. Research that previously required hours in the firm library can now be accomplished on a computer in a matter of minutes. Simply put, it's much harder, and much more mentally taxing, to reach the required number of billable hours today than it used to be—even if the hour requirement had remained unchanged, which it hasn't. Being a good lawyer, as we've tried to emphasize, takes a lot of thought. Like tea, good lawyers require steeping time, and modern practice doesn't allow that.

The massive upheaval the legal profession is now undergoing is only likely to accelerate in the future. We are likely to see a future with less face-to-face contact and more virtual hearings and online dispute resolution.[11] Most likely, a trend toward liberalization demanded by consumers who want more choices of where to go for legal advice will lead to changes in what is considered "the authorized practice of law" and new competition in the legal marketplace. We might expect to see the rise of Internet-based global legal businesses, online document production, outsourcing of legal services, and commoditized legal products.[12] With these changes, lawyers face the prospect of lower pay and reduced opportunities for thoughtful reflection about conventional legal problems. Richard Susskind, who has written extensively on the future of the legal profession, predicts "the emergence of a legal industry that will be quite alien to the current legal establishment."[13]

If good lawyers risk becoming an endangered species in the nation's largest law firms, is their critical habitat to be found elsewhere? Might good lawyers become concentrated in the public sector or in small to mid-size firms? Sadly, many of the same forces that have reduced time for both client contact and reflection in large firms have adversely affected other areas of practice as well. The increased concern among clients with the cost of legal services has hit small firms and solo practices, where lawyers often find themselves in a new competition with legal software and services provided over the Internet. Clients have reduced visits to law offices, relying more often on the cheaper alternatives to address many of their legal issues. Moreover, the recent recession and slow recovery has forced lawyers of all types to focus more on the bottom line. The financially pressed lawyer of today might forgo the leisurely (but sometimes very important) client counseling session and scoot the client out the door the minute he thinks he has enough information to proceed.

Not all trends are discouraging, however. Innovative legal technology now in the works "will empower lawyers to argue better and do more than ever before." According to Blake Masters, co-founder of the tech start-up Judicata, "Great legal technology will assist lawyers in exercising their skilled human judgment," free lawyers from some of their current drudgery, and move the legal industry forward.[14] Online marketplaces will make it easier for lawyers to share their skills, build reputations, and identify potential clients. Easier access to legal information will create a better-informed public and drive down the cost of basic legal services. For a new generation of nimble and tech-savvy lawyers, the brave new legal world can be an exciting place.

CREATING ENVIRONMENTS WHERE GOOD LAWYERS CAN FLOURISH

If we aimed to create environments where good lawyers could flourish, what changes would we be making in the practice? We could begin by not thinking of clients as profit centers. The culture of law firms needs to put first serving the true interests of clients. When pursuing those interests means less profit for the firm than an alternative strategy might have yielded, it is the profit and not the client's interests that must be sacrificed. Now, according to Patrick Schiltz, a federal judge in Minnesota, published surveys of incomes in big firms "are pored over by lawyers with the intensity of kids poring over statistics of their favorite baseball players."[15] The ABA, well aware of the problem, has urged that steps be taken to "resist the temptation to make the acquisition of wealth a primary goal of law practice."[16] Law firms must think of themselves as something more than mere businesses and unite around the common goal of providing high-quality legal services to clients.

Firms should change the way they evaluate the work of associates and partners. Rather than emphasizing performance goals, such as cases won versus lost or dollars brought into the firm, firms should stress mastery goals, such as whether lawyers have developed and are using the sorts of skills, virtues, and dispositions that we've considered in this book.

Firms should also consider ending some of the financial incentives that are designed to drive firm profits. Incentives generally do more harm than good because they "crowd out" both "the pleasure people can get from an activity" and "the moral motives that drive an activity."[17] By their very nature, incentives are designed to change behavior in certain ways, when the behavior we should really want is simply driven by an internal desire to do quality work.

Also, when it comes to evaluating attorneys, law firms should ditch their elaborate grading grids and scoring systems in favor of a more Gestalt-like process. What makes a good lawyer is far too complicated to be reduced to objectivizing criteria—criteria that almost invariably underweight "soft qualities" of good lawyers, such as an ability to listen well to clients or a habit of being honest and straightforward in dealings with other lawyers.

Law firms need to create supportive environments for lawyers—specifically, environments that encourage good work. Top-down structures rarely are as supportive as more decentralized structures. Firms should require supervising attorneys to provide regular feedback to associates, and associates should have the latitude to criticize superiors. Firms should strive to create an environment in which lawyers can feel free to ask for, and receive, frank criticism and suggestions as they work on projects. Small offenses should be pardoned, camaraderie encouraged, rules kept to a minimum, and decisions assessed in a long-term (not the typical short-term) framework.

Most importantly of all, law firms should treat different lawyers differently—as individuals, not as interchangeable parts. No two lawyers are alike in their strengths and skill sets, and every lawyer brings something different of value to a firm. The trick is to understand what those contributions might be, and then to give each lawyer the discretion needed to make them.

THE SCOURGE OF BILLABLE HOURS

> *I saw the best minds of my generation destroyed by madness, starving hysterical naked, dragging themselves through LSATs at dawn looking for job security, angelheaded hipsters burning for the ancient heavenly connection to the starry dynamo in the machinery of night and to partner-track slots at Skadden Arps, who in poverty and tatters and hollow-eyed and high sat up smoking in the supernatural darkness of cold-water flats floating across the tops of cities contemplating the idea of billing clients in 15-minute increments for the rest of their lives.*
>
> —Jeffrey Goldberg

Jeffrey Goldberg's take on the state of the modern legal profession, inspired by Allen Ginsberg's poem *Howl*, is too bleak in the extreme.[18] Lawyers, on the whole, are roughly as satisfied with their jobs as many other professionals, including doctors and accountants, ranking roughly in the middle in a survey of satisfaction in nearly 200 occupations.[19] But Goldberg is right in suggesting big firm associates are, on average, the least happy of lawyers, and that the prospect of "billing clients in fifteen-minute increments for the rest of their lives" has a lot to do with that.

At the top of a wish list of ways to make law practice both better and more humane would be abolition of billable hour requirements. Attempting to bill a staggering 2,100 or more hours a year means putting in fewer hours of pro bono work or other efforts that might benefit your community, a consequence Chief Justice William Rehnquist warned about more than two decades ago.[20] For some lawyers, the pressure to reach a billable hour requirement also is the beginning of a slippery slope that ends in a career of habitual corner cutting. Patrick Schiltz, in an article published by the *Vanderbilt Law Review*, presents a sobering view of what can happen to a lawyer who pads a time sheet:

> Maybe you will bill a client for ninety minutes for a task that really took only sixty minutes to perform. However, you will promise yourself that you will repay the client at the first opportunity by doing thirty minutes of work for the client for "free." ... And then what will happen is that it will become easier and easier to take these little loans against future work. And then, after a while you will stop paying back these little loans. You will convince yourself that...you did such good work that your client should pay a little more for it.[21]

Then, as Schiltz tells the story, dishonesty becomes a habit and you will tell a partner "you proofread a lengthy prospectus...even though you didn't," or you "you will find a document that would hurt your client's case...and you will simply 'forget' to produce it in response to your opponent's discovery requests." Eventually, your moral values will change and you will no longer care about what is "right or wrong," only about "what is profitable, and what you can get away with."[22]

Billable hours have another pernicious effect, also one related to what Professor Thomas Shaffer describes as the most serious ethical issue facing lawyers, their fondness for excessive remuneration for their services.[23] Not only do billable hour requirements encourage dishonesty and therefore breed the resentment of scrupulous lawyers; they also incentivize time-consuming strategies that might not be in a client's interest. What is best for your own count of billable hours might not be best for your client.

The perverse incentives of the billable hour system were on full display in recent litigation involving the world's largest law firm (4,200 attorneys strong), DLA Piper. When DLA Piper sued Adam Victor, an energy company executive, for unpaid legal bills relating to a bankruptcy filing for one of his companies, the

executive counterclaimed, accusing the firm of a "sweeping practice of overbilling" and demanding $22.3 million in punitive dam-
ages. Pretrial discovery proved embarrassing for DLA Piper when
e-mails surfaced that suggested—as a *New York Times* story on
the litigation put it—"a lax attitude about the size of Mr.Victor's
bill."[24] One e-mail exulted in the bill's massive run-up: "I hear
we are already 200K over our estimate—that's Team DLA Piper!"
Another lawyer at the firm predicted that now that a colleague
"has random people working full time on random research projects in standard 'churn that bill, baby!' mode," the bill "shall know
no limits."[25] The settlement agreement signed in 2013 included a
confidentiality provision, undoubtedly to spare the firm further
embarrassment.

Nothing, of course, requires firms either to have a billable
hour requirement for associates or to bill clients by the hour.
Compensation could be tied to seniority or be based on, for
example, an associate's mastery of certain skills. Clients could be
billed, in many cases, on either a contingency or flat fee basis.
Richard Susskind believes that "hourly billing may be reaching
the end of its natural life."[26] As Susskind sees it, clients sit at "the
center of the legal universe"—without clients, lawyers have nothing to do—and cost-conscious clients will demand the end of a
system that puts their economic interests into direct conflict with
those of the law firms they employ.

Law firms that seek to align their interests with those of their
clients, Susskind predicts, could "create enormous, even unprecedented, levels of confidence and would deserve the often mis-
placed honorific of 'trusted advisor.'"[27] He points to the example
of Cisco as a "case study in the future of legal services."[28] The large
tech company shifted almost all of its commercial litigation to
one firm for a fixed annual fee. Two years into the new arrange-
ment, the firm found that its revenues were being negatively
affected. The firm's solution was to devote more effort to anticipating Cisco's potential legal problems and doing what it could to

head them off. Lawyers for the firm began attending important corporate meetings, reviewing particular documents that carried legal risks, and securing "a level of access and involvement that litigators would not normally enjoy prior to problems arising."[29] The result was a win for the firm and a win for Cisco: reduced expenses for the law firm and less litigation for Cisco.

WHAT A GOOD LAWYER DOES

It is all too easy to drift off course. In *Good Work: When Excellence and Ethics Meet*, Howard Gardner, Mihaly Csikszentmihalyi, and William Damon conclude their exploration of quality work with words of advice to aspiring young workers in the professions. They warn that to "keep up professional values under the pressure of countervailing forces" it is necessary to be anchored in "the traditions of your domain, as embodied in the teachers, mentors, or paragons whom you admire." They also advise seeking the support of "allies," other professionals who share your purpose. Finally, they suggest, it is important to "resolve to stick by your principles," to make a commitment to doing your best work and following your own high standards.[30] Doing good work and doing it ethically is all about, as Bob Dylan reminds us in "Forever Young," having "a strong foundation when the winds of changes shift."

We've identified various virtues and abilities—and certainly not all of them that we might have—that contribute to good work, but only hinted at the characteristics of good work itself. Must we resort to the approach taken by Justice Potter Stewart in *Jacobellis v. Ohio* when, after years of trying to define hard-core pornography, he finally threw in the towel with his oft-quoted words, "I know it when I see it"?[31] Is it possible that the best that can be done is to point to examples of lawyers doing good work? Perhaps no Potter-like end-run is necessary, but describing a good lawyer isn't easy. Good lawyering has many dimensions—some obvious, some not.

Perhaps nothing so much marks good work as serving well the true interests of clients. Good lawyers engage clients in moral conversations that allow them to identify the clients' true interests, which often are quite different from the interests clients first express. Getting to the true interests of clients requires empathy, patience, experience, and sometimes a dose of humility. For a lawyer, the ability to read correctly a client's emotions can be as important as the ability to read correctly a statutory provision. Divining a client's true interest is an art, and a hard one at that.

Once having identified these true interests, the good lawyer then develops and implements strategies that help clients achieve their goals. In today's increasingly cost-conscious environment, that means both efficiently finding answers to important questions and sometimes having to engage in legal triage that might leave some potentially relevant questions unanswered. To serve clients well in our question-rich and information-rich environment, it is as critical to know what you do *not* know as what you do know. Some lawyers (public defenders, for example) have always practiced in a world of financial constraints; what is different today is that the vast majority of lawyers are without the luxury of time for study, reflection, debate, and "what-iffing" that used to play a central role in their day-to-day lives.

Good lawyers also attend to relationships within communities that matter. They understand that they will have differences, some never resolvable, with other members within the legal fraternity, but they commit to actions that prevent the fraying of that community. They aspire to view the actions of lawyers and judges in a favorable light and seek to avoid both gloating and sulking over outcomes. The good lawyer does this, of course, because he or she knows that maintaining respect within the fraternity is critical to the long-term health of the practice. In addition to the legal community, the welfare of the larger community to which both lawyers and clients belong is never far from the minds of good lawyers. Whenever possible, they look for "win-win" opportunities that advance both the interests of their clients and their communities. Recognizing when this is possible, and when it isn't, is a talent they try to develop. When the interests of clients and communities clash, good lawyers understand that the interests of clients trump—and, if the damage to community is unacceptable, they have the option of declining representation (Figure 10.1).

Maintaining relationships in the communities from which a lawyer draws sustenance is critical because without the support of these communities, it is almost impossible to maintain the emotional balance that good work requires. For some lawyers, sustenance comes from their religious congregations. When serving a client's interests brings them into tension with their religious communities, those tensions need to be resolved through honest dialogue. Other lawyers, including many lawyers of color, draw

"Daddy doesn't slay dragons, dear—he represents them."

FIGURE 10.1. Serving clients sometimes put lawyers into conflict with their community. Credit: Cartoon by Michael Maslin, Condé Nast.

emotional support from the ethnic communities of which they consider themselves members. When their obligations as lawyers put them in conflict with many members of their community—as Christopher Darden, the African American assistant prosecutor in the O. J. Simpson murder case discovered—they must find ways to deal with the anger and ostracism that comes from simply doing their jobs. In his book about the trial, *In Contempt*, Darden writes movingly of the pain suffered in his pursuit of justice for Nicole Brown Simpson and Ronald Goldman. He did his job, and did it with class, but it was hard—very hard.[32]

Serving the interests of your clients well may also, at times, create conflict within your own family. Legal work can be very demanding, and there may not be enough hours in some days to meet both your obligations as a lawyer and your obligations to your family. Your professional life can encroach on your personal life to the point that you can no longer bear it. One lawyer described feeling trapped and drained by the long hours demanded in her firm:

> My parents simply did not understand the enormous pressures created by my career. I remember a bad fight the day I had to work on Mother's Day, and my mother's angry question, "Doesn't your boss have a mother?" I remember my parents' incomprehension at my irritability, my unavailability, my hyper behavior.[33]

For that unhappy lawyer, the solution came in giving up partnership ambitions and making arrangements with her firm for a workweek that would not exceed forty hours. She found a way to continue to enjoy the intellectual stimulation of her work but "leave at five without a moment's regret."[34] For lawyers unable to find a satisfying work-life balance, the decision to move to part-time work, even if it means sacrificing career and financial goals, is far preferable to the alternative of cutting corners and doing less than 100% of what your clients reasonably expect from you.

It takes a lot to be a good lawyer: being a good counselor, being a good advocate, being a good member of the legal fraternity and your community, all the while maintaining the relationships necessary to keep the heart and mind working well. In fact, it is an impossible standard to meet all the time. You might be or become a good lawyer, but the truth is you won't be one all the time. Your prospects of good work, however, are improved when you have a job that is well suited to your strengths and values.

FINDING WORK THAT FITS YOUR STRENGTHS

Bill Gates would be a lousy actor. Meryl Streep might not cut it as the CEO of a major software company, although perhaps she could sell Prada. And both of these people, despite their undeniable success in their own fields, probably would be just so-so dentists.

Law is one of the most diverse professions, with hundreds of different types of positions. The "A's to Z's" of traditional practice range from admiralty law to a Zurich-based international banking practice. If you factor in nontraditional law-related jobs, from legal academia to human resources to legal journalism to business and foundation work, the numbers are even larger. There are some jobs on this long list that might make a happy fit for you. No doubt, also, you'd find yourself absolutely miserable in some others among these jobs. Most importantly, in some positions in law you have a real chance of becoming a good lawyer; in others, you have almost none.

So what makes you a good fit for some jobs and a poor one for others? The answer is many things, but the biggest determinants are your strengths and your values. (Ranking third, most likely, is how well your job allows you to fit comfortably into the communities that matter to you.) If you happen to be in a good place in the law, one that draws on your strengths and aligns with your values, then stay put by all means. But if you are not, finding such a position can be a big step toward becoming a good lawyer. (Yes, we know that is easier said than done.) Eighty-five percent of lawyers change jobs at least once,[35] so join the crowd. When you are well suited to your job you will be more committed, have more energy, be happier, and will not feel estranged from the communities you value. Although strengths are inherently difficult things to measure, Tom Rath, head of Gallup's consulting division (which works with corporations on employee strength matching), reports that people who use their strengths regularly on their job are "six times more likely to be engaged on the job and three times more likely to be happy with their lives in general."[36] Positive psychologist Martin Seligman notes that the kind of satisfaction that comes to people who find jobs well suited to their strengths is "authentic happiness," the most erosion-resistant kind.[37]

Getting to the right place first requires you to identify your strengths and your values. This used to be a surprisingly difficult assignment. Most people, it turns out, have a difficult time listing their own strengths and are uncertain about how to rank their values. And it's not their fault. We are complicated creatures. We are the products of thousands of years of evolution and are molded by our environments, our nurture, our education, and our family and friends. We have evolved mechanisms that are designed to fool ourselves—we are experts at self-deception. Our values seem to shift, if we can even understand what they are. We forget that our lives are mainly controlled by our emotions and intuitions, a fact that dooms many of our attempts to understand ourselves.

Fortunately, identifying strengths can be as easy now as going online and taking a thirty-minute assessment at either of two websites. Millions of people have done so already. The University of Pennsylvania's Positive Psychology Center offers its free Values-in-Action (VIA) Signature Strength Questionnaire, which can tell you whether "curiosity," "hopefulness," "bravery," or any of a number of other strengths are among your own.[38] Gallup's "StrengthsFinder" requires payment of a fee but has the advantage of being more focused on careers.[39] Gallup's questionnaire promises to tell you, for example, whether you are an "Activator" (a person adept at implementing ideas) or "Strategic" (a person who sees the big picture and plans well). Both the Positive Psychology Center's "Authentic Happiness" website and Gallup's site offer suggestions for using the results from your questionnaires to identify jobs that would be well served by your strengths. Of course, sometimes all the strengths in the world won't be enough when the legal deck is stacked against you.

IF YOU ARE A GOOD LAWYER, WHO WILL KNOW?

> *Whatever you do, do it well, as well as you can, and be aware of what you are doing.*
> —Janwillem Van De Wetering, *The Empty Mirror*

Alan Dershowitz describes the practice of law as "a lifelong series of exams by often inaccurate graders."[40] While this is truer for litigators than transaction lawyers, it is well to remember that whether you prevail in a courtroom is often not a measure of whether you did your job well. Judges and juries sometimes mess up and the law is only the law—it's not justice.

If there's little correlation between quality and the marks you get from judges, you have to be guided by criteria you develop internally to evaluate your work. You need to ask yourself if you turned over enough stones, honestly represented the law and the facts, acted ethically, tried hard to be persuasive, accurately sized up the case, and did the other things good lawyers do. If you have done those things, and if you are lucky, your client will understand and know you did your best. If not, you still will have satisfied the audience that matters most: You.

"Quality" can be synonymous with "excellence," but we see it equally as *the route* to excellence. By keeping focused on quality you stay on a path that ascends in the direction of your goal of excellence. Excellence might prove to be outside your reach, because sometimes things out of your control can get in the way, but at least your focus allows you to steadily gain elevation. Robert Pirsig in *Zen and the Art of Motorcycle Maintenance* saw quality as a sort of *process* that manifested itself in many positive ways; it was the unfolding "knife edge" of experience accessible to us all, if only we embrace it and apply it to our situations. To be a good motorcycle mechanic, Pirsig argued, required accepting both the wisdom of the heart and of the mind. Becoming a good lawyer requires no less.

AT CAREER'S END: REMEMBRANCE OF THINGS PAST

Let us end with a thought about your future. Whether you are a lawyer or a law student, likely the day will come when you close your last case and shut your office door behind you forever. There will follow times for reflection, times when you think back on your legal career and wonder what it all meant.

At career's end, all that will be left of your life in the law will be your memories, your story. But that's really quite a lot. "Memory is life," stated the director of a memory enhancement institute in a Saul Bellow novel.[41] Memory can be a powerful thing. It gives us an identity. It can make us weep, make us laugh, make us angry, or make us fearful.

Memory is not a literal recording of reality. Our memory systems are conveniently built so that we remember best the things that are most important in our lives, while the trivial events of day-to-day existence erode or fade out altogether. Most of our experiences, such as our ability to remember the seven digits of a phone number we recently looked up, exist only temporarily in our short-term, or working, memory. Experiences tinged with greater emotional significance, such as a sexual encounter or traumatic event, get encoded in such a way that they have a much better chance of being remembered months or years later. We remember precisely where we were and what we were doing when we learned of the September 11, 2001, attack on the World Trade Center, but we are highly unlikely to remember what we had for breakfast on September 10, 2001. As we think, write, or talk about a past experience, we encode it more deeply, much as frequently playing an old vinyl record deepens its groove.

Memory loss actually serves us well, at least to a point. If we stored forever every single experience, no matter how trivial (assuming, for a moment, we had storage capacity enough to do this), we might lose our ability to frame a coherent life story, over-whelmed as we would be with the details piling up from every page, paragraph, and sentence of our pasts. The very fragility of our memories helps shape how we see ourselves.

What are you likely to remember from the thousands of days that made up your career? Only a small percentage of your experiences as a lawyer are likely to be deeply etched. They are likely to be those intense experiences where your work aligned best with your values, where your strengths led to a workplace triumph, or where you shared a deep emotional connection with a client or a colleague.

From our memories we construct the story of our careers. The encoded fragments of our past experience, distorted and degraded over time, are woven together to form the core of our personal identity as a lawyer. These stories—these career autobiographies—are more about meanings than they are about facts. Our understanding of ourselves is an act of construction; it is a "subjective and embellished telling of the past."[42] We make the history of our career; it has no existence in the physical universe.

Our stories anchor us. They allow us to savor the past, fully experience the present, and anticipate the future. Without an ability to travel in time our lives would be, in the words of psychologist and neuroscientist Daniel L. Schacter, "psychologically barren—the equivalent of a bleak Siberian landscape."[43]

As we age, memories become ever more important parts of our lives. It is common for senior citizens to say that photographs are their most valued possessions, while it is uncommon for younger adults to make the same claim. As we advance through middle age, we become more focused on who we are (and have been) than on what we do. In the well-lived life, a certain age also brings with it a new sweetness. In the golden late-day light, infused with a lifetime of memories, experiences might lack the emotional intensity of our youth. Instead, experiences bathe in a subtle and emotionally complex stew—our present, our past, our coming end all contributing to the mix.

Society unfairly devalues the tendency of older people to "live in the past," even though the senior citizens most prone to reminiscing show increased mental health and reduced levels of depression compared to older adults who spend less time living in the past. Psychologists also speculate that the process of remembering our pasts prepares us for death.[44] Schacter points out that the memories that form our life stories, however imperfect they might be, "are all that stick with us from cradle to grave."[45]

This has been a book, in no small part, about how you can become the kind of lawyer who can someday look back with satisfaction on your legal career. It is not a guide to being a successful lawyer, if success is measured by win-loss records, fame, or financial reward. It also offers no promises of finding greater happiness in your career, though that might be a welcome side effect from following some of its suggestions. At career's end, you will ask yourself, "Was I a good lawyer?" Your memories will provide the answer. Your good work will create the memories.

Acknowledgments

WE ARE INDEBTED IN OUR EFFORT TO A GREAT MANY PEOple, too many to identify on one page or ten, but among them all, some stand out.

We especially would like to thank Kaitlin Woody for her cheerful, patient, and successful efforts in obtaining copyright permissions, as well as her work in providing other invaluable administrative assistance. Edward Cantu, Barbara Glesner-Fines, Steven Lubet, and Allen Rostron deserve great thanks for their constructive criticism and helpful advice concerning earlier drafts, or draft chapters. David McBride at Oxford Press proved to be a superb editor, ably assisted by Sarah Rosenthal. Thanks also to Jack Balkin, Steven Lubet, and Karen Mathis for providing the pithy praise that appears on the back jacket of this book. Librarian Lawrence D. MacLachlan we thank for his help in locating information that we often despaired might not be found. Thanks also to Greg Westfall and Trevor Goring for allowing us to use, without charge, their creative work (a photo in one case, and artwork in the other). Orville Bloethe, John Doar, Don Horton, James Ed

Horton, and Tony Luppino provided stories that we used in this book, and we thank them for doing so. Special thanks are owed to Professors John Kaplan and Thomas Shaffer for impressing on us early in our careers how certain virtues can make all the difference between being a good lawyer and being merely a lawyer—without their shared wisdom, this book would never have been written.

Finally, we wish most of all to thank our spouses (our own good lawyers and life companions) for the encouragement and support they provided in this project, as they have in so many others in each of our lives.

Notes

Preface

1. ROBERT M. PIRSIG, ZEN AND THE ART OF MOTORCYCLE MAINTENANCE: AN INQUIRY INTO VALUES xii (2009).
2. *Id.* at 66–67.
3. *Id.* at 76.
4. *Id.* at 67.
5. *Id.* at 329.
6. *Id.* at 352.
7. Jessica Lyons, *Disaster Déjà Vu*, METROACTIVE (July 28, 2010), http://www.metroactive.com/features/Dennis-Kelso.html.
8. David Lebedoff, *The Exxon Valdez's Endless Legal Voyage*, L.A. TIMES, Nov. 3, 2007, at 21.
9. Father Guido Sarducci (Don Novello), *Five Minute University*, Templar University, http://www.templaruniversity.com/guido.html (last visited Sept. 15, 2013).
10. Douglas Linder & Nancy Levit, *The Quest for a Satisfying Career in Law*, http://law2.umkc.edu/faculty/projects/ftrials/happylawyers/questions.html (last visited Sept. 15, 2013).
11. Douglas O. Linder, *Famous Trials*, http://law2.umkc.edu/faculty/projects/ftrials/ftrials.htm (last visited Sept. 15, 2013).
12. The psychological literature amply supports this idea that doing good work leads to the development of enduring well-being and satisfaction. *See, e.g.,* Michael F. Steger et al, *Being Good by Doing Good: Daily Eudaimonic Activity and Well-Being*, 42 J. RES. PERSONALITY 22 (2008).

Chapter 1

1. David Brooks, *The Limits of Empathy*, N.Y. TIMES, Sept. 29, 2011, *available at* http://www.nytimes.com/2011/09/30/opinion/brooks-the-limits-of-empathy.html?_r=0 (quoting STEVEN PINKER, THE BETTER ANGELS OF OUR NATURE: WHY VIOLENCE HAS DECLINED (2011)).

2. STEPHEN S. HALL, WISDOM: FROM PHILOSOPHY TO NEUROSCIENCE 128 (2010).

3. DANIEL GOLEMAN, EMOTIONAL INTELLIGENCE WHY IT CAN MATTER MORE THAN IQ (1996).

4. Daniel Goleman, *Winning the Battle for the Human Heart, in* PREDICTIONS 135, 137 (Sian Griffiths ed. 1999).

5. Richard J. Baskin, *My Story of Self Discovery at Gerry Spence's Trial Lawyer's College*, http://www.rjbaskin.com/self-discovery.php.

6. *Id.*

7. GERRY SPENCE, WIN YOUR CASE: HOW TO PRESENT, PERSUADE, AND PREVAIL—EVERY PLACE, EVERY TIME 9 (2006).

8. *Id.* at 10.

9. *Wild Horses* (2013), http://www.triallawyerscollege.com/ViewStory.aspx?g=72aa3bc0-35e0-44bf-a5dd-b3210e2f494e.

10. John Nolte, *About Saddles and Horses*, WARRIOR, Spring 2011, at 6, 8–9.

11. *Wild Horses, supra* note 9.

12. SPENCE, *supra* note 7, at 5.

13. Jessica Garrison, *Lawyers Tap Their Feelings to Connect with Jurors*, L.A. TIMES, Nov. 25, 2006, *available at* http://articles.latimes.com/2006/nov/25/local/me-psychodrama25.

14. *Id.*

15. *Id.*

16. JONATHAN HAIDT, THE RIGHTEOUS MIND: WHY GOOD PEOPLE ARE DIVIDED BY POLITICS AND RELIGION 75 (2012).

17. SIMON BARON-COHEN, THE SCIENCE OF EVIL: ON EMPATHY AND THE ORIGINS OF CRUELTY 16 (2011).

18. *Id.*

19. Kristin B. Gerdy, *Clients, Empathy, and Compassion: Introducing First-Year Students to the "Heart" of Lawyering*, 87 NEB. L. REV. 1, 8 (2008).

20. *Id.* at 9.

21. *Id.* at 7.

22. *Id.* at 11.

23. ANTHONY T. KRONMAN, THE LOST LAWYER: FAILING IDEALS OF THE LEGAL PROFESSION 130 (1993).

24. Gerry L. Spence, *Discovering the Story*, WARRIOR, Summer 2004, at 3.

25. *See* Jeffrey Abramson, *The Jury and Popular Culture*, 50 DEPAUL L. REV. 497, 497 n.1(2000); Shari Seidman Diamond et al., *The "Kettleful of Law" in Real*

Jury Deliberations: Successes, Failures, and Next Steps, 106 Nw. U. L. Rev. 1537, 1603–04 (2012).

26. Nancy Pennington & Reid Hastie, *The Story Model for Jury Decision Making, in* Inside the Juror: The Psychology of Juror Decision Making 205–06 (Reid Hastie ed., 1993).

27. *Id.* at 210–11.

28. *Id.* at 191–222.

29. Spence, *supra* note 24, at 6.

30. *Id.* at 8.

31. Baron-Cohen, *supra* note 17, at 187–95. *See also The Empathy Quotient,* Guardian News & Media Ltd. (2011), http://www.guardian.co.uk/life/table/0,,937442,00.html.

32. Baron-Cohen, *supra* note 17, at 19–26, 136.

33. *Id.* at 130.

34. Douglas O. Linder, *Jurors, Empathy and Race,* Tenn. L. Rev. 887, 894 (1996).

35. Glenn Loury, *The Impossible Dilemma,* New Republic, Jan. 1, 1996, at 21, 24.

36. Ronald Cohen, *Altruism: Human, Cultural, or What?, in* Altruism, Sympathy and Helping 89 (Lauren Wispé ed., 1978).

37. Bahar Gholipour, *Brain Surgery to Remove Amygdala Leads to Woman's 'Hyper Empathy,'* Huffington Post (Sept. 13, 2013), *available at* http://www.huffingtonpost.com/2013/09/13/brain-surgery-hyper-empathy-amygdala-remove-epilepsy_n_3920770.html?ir=Healthy+Living.

38. Baron-Cohen, *supra* note 17, at 27–41.

39. David Brooks, The Social Animal: The Hidden Sources of Love, Character, and Achievement 41 (2012).

40. *Id.* at 160.

41. *Id.*

42. *Id.* at 77.

43. Baron-Cohen, *supra* note 17, at 176.

44. Spence, *supra* note 7, at 77.

45. Jamil Zaki, *What, Me Care? Young Are Less Empathetic,* Sci. Am., Jan. 19, 2011, *available at* http://www.scientificamerican.com/article.cfm?id=what-me-care.

46. Sara H. Konrath et al., *Changes in Dispositional Empathy in American College Students over Time: A Meta-Analysis,* 15 Personality & Soc. Psychol. Rev. 180, 181 (May 2011).

47. *Id.* at 189–91.

48. Zaki, *supra* note 45.

49. Jeanna Bryner, *Today's College Students Lack Empathy,* LiveScience (May 28, 2010), http://www.livescience.com/9918-today-college-students-lack-empathy.html.

50. *Id.*

51. *Id.*

52. Michael F. Melcher, The Creative Lawyer: A Practical Guide to Authentic Professional Satisfaction 75–76 (2007) (referring to a study of more than 3,000 lawyers conducted by Larry Richard).

53. Gerdy, *supra* note 19, at 2 (quoting Karen J. Mathis, President, American Bar Association, Keynote Address at the Drexel University College of Law Inaugural Celebratory Dinner (Sept. 27, 2006), *available at* http://www.abanet.org/op/mathis/speeches/drexel_univ_ dinner_speech_0906.pdf).

54. Gerdy, *supra* note 19, at 3.

55. *Id.*

56. *Id.* at 35.

57. John Connolly, The Book of Lost Things 345 (2011).

58. Pam Bullock, *For Better Social Skills, Scientists Recommend a Little Chekhov*, N. Y. Times, Oct. 4, 2013, at A1, A3.

59. Gerdy, *supra* note 19, at 45–48.

60. Ian Gallacher, *Thinking Like Nonlawyers: Why Empathy Is a Core Lawyering Skill and Why Legal Education Should Change to Reflect Its Importance*, 8 Legal Comm. & Rhetoric: JALWD 109, 117 (Fall 2011).

61. Cheryl McCall, *For Country Lawyer Gerry Spence, It's Open Season on Big Corporations*, People, Aug. 24, 1981, *available at* http://www.people.com/people/archive/article/0,,20080055,00.html.

62. Natalie Angier, *Scientists Mull Role of Empathy in Man and Beast, in* The Science Times Book of Mammals 252, 255 (ed. Nicholas Wade 1999).

63. Linder, *supra* note 34, at 893 n.45.

64. Dan Ariely, The (Honest) Truth About Dishonesty: How We Lie to Everyone—Especially Ourselves 225 (2012).

65. Douglas O. Linder, *"The Chicago Seven" Trial, 1969–1970, Contempt Specifications Concerning Attorney William Kunstler*, Famous Trials, http://law2.umkc.edu/faculty/projects/ftrials/chicago7/kunstler.html (last visited Apr. 24, 2013).

66. *Id.*

67. *Id.*

68. Gerdy, *supra* note 19, at 22.

69. Emily P. Corwin et al., *Defendant Remorse, Need for Affect, and Juror Sentencing Decisions*, 40 J. Am. Acad. Psychiatry & L. 41 (Jan. 2012); Bryan H. Ward, *Sentencing without Remorse*, 38 Loy. U. Chi. L.J. 131, 131 (2006).

70. Linder, *supra* note 34, at 888.

71. *Id.* at 911.

72. Paul Bloom, *The Baby in the Well: The Case against Empathy*, New Yorker, May 20, 2013, *available at* http://www.newyorker.com/arts/critics/atlarge/2013/05/20/130520crat_atlarge_bloom?printable=true&currentPage=all.

73. Major Garrett, *Obama Pushes for Empathetic Supreme Court Justices*, FOX News, May 1, 2009.

74. *Id.*

75. Philip Elliott, *Kyl: Pick for Court Could Face Holdup*, ARIZ. REPUBLIC, May 25, 2009, *available at* http://www.azcentral.com/arizonarepublic/news/articles/2009/05/25/20090525kyl-supremecourt0525.html.

76. John Stanton, *Sessions Worried by Obama's "Empathy Standard" in Court Nomination*, ROLL CALL, June 9, 2009, *available at* http://www.rollcall.com/news/-35597-1.html (Alabama Senator Jeff Sessions in weekly Republican Address).

77. TINSLEY E. YARBROUGH, HARRY BLACKMUN: THE OUTSIDER JUSTICE 276 (2008).

78. *Id.* at 277.

79. 489 U.S. 189 (1989).

80. *Id.* at 192.

81. *Id.* at 195.

82. *Id.* at 202–03.

83. *Id.* at 212–13 (Blackmun, J., dissenting).

84. Kathryn Abrams & Hila Keren, *Who's Afraid of Law and the Emotions?*, 94 MINN. L. REV. 1997, 2005 (2010) (quoting Richard Posner, *Emotion versus Emotionalism in the Law, in* THE PASSIONS OF LAW 311 (Susan A. Bandes ed. 1999).

85. RICHARD POSNER, OVERCOMING LAW 381 (1995).

86. Charles A. Reich, *A Passion for Justice*, 26 TOURO L. REV. 393, 401 (2010).

87. *Id.*

88. Brooks, *supra* note 1.

89. *Id.*

90. *Id.*

91. Jesse J. Prinz, *Is Empathy Necessary for Morality, in* EMPATHY: PHILOSOPHICAL AND PSYCHOLOGICAL PERSPECTIVES 211, 221 (Amy Coplan & Peter Goldie eds. 2011).

92. *Id.* at 218.

Chapter 2

1. JOHN ADAMS, THE WISDOM OF JOHN ADAMS 208 (2003).

2. *Id.*

3. Yvonne Zacharias, *Legendary Civil Rights Activist to Speak*, VANCOUVER SUN (Canada), June 24, 2008, at E2 (quoting Maya Angelou).

4. Thomas Aquinas, *Treatise on the Virtues, in* SUMMA THEOLOGICA I–II, ¶¶ 49–67 (John A. Oesterle trans., 1966, Univ. of Notre Dame ed. 1984) (~1265–74).

5. CHRISTOPHER PETERSON & MARTIN E.P. SELIGMAN, CHARACTER STRENGTHS AND VIRTUES: A HANDBOOK AND CLASSIFICATION (2004).

6. *Id.* at 199.

7. Douglas O. Linder, *Bending toward Justice: John Doar and the "Mississippi Burning" Trial*, 72 MISS. L.J. 731, 760 (2002) (Interview with John M. Doar, prosecutor in *United States v. Price*, in Rockford, Ill. (Nov. 6, 1999)).

8. Douglas Linder, *Doar Pleading for Calm in Jackson after the Evers Assassination*, Famous Trials, http://law2.umkc.edu/faculty/projects/ftrials/price&bowers/Doar2.JPG (last visited Apr. 15, 2013).

9. Linder, *supra* note 7, at 734–35.

10. Brian Lamb, *John Doar, Former Assistant Attorney General for Civil Rights, 1965–67*, C-SPAN (Jan. 25, 2009) http://www.q-and-a.org/Transcript/?ProgramID=1216 (statement of Carl Fleming).

11. Craig Gilbert, *Doar Stood Tall in Fight for Civil Right in South*, J.-Sentinel (Milwaukee), Apr. 9, 2009, *available at* http://www.jsonline.com/news/statepolitics/52802372.html.

12. Linder, *supra* note 7, at 736.

13. Nadine Cohodas, *Remembering the Voting Rights Revolution*, N.J. L.J., Aug. 14, 1995, at 9.

14. Roy Reed, *Ubiquitous Rights Aide*, N.Y. Times, Sept. 2, 1963, at 26.

15. John Doar, *The Work of the Civil Rights Division in Enforcing Voting Rights under the Civil Rights Act of 1957 and 1960*, 25 Fla. St. U. L. Rev. 1, 10 (1997).

16. Linder, *supra* note 7, at 756.

17. *Id.* at 757.

18. *Id.*

19. *Id.*

20. Terry Keeton, Meridian Star, Oct. 18, 1967, at 1.

21. Walter Rugaber, *Trial of 18 Charged with Conspiracy in Mississippi Goes to All-White Jury*, N.Y. Times, Oct. 19, 1967, at 37.

22. United States v. Price, Crim. No. 5291, at 2363–64 (Summation of John Doar) (S.D. Miss. Oct. 11-21, 1967).

23. *See generally* William B. Huie, Three Lives for Mississippi 159 (1968).

24. Douglas O. Linder, *The Mississippi Burning Trial*, Famous Trials, http://law2.umkc.edu/faculty/projects/ftrials/price&bowers/account.html (last visited Apr. 15, 2013).

25. Ronald Maiorana, *Doar to Be Executive Director of Drive to Aid Brooklyn Slum*, N.Y. Times, Dec. 3, 1967, at 36.

26. Roy Reed, *Doar Resigns as Chief of the U.S. Civil Rights Division; Integration Leaders Term Action 'Gigantic Loss,'* N.Y. Times, Nov. 30 1967, at 35; Office of Congressman John Lewis, Congressman John Lewis Keynotes Ceremony Commemorating 40th Anniversary of the Civil Rights Division of Justice (Dec. 8, 1967).

27. Jimmy Breslin, John Doar: Doar Prize (Nov. 28, 2000), *available at* http://goprincetontigers.fansonly.ocsn.com/genrel/080100.aaj.html (last visited Jan. 6, 2003).

28. Wayne Washington, *Doar Honored for Quietly Seeking Justice*, Minneapolis Star Trib., Oct. 27, 1994, at 1B.

29. Linder, *supra* note 7, at 778.

30. Washington, *supra* note 28.

31. *Id.*
32. Linder, *supra* note 7, at 777.
33. *Id.*
34. *Id.* at 778.
35. ROBERT M. PIRSIG, ZEN AND THE ART OF MOTORCYCLE MAINTENANCE 81, 220 (1974).
36. Robert Ervin Cramer et al., *Subject Competence and Minimization of the Bystander Effect*, 18 J. APP. SOC. PSYCHOL. 1133 (1988).
37. Douglas O. Linder, *The Charles Manson (Tate-LaBianca Murder) Trial: Other Key Figures—Ronald Hughes*, Famous Trials http://law2.umkc.edu/faculty/projects/ftrials/manson/mansonothers.html (last visited Apr. 16, 2013).
38. James A. George, *A Plea for Civility: Lawyer's 10-Point Pledge*, TRIAL, May 1988, at 65, 65 (quoting Ernest Hemingway).
39. PETERSON & SELIGMAN, *supra* note 5, at 216–17.
40. Christopher R. Rate, et al., *Implicit Theories of Courage*, 2 J. POSITIVE PSYCHOL. 80, 92–93 (Apr. 2007).
41. PETERSON & SELIGMAN, *supra* note 5, at 214.
42. *Id.* at 228.
43. *Id.* at 222.
44. *Id.* at 225–27. *See also* Cynthia L.S. Pury, *Can Courage Be Learned?*, *in* POSITIVE PSYCHOLOGY: EXPLORING THE BEST IN PEOPLE 109, 118 (Shane J. Lopez ed. 2008).
45. JONATHAN HAIDT, THE HAPPINESS HYPOTHESIS: FINDING MODERN TRUTH IN ANCIENT WISDOM 195–200 (2006).
46. PETERSON & SELIGMAN, *supra* note 5, at 226.
47. ROBERT BISWAS-DIENER, THE COURAGE QUOTIENT: HOW SCIENCE CAN MAKE YOU BRAVER 9 (2012).
48. *Id.* at 55.
49. *Id.* at 79.
50. *Id.* at 81.
51. *Id.* at 113.
52. *Id.* at 127.
53. NORMAN VINCENT PEALE, THE POWER OF POSITIVE THINKING (2003).
54. Leslie E. Sekera & Richard P. Bagozzi, *Moral Courage in the Workplace: Self-Regulation as the Cornerstone to Virtuous Action*, *in* DIMENSIONS OF WELL-BEING: RESEARCH AND INTERVENTION 226, 229 (Antonella Delle Fave ed. 2006).
55. Jesse J. Prinz, *Is Empathy Necessary for Morality?*, *in* EMPATHY: PHILOSOPHICAL AND PSYCHOLOGICAL PERSPECTIVES 211, 212 (Amy Coplan & Peter Goldie eds. 2011).
56. *Id.* at 221.
57. *Id.*

58. Douglas O. Linder, *Law's Heroes—Dr. Lothar Kreyssig* http://law2.umkc.
    edu/faculty/projects/ftrials/trialheroes/HEROSEARCH7.html (last visited
    Apr. 16, 2013).

59. *Id.*

60. INGO MÜLLER, HITLER'S JUSTICE: THE COURTS OF THE THIRD REICH 193
    (1991).

61. MARK CURRIDEN & LEROY PHILLIPS, JR., CONTEMPT OF COURT: THE TURN-OF-
    THE-CENTURY LYNCHING THAT LAUNCHED A HUNDRED YEARS OF FEDERALISM
    136 (1999).

62. *Id.* at 139.

63. *Id.* at 5.

64. *Id.* at 8, 9, 12, 16.

65. *Id.* at 192.

66. *Id.* at 213–14.

67. *Id.* at 335.

68. *Id.* at 336.

69. *Id.* at 131, 132.

70. ROBERT D. PUTNAM & DAVID E. CAMPBELL, AMERICAN GRACE: HOW
    RELIGION UNITES AND DIVIDES US 461 (2012).

71. *Id.* at 473.

72. BISWAS-DIENER, *supra* note 47, at 14–16.

Chapter 3

1. Steven Pinker, *The Sugary Secret of Self Control*, N.Y. TIMES, Sept. 2, 2011, *available at* http://www.nytimes.com/2011/09/04/books/review/willpower-by-
   roy-f-baumeister-and-john-tierney-book-review.html?pagewanted=all.

2. ROY F. BAUMEISTER & JOHN TIERNEY, WILLPOWER: REDISCOVERING THE
   GREATEST HUMAN STRENGTH 2 (2011).

3. Kelly McGonigal develops this idea of the I will/I won't power distinction
   in her book. THE WILLPOWER INSTINCT: HOW SELF-CONTROL WORKS, WHY IT
   MATTERS, AND WHAT YOU CAN DO TO GET MORE OF IT 8–14 (2012).

4. ROBERT M. PIRSIG, ZEN AND THE ART OF MOTORCYCLE MAINTENANCE 296–
   304 (1974).

5. JOHN A. JENKINS, THE LITIGATORS: INSIDE THE POWERFUL WORLD OF AMERICA'S
   HIGH STAKES TRIAL LAWYERS 124 (1989).

6. *Id.* at 123.

7. *Id.* at 125.

8. *Id.* at 136.

9. *Id.*

10. *Id.* at 159.

11. *Id.* at 195.

12. *Id.* at 214 (emphasis in original).

13. *Id.* at 216.

14. *Id.* at 241.

15. McGonigal, *supra* note 3, at 51.

16. Baumeister & Tierney, *supra* note 2, at 62.

17. *Id.* at 63.

18. *Id.* at 77–78 (quoting David Allen).

19. Rick Morris, *The Marathon Wall—What It Is and How to Beat It*, Running Planet, http://www.runningplanet.com/training/marathon-wall-how-to-beat-it.html (last visited May 7, 2013).

20. McGonigal, *supra* note 3, at 186.

21. *Id.* at 196.

22. Baumeister & Tierney, *supra* note 2, at 10.

23. *Id.* at 11.

24. Christopher Peterson & Martin E.P. Seligman, Character Strengths and Virtues: A Handbook and Classification 230 (2004).

25. The Paper Chase (Twentieth Century-Fox Film Corp. 1973).

26. Peterson & Seligman, *supra* note 24, at 231. *See also* Jason M. Satterfield et al., *Law School Performance Predicted by Explanatory Style*, 15 Behav. Sci. & L. 95, 96 (1997).

27. Peterson & Seligman, *supra* note 24, at 231. *See also* Thomas Gilovich, *Biased Evaluation and Persistence in Gambling*, 44 J. Personality & Soc. Psychol. 1110 (1983).

28. Peterson & Seligman, *supra* note 24, at 232; Christopher Peterson & Lisa C. Barrett, *Explanatory Style and Academic Performance among University Freshmen*, 53 J. Personality & Soc. Psychol. 603 (1987); Christopher Peterson et al., *Explanatory Style and Helplessness*, 20 Soc. Behav. & Personality 1 (1992).

29. Peterson & Seligman, *supra* note 24, at 244.

30. Carol Dweck, Mindset: The New Psychology of Success 48–49 (2007).

31. *Id.* at 7.

32. *Id.* at 38.

33. *Id.* at 61.

34. *Id.* at 224.

35. *Id.* at 214–15.

36. *Id.* at 238.

37. *Id.* at 11 (quoting Howard Gardner, Extraordinary Minds (1997)).

38. *See, e.g.,* Kenneth L. Higbee, Your Memory: How It Works and How to Improve It (2001); Harry Lorayne & Jerry Lucas, The Memory Book: The Classic Guide to Improving Your Memory at Work, at School, and at Play (1996); Melissa Mullin, Flexible Thinking Program (2013).

39. Alina Tugend, Better by Mistake: The Unexpected Benefits of Being Wrong 31 (2012).

40. *Id.* at 30.

41. *Id.*

42. PETERSON & SELIGMAN, *supra* note 24, at 233. *See also* Debi M. Starnes & Otto Zinser, *The Effect of Problem Difficulty, Locus of Control, and Sex on Task Persistence*, 108 J. GEN. PSYCHOL. 249 (1983).

43. PETERSON & SELIGMAN, *supra* note 24, at 233.

44. BAUMEISTER & TIERNEY, *supra* note 2, at 136.

45. MCGONIGAL, *supra* note 3, at 143–45.

46. *Id.* at 83–87.

47. Sybil Dunlop, *When Willpower and Decision-Making Abilities Decline*, LAWYERIST, Jan. 29, 2013, http://lawyerist.com/when-willpower-declines/.

48. BAUMEISTER & TIERNEY, *supra* note 2, at 99.

49. Shai Danziger, et al., *Extraneous Factors in Judicial Decisions*, 108 PROC. NAT'L ACAD. SCI. 6889 (Apr. 26, 2011).

50. Alexander Lee et al., *Queue Position in the Endoscopic Schedule Impacts Effectiveness of Colonoscopy*, 106 AM. J. GASTROENTEROLOGY 1457 (Aug. 2011).

51. Melanie C. Wright et al., *Time of Day Effects on the Incidence of Anesthetic Adverse Events*, 15 QUALITY & SAFETY IN HEATH CARE 258 (2006).

52. MCGONIGAL, *supra* note 3, at 31.

53. BAUMEISTER & TIERNEY, *supra* note 2, at 49.

54. *Id.* at 51.

55. *Id.* at 45–46.

56. *Id.* at 59.

57. *Id.* at 60.

58. MCGONIGAL, *supra* note 3, at 46.

59. *Id.* at 42.

60. *Id.* at 11.

61. BAUMEISTER & TIERNEY, *supra* note 2, at 180.

62. *Id.*

63. MCGONIGAL, *supra* note 3, at 24–26.

64. PHILIP ZIMBARDO & JOHN BOYD, THE TIME PARADOX: THE NEW PSYCHOLOGY OF TIME THAT WILL CHANGE YOUR LIFE 156–57 (2008).

65. *See* MIHALY CSIKSZENTMIHALYI, FINDING FLOW: THE PSYCHOLOGY OF ENGAGEMENT WITH EVERYDAY LIFE (1997).

66. Harvey Mackay, *Don't Let Boredom Cramp Your Style*, July 21, 2011, http://harveymackay.com/column/don%E2%80%99t-let-boredom-cramp-your-style/.

67. Kevin Houchin, *Procrastination and Boredom, Evil Twins*, LAWYERIST, Jan. 31, 2011, http://lawyerist.com/procrastination-and-boredom-evil-twins/.

68. G. Andrew H. Benjamin et al., *The Prevalence of Depression, Alcohol Abuse, and Cocaine Abuse among United States Lawyers*, 13 INT'L J.L. & PSYCHIATRY 233, 236–41 (1990); *See also* Connie J. A. Beck, Bruce D. Sales, & G. Andrew H. Benjamin, *Lawyer Distress: Alcohol-Related Problems and Other Psychological Concerns among a Sample of Practicing Lawyers*, 10 J.L. & HEALTH 1, 5–6 (1996).

69. PETERSON & SELIGMAN, *supra* note 24, at 495.

70. Marina Krakovsky, *All about Willpower*, STAN. MAG., Sept.–Oct. 2011, at 29.
71. McGONIGAL, *supra* note 3, at 168.
72. STEPHEN S. HALL, WISDOM: FROM PHILOSOPHY TO NEUROSCIENCE 173 (2010).
73. *Id.* at 188.
74. McGONIGAL, *supra* note 3, at 237.
75. *Id.* at 178.
76. ZIMBARDO & BOYD, *supra* note 64, at 24.
77. *Id.* at 137.
78. *Id.* at 153.
79. *Id.* at 302.

Chapter 4

1. Stephen D. Easton, *My Last Lecture: Unsolicited Advice for Future and Current Lawyers*, 56 S.C. L. REV. 229, 237 (2004).
2. *Id.* at 51.
3. *See* WILLIAM LEE MILLER, LINCOLN'S VIRTUES: AN ETHICAL BIOGRAPHY 410–17 (2002).
4. Robert F. Blomquist, *The Pragmatically Virtuous Lawyer*, 15 WIDENER L. REV. 93, 115 (2009).
5. STEPHEN S. HALL, WISDOM: FROM PHILOSOPHY TO Neuroscience 138 (2010).
6. *Id.* at 140.
7. Blomquist, *supra* note 4, at 116 (quoting THE WIT AND WISDOM OF ABRAHAM LINCOLN: AN A–Z COMPENDIUM OF QUOTES FROM THE MOST ELOQUENT OF AMERICAN PRESIDENTS 115 (Alex Ayers, ed., 1992)).
8. Jonathon D. Brown & Chihiro Kobayashi, *Motivation and Manifestation: Cross-cultural Expression of the Self-enhancement Motive*, 6 ASIAN J. SOC. PSYCHOL. 85, 87 (2003).
9. CHRISTOPHER PETERSON & MARTIN E. P. SELIGMAN, CHARACTER STRENGTHS AND VIRTUES: A HANDBOOK AND CLASSIFICATION 474 (2004).
10. SUSAN CAIN, QUIET: THE POWER OF INTROVERTS IN A WORLD THAT CAN'T STOP TALKING 215 (2012).
11. *Id.* at 7–9.
12. *See generally* Yale Law School, *The Cultural Cognition Project*, http://www.culturalcognition.net (last visited May 24, 2013).
13. INSIDE THE SUPREME COURT (PBS 2006).
14. ROBERT M. PIRSIG, ZEN AND THE ART OF MOTORCYCLE MAINTENANCE 308 (1974).
15. Stephen S. Hall, *The Older-and-Wiser Hypothesis*, N.Y. TIMES, May 6, 2007, *available at* http://www.nytimes.com/2007/05/06/magazine/06Wisdom-t.html?pagewanted=all.
16. *Id.*
17. Erik P. Kimball, *Professionalism: The Road to Contentment*, AM. BANKR. INST. J. 52, 53 (Nov. 2011).

18. MODERN LITIGATION AND PROFESSIONAL RESPONSIBILITY HANDBOOK 279 (William H. Fortune et al. eds. 2001).

19. STEPHEN L. CARTER, CIVILITY: MANNERS, MORALS, AND THE ETIQUETTE OF DEMOCRACY 286 (1998).

20. *Id.*

21. Jonathan Macey, *Occupation Code 541110: Lawyers, Self-Regulation, and the Idea of a Profession*, 74 FORDHAM L. REV. 1079, 1081 n.6 (2005) (quoting Marvin E. Aspen, *The Search for Renewed Civility in Litigation*, 28 VAL. U. L. REV. 513, 518 (1994)).

22. Macey, *supra* note 21, at 1082.

23. Brian Sullivan, *The Last Word*, A.B.A. J., Jan. 2012, at 51, 52.

24. G. M. Filisko, *You're Out of Order! Dealing with the Costs of Incivility in the Legal Profession*, A.B.A. J., Jan. 2013, at 33, 37.

25. Milton S. Gould, *Oral Argument Losing Its Appeal*, 8 J. SEC. LITIGATION, A.B.A. 3 (Spring 1982) (quoting WILLIAM H. HARBAUGH, LAWYER'S LAWYER: THE LIFE OF JOHN W. DAVIS 127 (1973)).

26. HARBAUGH, *supra* note 25, at 482.

27. *Id.* at 60.

28. R. Michael Wells, *A Lawyer's Creation Story—John W. Davis*, Wells Jenkins (Mar. 10, 2011), http://www.wellsjenkins.com/legal-blog.asp?blog-id=705999490.

29. ANTHONY KRONMAN, THE LOST LAWYER: FAILING IDEALS OF THE LEGAL PROFESSION 93–101 (1993).

30. *Id.* at 93, 94.

31. *Id.* at 95.

32. *Id.* at 99, 101.

33. Adam Wahlberg, *Q & A: Ted Olson*, Washington DC Super Lawyers (May 2012), *available at* http://www.superlawyers.com/washington-dc/article/QandA-Ted-Olson/f9f423d9-a608-4dc4-a329-a0e85aa7c8a4.html.

34. Aspen Institute, *Sexual Orientation, Civil Rights, and American Opinion*, Aspen Ideas Festival 9, http://www.aspenideas.org/sites/default/files/transcripts/aif10_004.pdf (last visited Apr. 30, 2013).

35. Wahlberg, *supra* note 33.

36. *Id.*

37. Jo Becker, *A Conservative's Road to Same-Sex Marriage Advocacy*, N.Y. TIMES, Aug. 18, 2009, *available at* http://www.nytimes.com/2009/08/19/us/19olson.html?pagewanted=all&_r=0.

38. Nina Totenberg, *Ted Olson, Gay Marriage's Unlikely Legal Warrior*, Talk of the Nation, NPR (Dec. 6, 2010), *available at* http://www.npr.org/2010/12/06/131792296/ted-olson-gay-marriage-s-unlikely-legal-warrior.

39. Becker, *supra* note 37.

40. Robert Barnes, *Olson Surprises Many Conservatives by Seeking to Overturn Gay Marriage Ban*, WASH. POST, June 14, 2010, *available at* http://www.washingtonpost.com/wp-dyn/content/article/2010/06/13/AR2010061305057.html.

41. Totenberg, *supra* note 38.

42. Becker, *supra* note 37.

43. The Court ruled, after state officials refused to appeal a district court decision finding Proposition 8 to be unconstitutional, that proponents of the ban on gay marriage lacked standing to appeal. Hollingsworth v. Perry, 133 S. Ct. 2652 (June 26, 2013). *See also Paul Katami and Jeff Zarillo Wed Live on MSNBC*, Rachel Maddow Show (June 28, 2013), http://video.msnbc.msn.com/rachel-maddow-show/52346811#52346811.

44. Alan M. Dershowitz, Letters to a Young Lawyer 165 (2005).

45. Piers Morgan Tonight, *Interview with Antonin Scalia*, CNN, July 18, 2012, *available at* http://transcripts.cnn.com/TRANSCRIPTS/1207/18/pmt.01.html.

46. Jonathan Haidt, The Righteous Mind: Why Good People Are Divided by Politics and Religion 370, 129, 330 (2012).

47. Ryota Kanai et al., *Political Orientations Are Correlated with Brain Structure in Young Adults*, 21 Current Biology 677, 678 (Apr. 26, 2011).

48. Janet Fang, *Gray Matter: Liberal Brains vs. Conservative Brains*, Apr. 7, 2011, SmartPlanet, http://www.smartplanet.com/blog/rethinking-healthcare/gray-matter-liberal-brains-vs-conservative-brains/3896.

49. *Brain Structure Differs in Liberals, Conservatives: Study*, Agence France-Presse, Apr. 7, 2011, http://www.google.com/hostednews/afp/article/ALeqM5iISI7ifh-AjUE3ejyC1wQmwFrMFw.

50. Yoel Inbar et al., *Conservatives Are More Easily Disgusted than Liberals*, 23 Cognition & Emotion 714 (2009); Douglas R. Oxley et al., *Political Attitudes Vary with Physiological Traits*, Science, Sept. 19, 2008, at 1667.

51. Haidt, *supra* note 46, at 19.

52. *Id.* at 297, 306.

53. *See* Talia Bar & Asaf Zussman, *Partisan Grading*, 4 Am. Econ. J.: Applied Econ. 30 (Jan. 2012).

54. Haidt, *supra* note 46, at 297–309.

55. *The Credit Card Lobby, Wal-Mart's Politicking and More in Capital Eye Opener*, OpenSecrets Blog, Apr. 13, 2011, 2011 WLNR 7231347.

56. *Lawyers/Law Firms: Top Contributors, 2011–2012*, OpenSecrets, Mar. 25, 2013, http://www.opensecrets.org/industries/indus.php?ind=K01.

57. Haidt, *supra* note 46, at 312.

58. *Id.* at 90.

59. Ilona Bray & Richard Stim, The Judge Who Hated Red Nail Polish: and Other Crazy but True Stories of Law and Lawyers 25 (2010).

Chapter 5

1. Daniel Kahneman, Thinking Fast and Slow 11 (2011) (quoting Herbert A. Simon).

2. *See generally id.*

3. *Id.* at 79.

4. Jonathan Haidt, The Righteous Mind: Why Good People Are Divided by Politics and Religion 67 (2012).

5. Kahneman, *supra* note 1, at 103.

6. Haidt, *supra* note 4, at 81.

7. Douglas Linder, *The State of Ohio versus Sam Sheppard—October 18, 1954*, Famous Trials (2006), http://law2.umkc.edu/faculty/projects/ftrials/sheppard/1954 TrialAccount.htm.

8. Douglas Linder, *Dr. Sam Sheppard Trials: 1954 and 1966*, Famous Trials (2006), http://law2.umkc.edu/faculty/projects/ftrials/sheppard/samsheppardtrial. html.

9. F. Lee Bailey, The Defense Never Rests 109 (1971).

10. Douglas O. Linder, *The Dr. Sam Sheppard Trial*, Famous Trials (2006), http://law2.umkc.edu/faculty/projects/ftrials/sheppard/sheppardaccount.html.

11. *Id.*

12. *Id.*

13. Malcolm Gladwell, Blink: The Power of Thinking without Thinking 3–8 (2007).

14. David Brooks, The Social Animal: The Hidden Sources of Love, Character, and Achievement 88 (2011).

15. Elkhonon Goldberg, The Wisdom Paradox: How Your Mind Can Grow Stronger as Your Brain Grows Older 9 (2006).

16. William Arthur Wines, *Observations on Leadership: Moral and Otherwise*, 43 J. Marshall L. Rev. 159, 168 (2009).

17. Goldberg, *supra* note 15, at 154.

18. *Id.* at 155.

19. *Id.* at 212.

20. *Id.* at 213.

21. Barry Schwartz & Kenneth Sharpe, Practical Wisdom: The Right Way to Do the Right Thing 82 (2011).

22. Kahneman, *supra* note 1, at 105.

23. Thomas Gilovich, How We Know What Isn't So: The Fallibility of Human Reason in Everyday Life 84 (1991) (emphasis in original).

24. Haidt, *supra* note 4, at 90.

25. Ludwig Wittgenstein, On Certainty 3e (Gertrude Elizabeth Margaret Anscombe & George Henrik von Wright eds. 1969).

26. Kathryn Schulz, Being Wrong: Adventures in the Margin of Error 82 (2010).

27. *Id.* at 83.

28. Gregory R. Maio & Geoffrey Haddock, The Psychology of Attitudes and Attitude Change 49 (2010).

29. Haidt, *supra* note 4, at 76.

30. Keith E. Stanovich et al., *Intelligence and Rationality, in* The Cambridge Handbook of Intelligence 784, 792 (Robert J. Sternberg & Scott Barry Kaufman eds. 2011).

31. HAIDT, *supra* note 4, at 47.

32. ALAN W. WATTS, THE JOYOUS COSMOLOGY: ADVENTURES IN THE CHEMISTRY OF CONSCIOUSNESS 27 (1962).

33. CHRISTOPHER CHABRIS & DANIEL SIMONS, THE INVISIBLE GORILLA: AND OTHER WAYS OUR INTUITIONS DECEIVE US 31 (2010).

34. Christopher Chabris, *Missing the 200-Pound Gorilla in the Room*, June 23, 2010, at http://bigthink.com/videos/missing-the-200-pound-gorilla-in-the-room.

35. *See* BROOKS, *supra* note 14, at 95; John Kounios & Mark Beeman, *The Aha! Moment: The Cognitive Neuroscience of Insight*, 18 CURRENT DIRECTIONS IN PSYCHOL. SCI. 210, 212 (2009).

36. ROBERT A. BURTON, ON BEING CERTAIN: BELIEVING YOU ARE RIGHT EVEN WHEN YOU'RE NOT 187 (2008).

37. KAHNEMAN, *supra* note 1, at 87.

38. *Id.*

39. PAMELA CORLEY ET AL., THE PUZZLE OF UNANIMITY: CONSENSUS ON THE SUPREME COURT 96 (2013).

40. KAHNEMAN, *supra* note 1, at 324–25.

41. Amos Tversky & Daniel Kahneman, *Judgment under Uncertainty: Heuristics and Biases*, 185 SCIENCE 1124 (1974), *reprinted in* JUDGMENT UNDER UNCERTAINTY: HEURISTICS AND BIASES 14–16 (Daniel Kahneman et al. eds., 1982).

42. KAHNEMAN, *supra* note 1, at 331–32.

43. *See* IAT Corp., Project Implicit, https://implicit.harvard.edu/implicit/demo/ (last visited Apr. 10, 2013). *See generally* Brian A. Nose et al., *Harvesting Implicit Group Attitudes and Beliefs from a Demonstration Web Site*, 6 GROUP DYNAMICS 101 (2002) (reporting the results from more than 600,000 individual responses from takers of the Implicit Association Test).

44. *See, e.g.,* William A. Cunningham, et al., *Separable Neural Components in the Processing of Black and White Faces*, 15 PSYCHOL. SCI. 806 (2004).

45. INDICTMENT: THE MCMARTIN TRIAL (TV 1995).

46. HAIDT, *supra* note 4, at 59.

47. BURTON, *supra* note 36, at 159.

48. CAROL DWECK, MINDSET: THE NEW PSYCHOLOGY OF SUCCESS 213 (2007).

Chapter 6

1. Jane Goodman-Delahunty et al., *Insightful or Wishful: Lawyers' Ability to Predict Case Outcomes*, 16 J. PSYCHOL., PUB. POL'Y & L. 134, 135 (2012).

2. *Id.* at 139.

3. *Id.*

4. *Id.* at 141.

5. *Id.* at 142–43.

6. Lawrence R. Richard, *Psychological Type and Job Satisfaction among Practicing Lawyers in the United States*, 29 CAP. U. L. REV. 979, 1015 (2002).

7. Goodman-Delahunty et al., *supra* note 1, at 146–47.

8. *See* Daniel T. Gilbert et al., *Immune Neglect: A Source of Durability Bias in Affective Forecasting*, 75 J. PERSONALITY & SOC. PSYCHOL. 617, 619 (1998).

9. Goodman-Delahunty et al., *supra* note 1, at 134.

10. GERALD R. WILLIAMS, LEGAL NEGOTIATION AND SETTLEMENT 5v6 (1983).

11. Goodman-Delahunty et al., *supra* note 1, at 135.

12. *Id.* at 135

13. *Id.* (quoting Don A. Moore & Paul J. Healy, *The Trouble with Overconfidence*, 115 PSYCHOL. REV. 502, 504 (2008)).

14. *Id.* at 150.

15. *Id.*

16. *Id.* (quoting Elisha Babad et al., *Factors Influencing Wishful Thinking and Predictions of Election Outcomes*, 13 BASIC & APPLIED SOC. PSYCHOL. 461, 471 (1992)).

17. DANIEL KAHNEMAN, THINKING FAST AND SLOW 204 (2011).

18. *Id.* at 194.

19. KAHNEMAN, *supra* note 17, at 204–5.

20. *Id.* at 249.

21. *See* David A. Logan, *Libel Law in the Trenches*, 87 VA. L. REV. 503, 510, 513, 515 (2001).

22. KAHNEMAN, *supra* note 17, at 250.

23. *Id.*

24. *Id.* at 223.

25. *Id.* at 241.

26. MARJORIE CORMAN AARON, CLIENT SCIENCE: ADVICE FOR LAWYERS ON COUNSELING CLIENTS THROUGH BAD NEWS AND OTHER LEGAL REALITIES 162 (2012).

27. KAHNEMAN, *supra* note 17, at 231–32.

28. *See* Roy E. Hofer, *Supreme Court Reversal Rates: Evaluating the Federal Courts of Appeal*, 2 LANDSLIDE (Feb. 2010), *available at* http://www.americanbar.org/content/dam/aba/migrated/intelprop/magazine/LandslideJan2010_Hofer.authcheckdam.pdf.

29. Randall L. Kiser et al., *Let's Not Make a Deal: An Empirical Study of Decision Making in Unsuccessful Settlement Negotiations*, 5 J. EMPIRICAL LEGAL STUD. 551, 579 (2008); *see also* RANDALL KISER, HOW LEADING LAWYERS THINK: EXPERT INSIGHTS INTO JUDGMENT AND ADVOCACY (2011).

30. NATE SILVER, THE SIGNAL AND THE NOISE: WHY SO MANY PREDICTIONS FAIL—BUT SOME DON'T 66 (2012).

31. Brian Benton, *Lex Machina: "Law Machine" Helps Lawyers Predict Case Outcomes*, PALOALTOPATCH, July 30, 2012, *available at* https://lexmachina.com/2012/07.

32. Sharon Driscoll, *A Positive Disruption: The Transformation of Law through Technology*, STAN. LAW., Spring 2013, at 21.

33. *Id.*

34. *Id.*

35. *Id.*

36. Lex Machina, *Testimonials* (2012), https://lexmachina.com/testimonials/.

37. Tam Harbert, *Can Computers Predict Trial Outcomes from Big Data?,* Law.com, July 3, 2012.

38. Ron Friedmann & David Post, *Litigation Risk Analysis*, LEGAL TECH. NEWSL. (Dec. 1990), *available at* http://www.prismlegal.com/index.php?option=content&task=view&id=54&Itemid=58.

39. Amos Tversky & Daniel Kahneman, *Extensional versus Intuitive Reasoning: The Conjunctive Fallacy in Probability Judgment*, 90 PSYCHOL. REV. 293 (1983).

40. Kiser et al., *supra* note 29, at 566.

41. Amos Tversky & Daniel Kahneman, *Judgment under Uncertainty: Heuristics and Biases*, 185 SCIENCE 1124, 1129 (1974).

42. Friedmann & Post, *supra* note 38.

43. Deborah L. Cohen, *Not Playing Games*, 99 A.B.A. J. 25, 26 (Jan. 2013).

44. DANIEL GILBERT, STUMBLING ON HAPPINESS 4 (2007).

45. *Id.*

46. *Id.* at 76–83.

47. *Id.* at 16.

48. *Id.* at 15.

49. *Id.* at 19.

50. *Id.* at 3–24, 89–91, 105–6, 127–47, 175–84.

51. *Id.* at 162.

52. *See* David Lykken & Auke Tellegen, *Happiness Is a Stochastic Phenomenon*, 7 PSYCHOL. SCI. 186 (May 1996), *available at* http:// www.psych.umn.edu/psylabs/happness/happy.htm ("From 44% to 53% of the variance in [well-being], however, is associated with genetic variation. Based on the retest of smaller samples of twins after intervals of 4.5 and 10 years, we estimate that the heritability of the stable component of subjective wellbeing approaches 80%").

53. George A. Quattrone & Amos Tversky, *Contrasting Rational and Psychological Analyses of Political Choice, in* CHOICES, VALUES, AND FRAMES 451, 458 (Daniel Kahneman & Amos Tversky eds., 2000).

54. GILBERT, *supra* note 44, at 14.

55. STEPHEN S. HALL, WISDOM: FROM PHILOSOPHY TO NEUROSCIENCE 48 (2011).

56. GILBERT, *supra* note 44, at 223.

57. *Id.* at 224.

58. *Id.* at 223.

59. NANCY LEVIT & DOUGLAS O. LINDER, THE HAPPY LAWYER: MAKING A GOOD LIFE IN THE LAW 37–38, 44–45, 171–72 (2010).

60. *See, e.g.,* Hal Ersner-Hershfield et al., *Don't Stop Thinking about Tomorrow: Individual Differences in Future Self-Continuity Account for Saving*, 4 JUDGMENT & DECISION MAKING 280 (2009); Shane Frederick et al., *Time*

Discounting and Time Preference: A Critical Review, 40 J. ECON. LITERATURE 351 (2002).

61. HALL, *supra* note 55, at 184.

62. CHARLIE WILSON'S WAR (Paramount 2007).

63. John Meacham, *The Loss of Wisdom, in* WISDOM: ITS NATURE, ORIGINS, AND DEVELOPMENT 181 (Robert J. Sternberg ed. 1990).

Chapter 7

1. ANTHONY KRONMAN, THE LOST LAWYER: FAILING IDEALS OF THE LEGAL PROFESSION 123 (1993).

2. *Id.* at 129.

3. Interview with Orville Bloethe (Sept. 2012) (Names in this story have been changed).

4. THOMAS SHAFFER & ROBERT COCHRAN JR., LAWYERS, CLIENTS, AND MORAL RESPONSIBILITY 3, 40–54 (2009).

5. *Id.* at 30–39.

6. *Id.* at 4.

7. Steven J. Overman, *"Winning Isn't Everything. It's the Only Thing": The Origins, Attributions and Influence of a Famous Football Quote*, 2 FOOTBALL STUD. 77, 82–83 (Oct. 1999).

8. Tom Jones, *Winning*, ST. PETERSBURG TIMES, Mar. 13, 2011, at 2C.

9. THE GODFATHER (Paramount Pictures 1972).

10. SHAFFER & COCHRAN, *supra* note 4, at 12–13.

11. *Id.* at 9.

12. Monroe H. Freedman, *Personal Responsibility in a Professional System*, 27 CATH. U. L. REV. 191, 204 (1978).

13. Deborah L. Rhode, *Ethical Perspectives on Legal Practice*, 37 STAN. L. REV. 589, 623 (1985).

14. ROBERT BOLT, A MAN FOR ALL SEASONS 132 (Vintage Int'l ed. 1990).

15. SHAFFER & COCHRAN, *supra* note 4, at 29 (quoting RAND JACK & DANA CROWLEY JACK, MORAL VISION AND PROFESSIONAL DECISIONS: THE CHANGING VALUES OF WOMEN AND MEN LAWYERS 112 (1989)).

16. *Id.*

17. RICHARD SUSSKIND, THE END OF LAWYERS? RETHINKING THE NATURE OF LEGAL SERVICES 150 (2010) (emphasis in original).

18. *Id.*

19. SHAFFER & COCHRAN, *supra* note 4, at 40–54.

20. KRONMAN, *supra* note 1, at 299.

21. *Id.*

22. MARTIN BUBER, I AND THOU (Walter Kaufmann trans., 1970).

23. JAMES GLEICK, CHAOS: THE MAKING OF A NEW SCIENCE (1987).

24. Nelson P. Miller, *Meta-Ethical Competence as a Lawyer Skill: Variant Ethics Affecting Lawyer and Client Decision-Making*, 9 T. M. Cooley J. Prac. & Clinical L. 91, 110 (2007).

25. The Law Society of British Columbia, *2010 Law Society Commissioned Public Opinion Poll on Lawyers and Effectiveness of Law Society*, http://www.lawsociety.bc.ca/newsroom/2010lawsocietycommissionedpoll_table.pdf.

26. Lucie White, *Subordination, Rhetorical Survival Skills and Sunday Shoes: Notes on the Hearing of Mrs. G.*, 38 Buff. L. Rev. 1 (1990).

27. *Id.* at 32.

28. Russell Korobkin & Chris Guthrie, *Psychological Barriers to Litigation Settlement: An Experimental Approach*, 93 Mich. L. Rev. 107, 130 (1994) (citing Daniel Kahneman & Amos Tversky, *Prospect Theory: An Analysis of Decision under Risk*, 47 Econometrica 263, 263–64, 187, 197 (1979)).

29. William M. Sullivan et al., Educating Lawyers: Preparation for the Profession of Law 11 (2007) (the "Carnegie Report").

Chapter 8

1. Lawrence Lessig, *A Message to Law Grads: Instead of Corporations, Help Ordinary People*, Atlantic (May 31, 2012), *available at* http://www.theatlantic.com/national/archive/2012/05/a-message-to-law-grads-instead-of-corporations-help-ordinary-people/257945/.

2. *Be Heroes, Not Victims, Justice Thomas Tells UGA Grads*, Atlanta J.-Const., May 18, 2003, *available at* http://www.freerepublic.com/focus/f-news/913937/posts.

3. Judith Resnik & Dennis Curtis, Representing Justice: Invention, Controversy, and Rights in City-States and Democratic Courtrooms 126 (2011).

4. *Id.* at 373.

5. *Id.*

6. Randy Kennedy, *The Lady with the Scales Poses for Her Portraits*, N.Y. Times, Dec. 15, 2010, *available at* http://www.nytimes.com/2010/12/16/books/16justice.html?_r=0.

7. Resnik & Curtis, *supra* note 3, at 377.

8. 372 U.S. 335, 344 (1963).

9. Laurel Bellows, *The "Obvious Truth,"* A.B.A. J., Mar. 2013, at 8.

10. Mark Walsh, *Living Up to the* Gideon *Ideal*, A.B.A. J., Mar. 2013, 45, 46.

11. *Id.* at 48.

12. Lessig, *supra* note 1.

13. *Id.*

14. Deborah L. Rhode, *Access to Justice: An Agenda for Legal Education and Research*, 62 J. Legal Educ. 531 (May 2013).

15. Ethan Bronner, *No Lawyer for Miles, So One Rural State Offers to Pay*, N.Y. TIMES, Apr. 9, 2013, at 1.

16. Lessig, *supra* note 1.

17. Rhode, *supra* note 14, at 546.

18. *Id.* at 549.

19. *Id.* at 550.

20. NANCY LEVIT & DOUGLAS O. LINDER, THE HAPPY LAWYER: MAKING A GOOD LIFE IN THE LAW 50–53, 106–08 (2010); TOM W. SMITH, NATIONAL OPINION RESEARCH CENTER/UNIVERSITY OF CHICAGO, JOB SATISFACTION IN THE UNITED STATES (Apr. 17, 2007).

21. AMERICAN BAR ASSOCIATION, YOUNG LAWYERS DIVISION, ABA YOUNG LAWYERS DIVISION SURVEY: CAREER SATISFACTION 17 (2000), *available at* www.abanet.org/yld/satisfaction_ 800.doc.

22. Deborah Rhode, *Foreword: Personal Satisfaction in Professional Practice*, 58 SYRACUSE L. REV. 217, 224 (2008).

23. EDUARDO PUNSET, THE HAPPINESS TRIP: A SCIENTIFIC JOURNEY 41 (2007).

24. WALTER OLSON, SCHOOLS FOR MISRULE: LEGAL ACADEMIA AND AN OVERLAWYERED AMERICA 24 (2011).

25. *Deuteronomy* 16:21.

26. ALAN M. DERSHOWITZ, LETTERS TO A YOUNG LAWYER 50 (2005).

27. THOMAS L. SHAFFER & MARY M. SHAFFER, AMERICAN LAWYERS AND THEIR COMMUNITIES: ETHICS IN THE LEGAL PROFESSION 214 (1991).

28. *Id.* at 202–3 (emphasis in original).

29. ARTHUR WEINBERG & LILA WEINBERG, CLARENCE DARROW VERDICTS OUT OF COURT 312 (1963).

30. *Id.* at 428.

31. SMITH, *supra* note 20.

32. John W. Davis, Address at the 75th Anniversary Proceedings of the Association of the Bar of the City of New York, Mar. 16, 1946.

33. BERNHARD SCHLINK, SUMMER LIES 127 (2012).

34. THE THIN BLUE LINE (Miramax Films 1988).

35. *Id.*

36. KATHRYN SCHULZ, BEING WRONG: ADVENTURES IN THE MARGIN OF ERROR 240–41 (2010).

37. DERSHOWITZ, *supra* note 26, at 140.

38. *Id.* at 150.

39. JONATHAN HAIDT, THE RIGHTEOUS MIND: WHY GOOD PEOPLE ARE DIVIDED BY POLITICS AND RELIGION 192 (2012) (quoting CHARLES DARWIN, THE DESCENT OF MAN 156 (1871)).

40. *Id.* at 195 (quoting DARWIN, *supra* note 39, at 137).

41. *Id.* at 198.

42. *Id.*

43. David Brooks, *Nice Guys Finish First*, N.Y. TIMES, May 17, 2011, at A25.

44. Joshua D. Greene et al., *An fMRI Investigation of Emotional Engagement in Moral Judgment*, 293 SCIENCE 2105 (Sept. 14, 2001). *See also* Peter Saalfield, *The Biology of Right and Wrong*, HARV. MAG., Jan.–Feb. 2012, *available at* http://harvardmagazine.com/2012/01/the-biology-of-right-and-wrong.

45. Greene et al., *supra* note 44, at 2107.

46. THEODORE REIK, LISTENING WITH THE THIRD EAR vii (1949).

47. Douglas O. Linder, *Bending toward Justice: John Doar and the "Mississippi Burning" Trial*, 72 MISS. L.J. 731,748 (2002) (Telephone Interview with Howard A. Glickstein, Dean, Touro Law School (Sept. 25, 1999)).

48. *Id.*

49. Stephen Wizner, *Is Learning to "Think like a Lawyer" Enough?*, 17 YALE L. & POL'Y REV. 583, 583 (1998) (quoting Abraham Lincoln, *Fragment: Notes for a Law Lecture*, July 1, 1850, *in* 4 THE COLLECTED WORKS OF ABRAHAM LINCOLN 82 (Roy P. Basler et al. eds., 1953)).

50. *Honesty/Ethics in Professions*, Gallup Poll (Nov. 28–Dec. 1, 2011), http://www.gallup.com/poll/1654/honesty-ethics-professions.aspx.

51. John Day, *What It Takes to Be a Great Trial Lawyer—Part 6*, Day on Torts (Jan. 28, 2008), http://www.dayontorts.com/cat-what-it-takes-to-be-a-great-trial-lawyer.html.

52. DAN ARIELY, THE (HONEST) TRUTH ABOUT DISHONESTY: HOW WE LIE TO EVERYONE—ESPECIALLY OURSELVES 23 (2012).

53. Winston S. Churchill, *Speech at the House of Commons* (Nov. 11, 1947), *in* 2 WINSTON S. CHURCHILL: HIS COMPLETE SPEECHES, 1897–1963, at 7563, 7566 (Robert Rhodes James ed., 1974).

54. STEPHEN L. CARTER, INTEGRITY 112 (1996).

55. *Id.* at 120.

56. ARIELY, *supra* note 52, at 88.

57. *Id.* at 106.

58. *Id.* at 222.

59. *Id.* at 226.

60. *Id.* at 172

61. *Id.* at 130.

62. *Id.* at 50.

63. *Id.* at 215.

64. Powell v. Alabama, 287 U.S. 45 (1932).

65. F. Raymond Daniell, *New York Attacked in Scottsboro Trial*, N.Y. TIMES, Apr. 8, 1933; DECATUR DAILY, Apr. 8, 1933; BIRMINGHAM NEWS, Apr. 8, 1933.

66. F. Raymond Daniell, *Jury Out with Scottsboro Case; Judge Warns of Bigotry and Racial Issues*, N.Y. TIMES, Apr. 9, 1933.

67. F. Raymond Daniell, *Negro Found Guilty in Scottsboro Case; Jury Out 22 Hours*, N.Y. TIMES, Apr. 10, 1933.

68. DAN T. CARTER, SCOTTSBORO: TRAGEDY OF THE AMERICAN SOUTH 264 (1969).

69. Opinion of Judge Horton (reprinted in HAYWOOD PATTERSON & EARL CONRAD, SCOTTSBORO BOY 260–78 (2008) and on file with the Horton Files, Records of Judge Horton, Samford University, Birmingham).

70. *Id.*

71. JOHN TEMPLETON GRAVES II, THE FIGHTING SOUTH 208–9 (1943).

72. *Athens Lawyers Petition Judge Horton* (advertisement)(on file with the Horton Files, Records of Judge Horton, Samford University, Birmingham); *see also* Gillian W. Goodich, James Edwin Horton Jr.: Scottsboro Judge 21–25 (1974) (unpublished Master's thesis, University of Alabama-Birmingham) (on file with authors).

73. John Temple Graves II, *Scottsboro Judges Ask Re-Election*, N.Y. TIMES, Jan. 14, 1934, at 6.

74. Opinion of Judge Horton, *supra* note 69.

Chapter 9

1. *See, e.g.,* ROGER FISHER ET AL., GETTING TO YES: NEGOTIATING AN AGREEMENT WITHOUT GIVING IN (2d ed. 1991); BRYAN A. GARNER, THE WINNING BRIEF: 100 TIPS FOR PERSUASIVE BRIEFING IN TRIAL AND APPELLATE COURTS (2004); G. RICHARD SCHELL, BARGAINING FOR ADVANTAGE: NEGOTIATION STRATEGIES FOR REASONABLE PEOPLE (2d. ed. 2006); THE 12 SECRETS OF PERSUASIVE ARGUMENTS (JoAnne A. Epps et al., eds. 2010).

2. GERRY SPENCE, HOW TO ARGUE AND WIN EVERY TIME 202–4 (1995).

3. DAVID BALL, THEATER TIPS AND STRATEGIES FOR JURY TRIALS 41–56 (2003).

4. ROBERT B. CIALDINI, INFLUENCE: SCIENCE AND PRACTICE (2008).

5. *How to Be Persuasive*, WikiHow, http://www.wikihow.com/Be-Persuasive (last visited May 7, 2013).

6. *See, e.g.,* LAW AND NEUROSCIENCE: CURRENT LEGAL ISSUES (Michael Freeman, ed., 2010); Kathryn Abrams & Hila Keren, *Who's Afraid of Law and the Emotions?*, 94 MINN. L. REV. 1997 (2010); Susan A. Bandes, *The Promise and Pitfalls of Neuroscience for Criminal Law and Procedure*, 8 OHIO ST. J. CRIM. L. 119 (2010); E. Spencer Compton, *Not Guilty by Reason of Neuroimaging: The Need for Cautionary Jury Instructions for Neuroscience Evidence in Criminal Trials*, 12 VAND. J. ENT. & TECH. L. 333 (2010); Brent Garland & Paul W. Glimcher, *Cognitive Neuroscience and the Law*, 16 NEUROBIOLOGY 130 (2006); Daniel A. Martell, *Neuroscience and the Law: Philosophical Differences and Practical Constraints*, 27 BEHAV. SCI. & L. 123 (2009); Terry A. Maroney, *Adolescent Brain Science after Graham v. Florida*, 85 NOTRE DAME L. REV. 765 (2010).

7. Douglas O. Linder, *Bending toward Justice: John Doar and the "Mississippi Burning" Trial*, 72 MISS. L.J. 731, 748 (2002) (Telephone Interview with Howard A. Glickstein, Dean, Touro Law School (Sept. 25, 1999)).

8. SPENCE, *supra* note 2, at 47.

9. LOUIS NIZER, MY LIFE IN COURT 11 (1944).

10. Robert M. Gates, *Guarding against Politicization*, Central Intelligence Agency, Mar. 16, 1992, https://www.cia.gov/library/center-for-the-study-of-intelligence/kent-csi/volume-36-number-1/html/v36i1a01p_0001.htm (quoting Winston Churchill).

11. SPENCE, *supra* note 2, at 60.

12. BALL, *supra* note 3, at 25.

13. *Id.*

14. NIZER, *supra* note 9, at 12.

15. JONATHAN HAIDT, THE RIGHTEOUS MIND: WHY GOOD PEOPLE ARE DIVIDED BY POLITICS AND RELIGION 281 (2012).

16. SPENCE, *supra* note 2, at 175, 201.

17. *Id.* at 123.

18. BALL, *supra* note 3, at 4.

19. NIZER, *supra* note 9, at 524.

20. *Id.*

21. Clarence Darrow, *How to Pick a Jury*, ESQUIRE, May 1936, *available at* http://law2.umkc.edu/faculty/projects/ftrials/DAR_JURY.HTM.

22. HAIDT, *supra* note 15, at 48.

23. A handful of law schools are progressively ahead of the curve. *See, e.g.,* Lewis & Clark Law School, *Legal Persuasion Seminar*, Law Courses Catalog, http://law.lclark.edu/courses/catalog/law_498.php (last visited May 28, 2013); New York Law School, *Visual Persuasion Project*, http://www.nyls.edu/centers/projects/visual_persuasion (last visited May 28, 2013) (describing Prof. Richard K. Sherwin's course, Visual Persuasion in the Law); University of California—Berkeley Law, *Persuasion*, Courses@Boalt, http://www.law.berkeley.edu/php-programs/courses/coursePage.php?cID=9146 (last visited May 28, 2013); University of Virginia School of Law, *Persuasion* (Jan. 2013), http://lawnotes2.law.virginia.edu/lawweb/course.nsf/a4e1939f669b0adc8525714e006c83ee/195092f1fb6b45e585257a1c004262d8?OpenDocument.

24. *Id.* at 50.

25. ALAN DERSHOWITZ, LETTERS TO A YOUNG LAWYER 116 (2009).

26. *Interview with Antonin Scalia*, Piers Morgan Tonight (July 18, 2012), http://transcripts.cnn.com/TRANSCRIPTS/1207/18/pmt.01.html.

27. Jim McElhaney, *No Laughing Matter*, A.B.A. J., Nov. 2011, at 24, 24.

28. 4 THE SUPREME COURT (Ambrose Video 2007).

29. Nat'l Fed'n. Indep. Bus. v. Sebelius, 567 U.S. ___, 132 S. Ct. 2566 (2012).

30. Darrow, *supra* note 21.

31. *See, e.g.,* Gayle Herd, *Take Me to Your Leader: An Examination of Authoritarianism as an Indicator of Jury Bias*, 21 JURY EXPERT 14 (Jan. 2009), *available at* http://thejuryexpert.com/wp-content/uploads/TJEVol21Num1_Jan2009.pdf.

32. CLARENCE DARROW, THE ESSENTIAL WORDS AND WRITINGS OF CLARENCE DARROW 234 (Edward J. Larson ed. 2007).

33. Williams J. Bryan & Mary Baird Bryan, Memoirs of William Jennings Bryan (1925) 555 (2003). Bryan was denied the opportunity to deliver his closing argument, which he had labored over for weeks, when Darrow utilized a rule of Tennessee criminal procedure which barred prosecutors from giving closing arguments when the defense waives its right to a closing argument and asks the court to instruct the jury to find the defendant guilty.

34. Michael Berman, *A Few Words on Story-telling*, Humanizing Language Teaching Mag. (May 2003), *available at* http://www.hltmag.co.uk/may03/pubs4.htm.

35. Spence, *supra* note 2, at 131.

36. Nizer, *supra* note 9, at 7.

37. Sonia Sotomayor, My Beloved World 211 (2013).

38. The Trial of Bernhard Goetz (Aae Films, 1988).

39. Hal Higdon, Leopold and Loeb: The Crime of the Century 238 (1975).

40. Cheryl L. Grady et al., *Neural Correlates of the Episodic Encoding of Pictures and Words*, 95 Proc. Nat'l Acad. Sci. 2703 (Mar. 3, 1998).

41. Ball, *supra* note 3, at 23.

42. Spence, *supra* note 2, at 105.

43. Adam L. Rosman, *Visualizing the Law: Using Charts, Diagrams, and Other Images to Improve Legal Briefs*, 63 J. Legal Educ. 70, 71 (2013).

44. *Id.* at 71.

45. Amos Tversky & Daniel Kahneman, *Judgment under Uncertainty: Heuristics and Biases*, 185 Science 1124 (1974), *reprinted in Introduction*, Judgment under Uncertainty: Heuristics and Biases 1, 14–16 (Daniel Kahneman et al. eds., 1982).

46. Nizer, *supra* note 9, at 8.

47. Spence, *supra* note 2, at 129.

48. Nizer, *supra* note 9, at 8.

49. Dershowitz, *supra* note 25, at 109.

Chapter 10

1. Eric Posner, *The Real Problem with Law Schools: They Train Too Many Lawyers*, Slate (Apr. 2, 2013), http://www.slate.com/articles/news_and_politics/view_from_chicago/2013/04/the_real_problem_with_law_schools_too_many_lawyers.html. Median starting salaries fell from $72,000 in 2009 to $60,000 in 2012. *Id.*

2. Ethan Bronner, *Law School Applications Fall as Costs Rise and Jobs Are Cut*, N.Y. Times, Jan 30, 2013, *available at* http://www.nytimes.com/2013/01/31/education/law-schools-applications-fall-as-costs-rise-and-jobs-are-cut.html?pagewanted=all&_r=0.

3. William D. Henderson & Rachel M. Zahorsky, *The Pedigree Problem: Are Law School Ties Choking the Profession*, A.B.A. J., July 1, 2012, at 36.

4. *Id.* at 39.

5. *Id.* at 40. *See* Marjorie M. Shultz & Sheldon Zedeck, Final Report: Identification, Development, and Validation of Predictors for Successful Lawyering (2008), *available at* http:// www.law.berkeley.edu/ files/LSACREPORTfinal-12.pdf.

6. Henderson & Zahorsky, *supra* note 3, at 40.

7. *Id.*

8. Sam Spiewak, *Studying the Legal Profession*, Stan. Law., Spring 2011, at 9.

9. Bronner, *supra* note 2.

10. Reginald F. Davis, *Reality Sinks in*, A.B.A. J., Aug. 2012, at 36.

11. *See, e.g.,* Ethan Katsh & Janet Rifkin, Online Dispute Resolution: Resolving Conflicts in Cyberspace (2001); Susan Nauss Exon, *The Next Generation of Online Dispute Resolution: The Significance of Holography to Enhance and Transform Dispute Resolution*, 12 Cardozo J. Conflict Resol. 19 (2010).

12. *See, e.g.,* Jayanth K. Krishnan, *Outsourcing and the Globalizing Legal Profession*, 48 Wm. & Mary L. Rev. 2189 (2007); Milton C. Regan Jr. & Palmer T. Heenan, *Supply Chains and Porous Boundaries: The Disaggregation of Legal Services*, 78 Fordham L. Rev. 2137 (2010); Sedona Conference, *Database Principles Addressing the Preservation and Production of Databases and Database Information in Civil Litigation* (Apr. 2011), *available at* https://thesedonaconference.org/download-pub/426; Carole Silver, *The Variable Value of U.S. Legal Education in the Global Legal Services Market*, 24 Geo. J. Legal Ethics 1 (2011).

13. Richard Susskind, Tomorrow's Lawyers: An Introduction to Your Future xv (2013).

14. Sharon Driscoll, *A Positive Disruption: The Transformation of Law through Technology*, Stan. Law., Spring 2013, at 23–24.

15. Patrick J. Schiltz, *On Being a Happy, Healthy, and Ethical Member of an Unhappy, Unhealthy, and Unethical Profession*, 52 Vand. L. Rev. 871, 914 (1999).

16. *Id.* at 888 n.118 (citing Commission on Professionalism, American Bar Ass'n, "...In the Spirit of Public Service": A Blueprint for the Rekindling of Lawyer Professionalism, 112 F.R.D. 243, 265 (1986)).

17. Barry Schwartz & Kenneth Sharpe, Practical Wisdom: The Right Way to Do the Right Thing 195 (2010).

18. Jeffrey Goldberg, *What's Your Problem?*, Atlantic, Mar. 9, 2010, *available at* 2010 WLNR 26390454.

19. Tom W. Smith & National Opinion Research Center/University of Chicago, Job Satisfaction in the United States (Apr. 17, 2007).

20. William H. Rehnquist, *The Legal Profession Today: Dedicatory Address*, 62 Ind. L.J. 151, 153 (1987).

21. Schiltz, *supra* note 15, at 917.

22. *Id.* at 918.

23. Robert F. Blomquist, *The Pragmatically Virtuous Lawyer*, 15 WIDENER L. REV. 93, 120 (2009).

24. Peter Lattman, *Settling a Billing Dispute, a Law Firm Denounces In-House "E-Mail Humor,"* N.Y. TIMES, Apr. 18, 2013, *available at* 2013 WLNR 9412913.

25. *Id.*

26. RICHARD SUSSKIND, THE END OF LAWYERS: RETHINKING THE NATURE OF LEGAL SERVICES 151 (2008).

27. *Id.* at 148–49.

28. *Id.* at 153.

29. *Id.* at 152.

30. HOWARD GARDNER ET AL., IN GOOD WORK: WHEN EXCELLENCE AND ETHICS MEET 248–49 (2001).

31. 378 U.S. 184, 197 (1964) (Stewart, J., concurring).

32. CHRISTOPHER A. DARDEN, IN CONTEMPT (1996).

33. Thomas L. Shaffer & Mary M. Shaffer, *Character and Community: Rispetto as a Virtue in the Tradition of Italian-American Lawyers*, 64 NOTRE DAME L. REV. 838, 852 (1989).

34. *Id.* at 853.

35. John Monahan & Jeffrey Swenson, *Lawyers at Mid-Career: A 20-Year Longitudinal Study of Job and Life Satisfaction*, 6 J. EMPIRICAL LEGAL STUD. 451, 452 (2009).

36. Tom Rath, *New Book Continues the Strengths Revolution*, GALLUP BUS. J. (Feb. 12, 2007), http://businessjournal.gallup.com/content/26512/new-book-continues-the-strengths-revolution.aspx.

37. MARTIN E. P. SELIGMAN, AUTHENTIC HAPPINESS: USING THE NEW POSITIVE PSYCHOLOGY TO REALIZE YOUR POTENTIAL FOR LASTING FULFILLMENT (2002).

38. Martin Seligman, *Authentic Happiness*, http://www.authentichappiness.sas.upenn.edu/Default.aspx (last visited May 9, 2013).

39. Gallup, Strengths Center, http://strengths.gallup.com/default.aspx (last visited May 9, 2013).

40. ALAN DERSHOWITZ, LETTERS TO A YOUNG LAWYER 71 (2009).

41. DANIEL L. SCHACTER, SEARCHING FOR MEMORY: THE BRAIN, THE MIND, AND THE PAST vii (1996) (quoting SAUL BELLOW, THE BELLAROSA CONNECTION, COLLECTED STORIES (1989)).

42. *Id.* at 93.

43. *Id.* at 149.

44. *Id.* at 297.

45. *Id.* at 95.

Index